ENGLISH H

Highlight 5

Ausgabe A

Cornelsen

ENGLISH H
HIGHLIGHT
BAND 5   AUSGABE A

Im Auftrage des Verlages herausgegeben von
Roderick Cox, Aachen ▪ Raymond Williams, York

Erarbeitet von
Roderick Cox, Aachen
unter Mitwirkung von David W. Bygott, Oxford ▪ John Eastwood, Street
Iris Sprankling, Woodbridge ▪ Sydney Thorne, York

Verlagsredaktion
Frank Donoghue (Projektleitung)
Marie Keenoy (verantwortliche Redakteurin)
Jenny Dames, Barbara Jung *und* Birgit Herrmann, Aachen (Außenredaktion)

Beratende Mitwirkung

Hans Bebermeier, Bielefeld ▪ Johannes Berning, Münster ▪ Willibald Bliemel, Gelnhausen
Gisela Feldmann, Haltern ▪ Prof. Dr. Heinz Helfrich, Kaiserslautern
Prof. Dr. Liesel Hermes, Karlsruhe/Koblenz ▪ Prof. Dr. Peter W. Kahl, Hamburg
Karen Kreibohm, Berlin ▪ Gunhild Krekeler, Dortmund ▪ Tilbert Müller, Herxheim
Dr. Wolfgang Soldan, Brownsville, Texas ▪ Ute Spreckelsen, Lübeck
Ruth Williams, Alexandria, Virginia ▪ Herbert Willms, Herford

Grafik

Donald Gott, London ▪ Bob Jones/Artworks, New York City ▪ Roy Schofield, Cheam
Gabriele Heinisch, Berlin ▪ Dr. Hans-Joachim Kämmer, Berlin ▪ Skip G. Langkafel, Berlin
Constanze Schargan, Berlin ▪ Sue Tewkesbury, Penton Mewsey ▪ Katharina Wieker, Berlin

Umschlaggestaltung
Knut Waisznor

Gestaltung und technische Umsetzung
Heike Freund, Berlin

Bildquellen
s. Verzeichnis auf Seite 160

Zusatzmaterialien zum vorliegenden Schülerbuch
Workbook (Best.-Nr. 78787)
Workbook Lehrerfassung (Best.-Nr. 78795)
Cassetten zum Schülerbuch (Best.-Nr. 70670)
CDs zum Schülerbuch (Best.-Nr. 70689)
Arbeitsfolien (Best.-Nr. 70697)
Auf weitere Bestandteile wird im Handbuch für den Unterricht (Best.-Nr. 78809) verwiesen.

1. Auflage €✔   Druck 5 4 3 2   Jahr 02 01 2000 99

Alle Drucke dieser Auflage können im Unterricht nebeneinander verwendet werden.

Druck: CS-Druck Cornelsen Stürtz, Berlin

ISBN 3-464-07877-9 – broschiert
ISBN 3-464-08471-X – gebunden

Bestellnummer 78779 – broschiert
Bestellnummer 84710 – gebunden

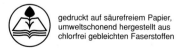

gedruckt auf säurefreiem Papier,
umweltschonend hergestellt aus
chlorfrei gebleichten Faserstoffen

INHALT

[ ] Rezeptiv: Strukturen, die nur verstanden
   werden sollen
 * Fakultativ: wahlfreie Bestandteile

4

Differenzierungshinweis

☐ Leichtere Übung
■ ■ Schwierigere Übung

UNIT ONE

Media USA

American media are all over the world. Hollywood films are in cinemas from Alaska to Zimbabwe, American TV comes into people's homes, and music from the USA is in every CD shop.

■ **Quiz: Look at these US logos. Which logos and sentences belong together?**

1 News, news and more news!
2 You can't use most computers if you don't have this.
3 This firm makes computers.

4 This firm makes films.
5 Watch videos and listen to music on your TV.

■ **Web sites: The Internet started in the USA. What can you find at the following US web sites?**

| birthday cards ▪ cinema tips ▪ jeans |
| music news ▪ restaurant tips ▪ world news |

www.levi.com
www.cnn.com
www.777.film.com
www.menusonline.com
www.rocktropolis.com
www.americangreetings.com

Perhaps you can go online and visit one of them.

■ **Word pool: Media**

books · cassettes · CDs · CD-ROMs · cheap · cinema-goers · dangerous · exciting expensive · films · important · Internet · listen to · listeners · magazines · newspapers popular · radio · read · readers · surf · surfers · TV · use · videos · viewers · watch

Tip: You can find new words in the *Dictionary* (page 138).

Find words that tell you …
– what the media are: books, …
– what people do with the media: listen to, …
– what you call the people: cinema-goers, …
– what the media are like: cheap, …

You and the media
I often watch TV / read books / …
I don't go to the cinema / buy CD-ROMs / …
… is my favourite video / web site / …

W 1, 1-2*

* Die blau gedruckten Verweise bezeichnen den frühestmöglichen Einsatzort der Übungen im Workbook.
W 1, 1-2 = Workbook Seite 1, Übungen 1-2

* SONG 🎧 Radio ga ga

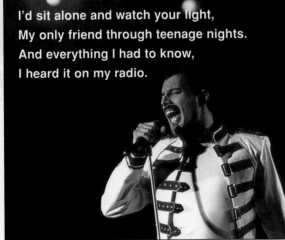

I'd sit alone and watch your light,
My only friend through teenage nights.
And everything I had to know,
I heard it on my radio.

You had your time, you had the power.
You've yet to have your finest hour.
Radio.

All we hear is radio ga ga,
Radio goo goo, radio ga ga.
All we hear is radio ga ga,
Radio blah blah.
Radio, what's new?
Radio, someone still loves you.

* CLASS PROJECT Pop "standards"

Radio ga ga isn't a new song. It's a "standard", an old song that DJs often play on the radio and at discos. Make a list of your top five "standards" and say why you chose them. Put all the lists on the classroom wall (or write them on a computer).
Now you can make a top five for your class.

Say why you chose each song:
- ► It's a good song for dancing / aerobics / cheering people up / listening to alone / ...
- ► It has a good beat / an interesting message / great words / super guitar work / ...
- ► Everybody likes/knows the song.

A Music is a big industry in the USA. Lots of young people try to get a job in the music business.

So you want to start a group?

David Ellefson, guitarist for *Megadeth*, wrote a book for young people who want to work in the music industry.

In his book he says, "You don't suddenly become a star. It doesn't just happen. You must work hard. You need talent, lots of energy – and a little
5 luck." He says that all he can do in his book is tell young groups what he has learned in his career. He mentions that being in the right place at the right time is very useful. But he adds, "Being different and interesting are the two most important things."

What tips does he give for the first years of a band's career?

10 *"One: Write your own music. Two: Play in front of people as often as you can."* David explains that he doesn't just mean concert halls and clubs. He says that young musicians should play at birthday parties and church discos. He tells his readers that this is the only way of learning to play better in front of people.

15 *"Three: Tell people who you are and what you do."* David says that you shouldn't think that suddenly an agent will get you work and help you to become famous. He points out that when he played in his first bands, he spent a lot of time hanging up posters in his small town.

"Four: Decide who's in the team and what their jobs are." He says that every group needs a boss. He remarks that everybody should only do their own job.

20 *"Five: It's important to get the help of a manager, somebody who organises your work."* David tells his readers that later, maybe, they'll need an agent, too.

And what are the last words in the book? – *"Good luck!"*

EXERCISE 1 □ What are the adjectives/ adverbs?   Tip: The text will help you.
1 Musicians have to work DRAH.
2 They must be TERENFIDF and interesting.
3 They have to learn how to play TETREB.
4 They won't suddenly become SUOMAF.
5 A manager is very PORMINTAT.

EXERCISE 2 ■ Find the words in the text.
1 A big place where bands play.
2 Somebody who makes music.
3 Somebody who organises people's work.
4 Somebody who says what others have to do.
5 Somebody who gets work for people.
6 Another word for "perhaps".

EXERCISE 3 ■ Find the other verbs.
You could write:
David says that being in the right place at the right time is useful.
But the text has:
David mentions that being in the right place at the right time is useful.
Find 5 other verbs like this in the text.

EXERCISE 4 ■ What's the wrong word in each group?
1 learn – know – find out – hope
2 talent – decide – luck – energy
3 mistake – career – job – work
4 happy – famous – popular – fed up
5 letter – worker – poster – picture
6 manager – boss – agent – equipment

EXERCISE 5 ■■ So you want to …?
Ask a partner for 5 tips about something you want to do. Then tell the class what he/she says: … says I should …

meet a boy/girl • learn inline-skating
get a weekend job • save money • …

W 2, 4

8

B A job in the music business isn't easy. What do you think are the problems?

The music business

Being a musician doesn't just mean writing songs and playing them. We asked musicians about other things that they do.
David Ellefson of *Megadeth* told us that musicians couldn't do everything themselves. He said that managers, for example, got
5 about 20 per cent of a musician's money.
Singer **Tori Amos** said that everybody in the business wanted something for their money. She said people were only your friends sometimes, but usually they were just business partners. She told us you had to know how the business worked.
10 But **Chrissie Hynde**, singer and guitarist for the *Pretenders,* didn't like this idea. She said she never thought about business things. She paid other people to do that.
Every band needed publicity, **Slash** of *Guns N' Roses* told us. He thought TV and radio would always be important. But the Internet
15 was very useful, too – and not just for publicity. He said you could sell your CDs through the Internet.
Bob Mothersbaugh, guitarist for *Devo*, told us that all musicians had to be careful with people from music companies. He told us what happened when a woman from a music company wanted to
20 give the band a recording contract. She said there would be very little money. So the members would all need girlfriends with jobs who could pay for them! Bob told her that they would wait for a better contract. Bob said that you learned new things about the music business every day – if you watched and listened.

❝You can't do everything yourself.❞
David Ellefson

❝They're only your friends sometimes.❞
Tori Amos

❝I never think about business things.❞
Chrissie Hynde

❝TV and radio will always be important.❞
Slash

EXERCISE 6 ☐ Who said it?

1 "Musicians can't do everything themselves."
2 "All musicians have to be careful."
3 "I never think about business things."
4 "You learn new things every day."
5 "You can sell your CDs through the Internet."
6 "You have to know how the business works."

EXERCISE 7 ■■ What were their words?

1 He said that managers … about 20%. *(line 4)*
 He said, "Managers *get* about 20%."
2 She said people … just business partners. *(line 8)*
 She said, "People …"
3 She said she … other people to do that. *(line 12)*
4 He said every band … publicity. *(line 13)*
5 He said the Internet … very useful. *(line 14)*

W 2, 5

wilhelm

C ## LISTENING 🎧 A film star

Two reporters from a magazine are talking. Listen.

EXERCISE 8 ■ What three things tell you the star's name and the film he almost won an Oscar for?

His second name ▪ The name his mother thought of ▪ His mother's name ▪ His father's name ▪ A boy's name ▪ A ship's name

EXERCISE 9 ■■ Listen again. Make notes about the work the star did before the big film in 1997.

Tip: Listen to the cassette/CD again and check your answers.

STORY 🎧

Why do people often want to be on TV?

"The Window on the World"

NBC TV have a studio on 49th Street in New York that you can look into from the street. They call it *The Window on the World*. It's where they make the breakfast show *Today*. As part of the programme the show's stars come out and talk to some of the people who are looking through the window or watching on TV screens outside. If they're lucky, they can say "Hi" to their friends on breakfast TV.

It was only 7 o'clock in the morning, but it was already warm. Another hot August day in Manhattan. Kay Norton and Pat Butler, two friends on a trip to New York, "The Big Apple", were at
5   *The Window on the World*. They wanted to say "Hi" to their friends in San Diego, California. They waited outside the studio for almost two hours. The stars came out a few times, but they didn't come and talk to Kay and Pat.
10 One of the things on the programme that morning was an interview with an English boy, Dave Kelly. He was in the USA to look for his girlfriend. He hoped that the TV viewers could help him to find her.
15 "He looks nice," said Kay. "What a sad story. Do you think his girlfriend is watching the programme? Look, there's a photo of her." But Pat wasn't watching the TV screen. She was watching the door the stars came through.
20 "I don't think people should tell him where she is. If she wants to live without him, that's her decision," said Pat. "And – look. Matt is coming out!" The people outside the studio started to shout.
25 "Come here! Hi, Matt! Come and talk to us!" Kay and Pat shouted, too, and they showed their sign *Hi! from San Diego*. But the star talked to a group from Brownsville, Texas. Pat thought it wasn't fair. The group had the least interesting
30 sign. Then Matt quickly went back into the studio. Two minutes later the programme was over.

"No problem," said Pat. "We aren't flying home till tomorrow evening, so we can come here again tomorrow morning. I'd really like to be on TV."
35
"I'm not coming to this stupid studio again," said Kay. "It's the worst place in New York. Come on. Let's go to Greenwich Village now. There are some cheap music shops there, with the latest CDs."
40
They took the subway to Bleeker Street and spent the morning in Greenwich Village. They bought two CDs. Then they were hungry and tired. Kay had an idea for a good snack bar. "This book says *Gray's Papaya*
45
has the best – and cheapest – hot dogs in town," said Kay. "And it's just a little farther down this street."
"OK," said Pat. "Let's go."

50 "Great," said Kay. "The best hot dog I've ever eaten."

"Yes," said Pat. "And this sauerkraut is fantastic. – You know, Kay, I've thought a lot about that English boy on the *Today*
55 programme."

"Yes, he looked really nice," said Kay. "I'd like to help him."

"I told you this morning," said Pat, "I think the media should stay out of other people's
60 lives. If that English girl doesn't want to come home, that's her decision. I don't think the TV viewers should help her boyfriend. They'll only make things worse."

A young man came and stood next to her and
65 started to eat his hot dog. Suddenly she saw the photo he was looking at. Funny! It looked just like the young woman who worked in the café near the beach in San Diego. She looked at the young man.

70 "Well, I think people sometimes don't really know what they're doing," Kay was saying. "And then you have to help … What's the matter?"

"It's him," Pat whispered. "The English boy.
75 And he has a photo of his girlfriend. I've seen her in San Diego. She works in José's restaurant."

Kay smiled and whispered to her friend.

"You could be on TV tomorrow. Not *outside*,
80 but *inside* the studio. Are you going to tell him?"*

---

* Did Pat tell Dave? You can find out more in *Point of no return*. It starts on page 18.

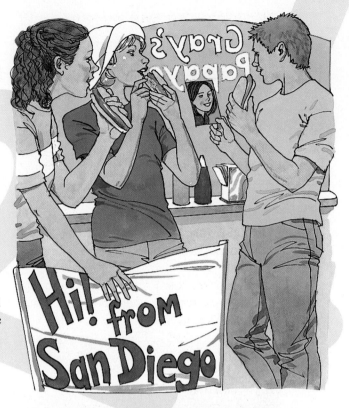

TASK A □ What's …?
1 *The Window on the World*
2 *Today*
3 "The Big Apple"
4 *Hi! from San Diego*
5 *Gray's Papaya*
6 *José's*

TASK B ■ Who said it: Pat or Kay?
1 He looks nice. What a sad story.
2 I don't think people should tell him where she is.
3 We can come here again tomorrow morning.
4 I'm not coming to this stupid studio again.
5 The best hot dog I've ever eaten.
6 I'd like to help him.
7 I think the media should stay out of other people's lives.
8 People sometimes don't really know what they're doing.
9 Are you going to tell him?

TASK C ■■ What could Pat say to Dave?
San Diego – visit New York – studio – saw you – girlfriend – restaurant – …

ACTIVE ENGLISH

ACTIONS TV and the cinema

Two friends are planning their evening.

What are the boys going to do first – watch TV or go out?

JAMES Oh no! Tom Getty is on *The Tonight Show*
and we're going out. Can you record it?

JOE Is that an NBC programme?

JAMES Yes, it is.

JOE When's the programme on?

JAMES From 10 pm till 11 pm.

JOE OK. I'll programme the video-recorder.

EXERCISE 1 ■ Make dialogues.

YOU Can you record … this evening?

A PARTNER Is that a/an … programme?

YOU Yes, it is.

A PARTNER When's the programme on?

YOU From … till …

| *Married … with children* | *Roseanne* | *Malibu Shores* | *David Letterman* |
| CBS, 6 pm – 6.30 pm | ABC, 6.30 pm – 7 pm | NBC, 8 pm – 9 pm | CBS, 10.30 pm – 11.30 pm |

ⓘ WHAT'S ON TV?

- Most newspapers have a – very full! – page with the TV programmes. Or you can buy "TV Guide", one of the most popular magazines in the country. It isn't in colour inside, it doesn't have many photos – and there isn't much information about the programmes.

- Letters and numbers after the name of a programme (see the box on the right) tell parents if a programme is OK for children.

- Some films get a "bad letter" because they show violence. But there's violence in news programmes, too – and they don't get letters. And "bad letters" can even make a programme more attractive!

- With modern technology (see photos) parents can be sure that their children don't watch programmes with "bad letters".

Y 7	Children 7 and older
PG	Parental guidance suggested
14	Inappropriate for children under 14
M	For adults **S** Sex **V** Violence

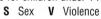

Do these cinema-goers like the same stars?

BOY Do you like Helen Labone?

GIRL Yes, I do. She's great.

BOY Everybody says that. She's OK, but I didn't like her last movie. Shauna Hart is much better. She's brilliant!

GIRL Shauna Hart? Oh, I don't really like her. I hope she isn't in *California Sun*.

BOY Don't worry, she isn't. – Two tickets for Screen 8, please. *California Sun*.

WOMAN Is it for tonight?

BOY Yes, 8.00, please.

WOMAN That's $12.

EXERCISE 2 ■ At the cinema: Make six dialogues.

YOU Two tickets for Screen 1, please.

A PARTNER *Beach Games*?

YOU That's right.

A PARTNER Is it for tonight?

YOU Yes, 8.00, please.

A PARTNER That's $12.

Screen 1			Screen 2		
BEACH GAMES			MY LEFT FOOT		
6:00	8:00	10:10	5:30	7:40	9:50
Screen 3			Screen 4		
THE BIG HEADACHE			YOU CAN'T TALK TO A DENTIST		
5:45	7:55	10:00	6:15	8:15	10:15
Screen 5			Screen 6		
AIRPORT DISASTER			AS COLD AS ICE		
6:10	8:00	10:00	5:20	7:30	9:40

EXERCISE 3 □ You want to watch TV later. Make a dialogue with a partner.

Frage, ob er/sie *Explosiv* aufzeichnen kann.

Frage, ob das eine Pro 7-Sendung ist.

Sage nein. Es ist eine RTL-Sendung.

Frage, wann die Sendung läuft.

Sage, dass sie von 19 Uhr bis 19.30 Uhr läuft.

Tip: Look at page 12.

EXERCISE 4 ■■ Make a dialogue about film stars.

Sage, dass Rick Day dein Lieblingsfilmstar ist.

Frage, ob er/sie Ricks neuen Film kennt.

Sage, dass du ihn dreimal gesehen hast und dass er sehr gut ist.

Sage, dass dir der Film nicht gefallen hat. Sage, dass Jeff Bruce viel besser ist.

Sage, dass er furchtbar ist.

W 4, 9-10

PRACTICE PAGES

STRUCTURES

EXERCISE 1 ■ US newspapers: What are the missing words?

best (2x) ▪ farther ▪ less ▪ more ▪ worse

The New York Times is one of the world's (1) … newspapers. Like all US newspapers, it has (2) … news about the USA than about other countries in the world. There's (3) … news about Holland, for example, than in a German newspaper. But the USA is much (4) … away from Holland. And Holland is smaller than most US states! So it's unfair to say that US newspapers are (5) … than European ones. If you're in the USA and you want to find out what's happening in Germany, it's (6) … to go to an Internet café and read a German newspaper – online!

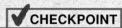

> ✔ **CHECKPOINT**
>
> **Unregelmäßige Steigerungsformen**
> bad/badly – worse – worst
> far – farther – farthest
> good/well – better – best
> little – less – least
> much – more – most

EXERCISE 2 ■ A brilliant musician: What are the right words?

Peter Lewis is a very (good/well) guitarist. He always plans his concerts very (careful/carefully). His concert in New York last weekend was (brilliant/brilliantly). When I bought my ticket I was (angry/angrily) that it was so expensive, but I (quick/quickly) forgot that when he started to play. Peter played all the songs from his new CD, of course, and lots of old ones. But he played them so (different/differently) last weekend. He didn't just play (good/well). He played (brilliant/brilliantly).

> ✔ **CHECKPOINT**
>
> **Adjektive beschreiben, wie jemand ist:**   **Adverbien sagen, wie jemand etwas macht:**
> Sarah is a careful driver.   Sarah drives carefully.
> **Viele Adverbien enden auf *-ly*:** quick – quickly, angry – angrily, nice – nicely
> ⚠ **Beachte aber:** good – well, fast – fast, hard – hard

EXERCISE 3 ■■ Reporters and stars   Tip: Look at page 114 first.

I did an interview with Tom Delaney last week. He told me that he would start work on a new film next month. Liz Logan would be in the film, too. He said he couldn't tell me too much because the film company was planning a surprise. He said that he always enjoyed working with Liz. She was one of the best movie stars in the USA, if not the world. He said people often wrote stupid things about her. He couldn't understand this. He thought she was brilliant – and she was his wife!
Later the reporter listened to the cassette of his interview. What were Tom Delaney's words?
"I'll start work on a new film next month. Liz Logan …"

EXERCISE 4 ☐ The media in the future. What do some people say will happen?

1 There (be) even more TV stations.
There *will be* even more TV stations.
2 Everybody (have) the Internet on their TV.
3 Some people (read) newspapers online.
4 All letters (go) by e-mail.
5 Shops (not sell) small TVs.
6 Computers (do) exercises like this one!

EXERCISE 5 ■ Matt's notes for tomorrow's show. What does he say?

Interview with Jon Brain
Meet the stars of "Frankie's Farm"
Find out about the new Cybersoft CD-ROM
Tell viewers about our new quiz
Show part of the Sandra Heffer movie
Hear the new Vince Dobson song

"Tomorrow we're going to have an interview with Jon Brain. Then we're …"

WORDPOWER

WORDPOWER 1 ■ What's the right word?

1 Where's the *next/nearest* CD shop?
2 When's the *next/nearest* concert? – In May.
3 "Let it be" was the Beatles' *last/latest* CD.
4 What's the *last/latest* news about Kay Lee?
5 Let's sit on a *bench/bank* and listen to CDs.
6 I'm going to the *bench/bank*. I need money.

WORDPOWER 2 ■ Find the preposition that belongs to each group of words.

1 ? + bus, bike, car, train
2 ? + Sunday, TV, holiday, the left, March 1st
3 ? + the country, my photo, town, time
4 ? + lunch, example, a long time, 10 years
5 ? + 6 o'clock, home, least, night, school

WORDPOWER 3 ■ German media: Explain these things to a visitor from the USA.

1 RTL? – It's a TV company.
2 Guten Morgen, Deutschland? – …
3 VIVA? – …
4 Hör Zu?
5 Bild?
6 Tatort?
7 Lindenstraße?
8 Thomas Gottschalk?

WORDPOWER 4 ■■ Make a word web.

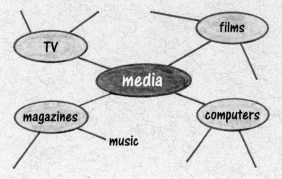

WRITING

EXERCISE ■■ A letter to a newspaper

Schreibe einen Brief von David Chan an die *Santa Barbara News*. Du schreibst, dass du manchmal die Zeitung deiner Eltern liest. Es gibt aber nicht genug Nachrichten für junge Leute in der Zeitung. Schreibe, dass junge Leute sich für andere Themen interessieren *(other topics)*. Du würdest gern Artikel über örtliche Musikgruppen lesen *(local bands)*. Und nicht alle jungen Leute haben genug Geld für Zeitschriften. Schreibe, dass die Zeitungsfirma sicher an neuen Leserinnen/Lesern interessiert ist. Später werden die jungen Leute von heute selbst eine Zeitung kaufen. Frage, welche Zeitung sie sich dann wohl kaufen werden *(And which newspaper do you think …?)*.

PRACTICE PAGES

READING A letter to a newspaper's problem page

BEFORE YOU READ ■ What do people write to problem pages about?

The Problem Page

I'm Jane Franklin, and I'm here to help you with your problems. So write to me at The Weekly News. I'll do my best to help.

Dear Jane,

One of my problems is that I don't have a boyfriend at the moment. I had one last year, but we broke up. At my school all the boys of the right age are ugly or stupid. My friend Amber has a boyfriend. She met him about six weeks ago. His name is Paul. They're always together. This means I don't see so much of Amber because I can't go out with them all the time. And I don't have many other friends. Well, Amber is my *only* friend. Now I think I'm in love with Paul. He's so nice. I'm sure he likes me. He never says I should go away. He never says he wants to be alone with Amber. Maybe he's getting tired of her and he wants to be with me. I get a really strange feeling when he looks at me. It makes me happy. I wish he was my boyfriend. So now you know the big problem. How can I get Paul and still have Amber as my friend? I don't want to hurt her.

Lisa (16)

Dear Lisa,

The answer to your problem is easy, but you won't like it. Don't try to take Paul away from Amber. Amber is your best friend. If you try to steal her boyfriend, she won't be your friend much longer. And you'll hate yourself for it. Friends are very important. Boyfriends can be important, too, but they come and go. Paul really is a nice boy. He's friendly, but that doesn't mean he loves you. I think this is just a dream – an idea you've thought of for yourself. I know it won't be an easy thing to do, but you should forget this silly idea. The other boys you know can't all be stupid or ugly. Try to make friends with some of them and I hope you'll get a nice surprise. You never know when you're going to find romance.

Jane

Tip: You can find new words in the *Dictionary* (page 138).

EXERCISE 1 ☐ **Basic reading:** *Right, Wrong* or *Not in the text*?

1 Paul is Lisa's boyfriend.
2 Amber knows that Lisa is interested in Paul.
3 Jane says Lisa should try to get Paul.
4 She says Lisa should forget her silly idea.

EXERCISE 2 ■ **Reading for details: What's wrong with these sentences?**

1 Lisa had a boyfriend two years ago.
2 Amber met Paul about six months ago.
3 Lisa: "Amber never says I should go away."
4 Jane: "People will hate you if you steal Paul."
5 Jane: "Friends come and go."
6 Jane: "Other boys must all be stupid or ugly."

EXERCISE 3 ■ **Language tasks**   Tip: All the words are on page 16.

1 Find the opposites: a) next; b) beautiful; c) clever; d) together; e) difficult; f) love; g) remember.
2 Find the words in the text for: a) im Augenblick, vor sechs Wochen, die ganze Zeit;
b) sich trennen, sich kennen lernen, sich anfreunden.

EXERCISE 4 ■■ **What do you think?**

1 Why does Lisa have only one friend?
2 Is it OK that she's often with Paul and Amber?
3 Why doesn't Paul say Lisa should go away?
4 Is Jane's answer good? Why / Why not?

EXERCISE 5 ■■ **Writing**

Write your own answer to Lisa's letter.

LISTENING 🎧 My favourite magazine

You're going to hear some teenagers. They're talking to a reporter about their favourite magazines. Listen.

EXERCISE 1 ■ **Right or wrong?**

1 Paula's favourite magazine is about sport.
2 Joe reads about – and plays – music.
3 Monica doesn't have a mountain bike.
4 Kate knows a lot about computers.
5 Sam's mother pays for his magazine.

EXERCISE 3 ■■ **Listen again. Find …**

1 something Paula likes to read about.
2 two things Joe does in his free time.
3 three tips that are useful for Monica.
4 four things Kate uses her computer for.
5 something Sam is interested in.

EXERCISE 2 ■ **Listen again. What are the names of these magazines?**

Tip: Listen to the cassette/CD again and check your answers.

Weitere Fragen: W 52

*SERIAL
Point of no return (1)

Tip: You can find new words in the *Dictionary* (page 138).

point of no return: when you know that you must go on with what you're doing and you can't stop

The postman! Dave Kelly ran to the door. He looked at the letters: Mrs Kelly, Mr and Mrs Kelly, adverts, adverts ... Dave Kelly! A letter for
5 him! Dave read it.

Flying to America

Thank you very much for your letter to the "TeenScene" problems page. You'll see Jackie Trent's answer in the April magazine. But I don't
10 *think you'll like it. If your girlfriend has gone to the USA and doesn't want to tell people where she is, that's her decision. But I'm writing to you privately to give you another tip. I have*
15 *a sister in New York. She works on the "Today" programme. It's a breakfast TV show that people all over the USA watch. There are often guests on the show. And they aren't always stars.*
20 *A boy from England who's looking for a girl from England in the USA would be a different story for the show. If you like, I'll phone my sister. If it's OK, she'll phone you. Let me know what*
25 *you think. Good luck.*
Charles Shrimpton (Jackie Trent).

Dave had known all the time that *TeenScene* couldn't help him to find Sharon, the girl-
30 friend who had left him for that American boy last summer. But it was nice of "Jackie Trent" to write to him. Now, what was the telephone number? As if
35 those people in New York would be interested in Dave Kelly from England. Two weeks later Dave got a phone call ...

Terry

"Ladies and gentlemen. We're at the point of no return on this British 40 Airways flight from Manchester to New York. Yes, we're halfway across the Atlantic. The weather in New York: sunny, 75 degrees Fahrenheit. That's 25 degrees Celsius." 45

Now he really couldn't go back. He looked at the screen in the 747. They were showing the latest Sally Strong movie, *Dynamic*. Everybody knew the song from the film, "I'll stay with 50 you". Well, Sharon hadn't stayed with him. It had all started at that big party at Grove School for the students who were leaving, when they had danced 55 together all evening and walked back to Elm Road hand in hand. Then they had kissed for the first time, outside 60 Sharon's house. (And Sharon's dog Terry had started barking and had woken up all her family – and the neighbours!) 65

Then he had gone to Midland College in Birmingham for the car mechanic's course and she had started her secretarial course at Chester College. His aunt lived in Birmingham and he had stayed with her in the week. How he had looked forward to the weekends in Chester and the long summer holidays! He and Sharon had always been together then. His friend Asif Ahmed had often complained that

Dave never had time for him, never came to Manchester United's home games with him. Now it was *his* turn to complain. Asif and his girlfriend Nasreen went everywhere together. And he was alone …

"Ladies and gentlemen. We're almost at John F. Kennedy Airport, New York. Please fasten your seat-belts."

This was it. Almost there. The show was tomorrow morning. Time to tell America his story.

Dave arrived at the hotel on 47th Street. His room wasn't very big, but it was clean – and the hotel was only two blocks from the NBC Studios. He could walk there for the programme on Thursday morning. NBC had been really nice. They had said he could have three minutes on the *Today* programme. They had paid for his flight and one night in the hotel. He was tired. In England it was already 11 pm. But here in New York it was still only 6 pm.

Chester

19

He walked out of the hotel and along Sixth Avenue till he came to 49th Street. The street wasn't very busy at this time of the day. He walked over to the big window of the studio where *Today* was made – "The Window on the World". He looked into the studio. It was dark inside.

It was hard to imagine that tomorrow morning this studio would be full of activity, that the street outside would be full of people who wanted to see their favourite TV stars and that he, Dave Kelly from Chester, England, would be on the sofa over there, telling his story, hoping that the TV viewers could help him.

The TV studios

He planned to stay in a cheap bed and breakfast in Harlem for three weeks after the programme. His aunt in Birmingham had given him the money. "I was in love, too, a long time ago," she had said. "Sometimes you just have to follow your heart."

"**Well,** Dave. That's very interesting," said Katie Couric, one of the *Today* show's stars. "But if your ex-girlfriend wants to come to the USA, that's her decision."
"Yes, of course it is," said Dave. "But six months after Sharon arrived in the USA, I got a letter from her. Can I read it?"
"OK, Dave," said Katie. Dave took out the letter he always carried with him. Before the show he had been so nervous. Now he just forgot about the people in the studio, the tourists outside the studio and the millions who were watching on TV. He wanted to find Sharon.

Sixth Avenue, New York City

"Wayne has left me and told me to go back to England, but I can't. I've never been so unhappy in my life. But there's no going back. I don't want to come home after what has happened. Goodbye, Dave.
PS Say hallo to Boris for me."

"Boris?" said Katie. "Another boyfriend?"
"Er, no," said Dave. "My cat."
"Well," said Katie. "We've heard a sad story. This young English guy lost his girlfriend, the girl he went to school with, to an American guy. And now *she's* alone, too. She's somewhere in America. If she wants to come home, no problem. Dave has forgiven her a thousand times, he says. And if she wants to stay in the USA, he'd just like to know she's OK. Then he'll go home and try to forget her. Is that right, Dave?"
"Yes, it is. I love you, Sharon."
"Dave will be in New York for another three weeks. Here's a photo of Sharon. If you have news about her, please phone NBC."

Katie Couric

The red light on the camera went off. Katie said, "Thanks, Dave. All of us here at NBC wish you all the luck in the world. But, privately, I don't think it will work. I think you should forget Sharon and just enjoy New York." Dave looked at Katie. Perhaps she was right.

(To be continued)

W 8,9, 17-20

UNIT TWO
People in the USA

The families of the people who live in the USA today came from all over the world. People still come to live in the USA. Most immigrants now come from Latin America and different Asian countries.

■ **Where do the family names of these American teenagers come from?**

China · England · France
Germany · Mexico · Poland

Pete Meyer

Angie Dupont

Jeff Chang

Sal Gonzalez

Tom Smith

Helen Kovak

■ **Two groups have been in the USA for a long time: American Indians and Blacks. Which group is each of these texts about?**

A This group lived in North America long before white people came. White people put them on reservations. Today less than 1% of Americans belong to this group. They call themselves Native Americans or ...

B This group was brought to the USA by ship from Africa more than 200 years ago. They were sold to white people. Many years later they became free. Today about 12% of Americans belong to the group. They call themselves African Americans or ...

■ **Word pool: People**

American · angry · beautiful · blond · boring · careful · clever · cook · cry · dance
dark-haired · drink · eat · English · famous · fit · French · friendly · funny · German
happy · hate · hope · interesting · Irish · laugh · learn · like · live · love · Mexican · nice
old · plan · play · polite · poor · popular · proud · rich · run · sad · Scottish · sing · small
smile · Spanish · talk · tall · think · tired · understand · walk · Welsh · work · young

Tip: You can find new words in the *Dictionary* (page 138).

Find words that ...
– tell you which country people come from: He's/She's American, ...
– describe people: angry, ...
– tell you the things people do: cook, ...

| **How can you describe yourself?** |
| I'm 14/15/16/... ▪ I'm German/... ▪ I'm tall/... ▪ I'm blond/dark-haired. |
| I have blue/... eyes. ▪ I'm friendly/... ▪ I like/love ... ▪ I don't like/hate ... |

W 12, 1-2

ℹ️ POOR PEOPLE IN THE USA

- America is a rich country, but 15% of the people there (about 40 million) are poor.
- Blacks are usually poorer than Whites, and most American Indians are poor, too.
- Immigrant families have less money than families that were born in the USA. Many of them are poor. But they were often even poorer in their home country.
- More than 5 million children under 12 don't get enough food. And 30% of homeless people are children.
- Single-parent families are poorer than two-parent families. 38% of families with only one parent, usually the mother, are poor.
- The poorest group in the country are black, single-parent families.

And you?
- What do you think being poor means?
- Why do people leave their home country?
- What problems do you think immigrants often have?

* SONG 🎧 Black and white

The ink is black, the page is white.
Together we learn to read and write,
To read and write.

A child is black, a child is white,
The whole world looks upon the sight,
One beautiful sight.

And now a child can understand,
This is the law of all the land,
All the land.

The world is black, the world is white,
It turns by day and then by night.
A child is black, a child is white,
Together they grow to see the light,
To see the light.

* CLASS PROJECT How we spend our money

Poor families have to be especially careful with money. They buy food and other important things with it.

But what things do teenagers buy with their money? Are they all important?
- Make a list of things that people in your class bought with their pocket-money last month.
- Then find out what things people could most easily do without and make another list.

A The Navajos have found a way of being Indians *and* Americans.

The Navajo reservation

The biggest reservation in the USA is the Navajo reservation in Arizona.

Most people on the Navajo reservation live in modern houses, but some people have a traditional Indian house – a hogan, not
5 a wigwam! – next to their modern house. The Navajos have their own shops, banks, police stations, restaurants, camp-sites and motels.

In Navajo schools children learn English and the Navajo language. Their radio station, KTNN, has Navajo programmes in the morning
10 and English programmes in the afternoon. Window Rock is the reservation capital. There's a big fair there every summer. You can watch traditional Indian rodeos and dances. You can take some great photos, too. But always ask if it's OK, *before* you take a photo of an Indian. And you might like to give a tip.

15 There aren't enough jobs on the reservation, so many Indians are out of work and they often drink too much or take drugs. Some get money from tourists. For example, they make and sell traditional Indian art and modern souvenirs. Or they look after famous tourist attractions on the reservation, like Monument Valley. It has been
20 in many cowboy films and lots of adverts. Today the Navajos take tourists there, in jeeps – not only on horses!

A Navajo

A hogan

Monument Valley

EXERCISE 1 ☐ **Right or wrong?**
1 The Navajos live in wigwams.
2 Navajo children learn two languages.
3 The Navajos have a big fair every summer.
4 Tourists should never give Navajos tips.
5 Most Navajos have lots of money.
6 Monument Valley hasn't been in many cowboy films.

EXERCISE 2 ■ **What is it?**
1 A reservation?
2 A hogan?
3 A camp-site?
4 KTNN?
5 Window Rock?
6 A souvenir?
7 Monument Valley?
8 A jeep?

EXERCISE 3 ■ ■ **Modern or traditional?**
Make two lists.
Modern: reservations, …
Traditional: hogans, …

EXERCISE 4 ■ ■ **Adverts**
Write more slogans for adverts that use this photo of Monument Valley.

Feel free with Country Cola!

W 13, 3

24

B Many people speak two languages. In the USA lots of people speak English and Spanish.

Meet a Mexican-American

My name is Blanca Molina and I'm 16. I live in Brownsville,
Texas, and I go to Lopez High School there. My family comes
from Mexico, but I was born in Brownsville, so I'm American.
Most students at our school are Mexican-Americans. In
5 classes we have to speak English, but some of us speak it
with an accent. That's because we speak Spanish at home.

My mother doesn't speak much English so I often have to
translate things for her. I sometimes help my parents with
letters in Spanish because they aren't very good at writing. I go to Spanish classes at school. We always
10 spend the summer with our grandparents in Mexico. My sister and I usually speak Spanish there, but we
have English as our secret language. I like my two languages.

EXERCISE 5 ■ What words are missing?

1 Blanca … in Brownsville.
2 She … to Lopez High School.
3 Her family … from Mexico.
4 She … English and Spanish.
5 She often … things for her mother.
6 She … her two languages.

EXERCISE 6 ■■ Secret languages

Where can a secret language (English, for
example) be useful?
– In a shop, when you're talking about the
assistant. / At a disco, … / At a party, … /
At school, … / …

W 13, 4

---

i SPANISH IN THE USA

● There are about 30 million Spanish-speaking people – Hispanics – in the USA. About a quarter
of all the people in New York speak Spanish at home.
● Hispanics come from many countries, for example: Mexico, Puerto Rico or Cuba. They'll soon
be the biggest minority group in the USA – bigger than the African-Americans.

Find out:
● What are the names of other countries in the world where people speak Spanish?

C ## LISTENING 🎧 From San Juan to New York

Two high school students in New York, Jennifer Blake and Daniel Santiago, are talking. Listen.

EXERCISE 7 ■ Right or wrong?

1 Daniel lives in Puerto Rico.
2 Daniel's parents were poor.
3 Daniel's parents went to America because
they wanted to get more money.
4 Daniel's parents can only speak Spanish.
5 Daniel doesn't want to live in Puerto Rico.

**EXERCISE 8 ■■ Listen again. Make
notes about Daniel's parents:**

– home in Puerto Rico
– jobs in Puerto Rico
– first jobs in New York
– home in New York
– jobs in New York today

Tip: Listen to the cassette/CD again and check your answers.

STORY 🎧

What problems do single-parent families sometimes have?

I have my reasons

New Orleans is a big city on the Mississippi River in the south of the USA. It's the place where jazz began. Tourists like to visit the old part of the city, the French Quarter. Or they look at the beautiful old houses. But New Orleans has problems, too. There are lots of poor families – and many of them are black.

It was a Sunday afternoon in New Orleans. Two teenagers left the cinema together.
"Let's have a pizza now," said Paul DeVille.
"Sorry, I can't," said Wendy Dubois. "I still
5 haven't done my weekend homework."
"Well, maybe I could help you."
"I told you before. Mom doesn't like it when I bring people home."
"OK. Then come to my house. My parents are
10 away again for a few days."
"That's the problem. Who knows what might happen when we're alone! Hey, I'll miss my bus if I don't hurry. Bye! See you tomorrow."

When Wendy walked to the bus-stop, she
15 thought about her new boyfriend, about the day when they first saw each other at *Roger's* restaurant, and about how happy they were together. The only problem was that Paul's family was so different from her own.
20 Paul's parents were dentists. He always got enough money from them to buy things. It was different in Wendy's family. Her mom didn't always have a job, so there were often money
25 problems. It was good that Wendy worked at *Roger's* at weekends and in the holidays. She sometimes helped her mom out with a few dollars.

A car stopped next to her. It was Paul.
"Surprise, surprise! Do you like my new car? 30 It's an early Christmas present from my mom. Come on! Let's go to the lake. You can do your homework later."
They drove out to Lake Pontchartrain. It was good to be out of the city. Paul stopped the car 35 in a quiet car park next to the lake. He looked into Wendy's eyes and then he said, "It's very quiet here this afternoon. What do you think? Maybe we could have some fun?"
"No," said Wendy. "Let's go back to the city 40 now. You can take me to the bus station."
"Come on, Wendy. We've been together for two months now."
Wendy looked at him. Maybe it would be OK. No! No! No! 45
"I have my reasons," she said. "Let's go!"

Paul drove back to the city. They didn't speak to each other for a few miles. Then Paul said, "So what are your reasons?"

50 Wendy didn't answer.

"I thought you liked me," said Paul.

"Of course I like you," Wendy said angrily.

"OK! Don't take me to the bus station. Drive me home. I'll show you my reasons."

55 Half an hour later they arrived in Wendy's street, in a poor part of town.

"OK. Stop here. This is it. Number 2098. I think your nice car will be OK for a few minutes."

60 They went into the building. The lift was broken. They started to walk up five storeys.

"We should be happy the elevator is broken again," said Wendy. "The

65 smell there is even worse."

Two minutes later Wendy opened the door. In the living-room of the small apartment a young woman was asleep on the couch. Paul and

70 Wendy looked at each other.

"Wendy, I know you aren't rich," said Paul. "But that isn't important. You're important. Listen, I'll see you tomorrow. I don't want to wake your sister."

Wendy looked at him. 75

"That isn't my sister," she said. "She's out with my younger brother."

"What! You mean, that's …?" Paul said.

"Yes, that's my mom, my poor tired mom. She was 14 when I was born. And 16 when 80 my sister arrived. Now do you see why I have my reasons?"

TASK A ☐ Who?

1 Who went to the cinema with Paul?
2 Who gives Paul money to buy things?
3 Who has a new car?
4 Who suddenly wanted to go back to the city?
5 Who lives in a poor part of town?
6 Who was the young woman on the couch?

TASK B ■ Tell the story.

But it was her mom!
They drove to Wendy's apartment.
Wendy didn't want to stay in the car park.
It was very small.
Paul thought it was Wendy's sister.
➡ Wendy didn't want to go to Paul's house.
They drove to the lake in Paul's new car.
A young woman was asleep on the couch.

TASK C ■■ On the next day Paul sent Wendy a letter. What did he write?
Use the ideas in A *or* B and write the letter.

A understand your reasons – still want to be your boyfriend – we can wait –
meet your mom – Let's …

B don't understand your reasons – finish – want fun – families different – I …

W 14, 5-7

ACTIVE ENGLISH

ACTIONS Going to a party

What can Jack do to help?

JACK I'm looking forward to your party next Friday, Anna. Thanks again for the invitation.

ANNA You're welcome.

JACK What can I do to help?

ANNA Could you come at 6 o'clock and help me with the decorations?

EXERCISE 1 ■ What can I do to help?
Make dialogues.

YOU Thanks again for the invitation to your party next …

A PARTNER You're welcome.

YOU When should I be there?

A PARTNER At …

YOU What can I do to help?

A PARTNER Could you …?

be the DJ ▪ bring some CDs
look after the music/barbecue/…
help me with the decorations/…
help me to clean up after the party
make a salad / some sandwiches
dance with lots of my friends

How's Adam getting home after the party?

DIANA How are you getting home after Anna's party?

ADAM I don't know yet.

DIANA You can come with us if you like. My mother is picking me up at 11.30.

ADAM That would be great. Thanks.

EXERCISE 2 ■ Getting home: Make dialogues.

YOU How are you getting home after …?

A PARTNER I don't know yet.

YOU You can come with us if you like. … is picking me up at …

A PARTNER That would be great. Thanks.

…'s party ▪ the fair ▪ the football game
the cinema ▪ the concert ▪ the school
dance ▪ the computer show ▪ …

W 15, 8

ℹ GOING OUT IN THE USA

● There are often school and church dances or parties. Parents and teachers check that nobody drinks or smokes. Discos sell alcohol, so teenagers in the USA can't go to them.

● There are lots of rules for American teenagers. In some cities they can't even be "outside the home" without a parent from late evening till the morning. This is because of the teen curfew (= Ausgangssperre). "Outside the home" means on the streets, at the cinema or a football game – even in their own car! This helps to keep teenagers out of trouble.

● The police can stop teenagers they see in curfew time. Then they might give them a warning and send them home. Or the teenagers might have to pay $50 or more. Teenagers who often break the curfew might have to pay $1,000 – or go to jail for 90 days!

W 15, 9

What's Anna's present from Jack?

JACK Happy birthday, Anna! I like your earrings.

ANNA Thank you very much, Jack. They're new.
I got them from my mom today.

JACK Aren't you going to open your present?

ANNA Hey! *Monsters!* How did you know I like
Stacy Queen books? What a great present!
Thanks.

JACK You're welcome. You're a special friend.

EXERCISE 3 ■ Make dialogues about presents.

- Happy birthday, …
- Aren't you going to open your present?
- You're welcome. You're a special friend / my best friend / …

- Thank you very much.
- Hey! …! How did you know I like …? What a great present! Thanks.

EXERCISE 4 □ Make a dialogue about an invitation to a party.

Bedanke dich für die Einladung.

▼

Sage, dass es nichts zu danken gibt.

▼

Frage, wann du da sein sollst.

▼

Gib eine Zeit an.

▼

Sage, dass du dich auf die Party freust.

▼

Sage, dass du dich auch auf die Party freust.

Tip: Look at page 28.

EXERCISE 5 ■■ Make a dialogue about a party.

Bedanke dich für das Computerspiel. Sage, dass es ein tolles Geschenk ist.

▼

Sage, dass es nichts zu danken gibt. Sage, dass du dich auf die Party heute Abend freust. Biete deine Hilfe an.

▼

Frage, ob er/sie früher kommen und dir bei den Sandwiches helfen könnte.

▼

Sage, dass das kein Problem ist. Frage, ob du einige deiner CDs mitbringen sollst.

▼

Sage ja. Seine/Ihre CDs sind besser als deine.

W 15, 10

PRACTICE PAGES

STRUCTURES

EXERCISE 1 ☐ What are the missing words?

buy ▪ eat ▪ go ▪ read ▪ smoke ▪ watch

People like different things in different parts
of the USA. Here are some examples:
1 More people in the west … jogging.
2 People in the west … the most rock CDs.
3 More people in the west … books.
4 And more people in the north … apples!
5 Not many people in the north … MTV.
6 Very many people in the south …

✔ **REVISION**

Simple present form
Für Gewohnheiten, Zustände, Vorlieben
und Abneigungen, Berufe und Hobbys
Tip: Look at page 115, too.

EXERCISE 2 ■ Chinatown, Manhattan: Write the sentences.

1 The Chongs (live) in Chinatown, Manhattan.
2 Mr Chong (sell) coffee from a stall.
3 Mrs Chong (work) in a clothes shop.
4 Their children (go) to school in Canal Street.
5 The Chongs (like) New York. It isn't so different from their
   old home.
6 It even (look) like Hong Kong!

EXERCISE 3 ■ At an American airport

When you arrive at an American airport, an officer from *US Immigration*
usually wants to know what your plans are. Help these German tourists.
1 Wir verbringen eine Woche in Arizona.
   We're spending a week in Arizona.
2 Ich besuche meine Tante in Milwaukee.
3 Wir mieten ein Haus in Miami.
4 Ich treffe eine Freundin in New York.
5 Wir nehmen Route 66 von Chicago nach LA.
6 Ich verlasse den Flughafen nicht. Ich fliege
   in zwei Stunden nach San Diego.

✔ **REVISION**

Present progressive form
Hiermit sagst du, was gerade geschieht –
aber auch über Pläne und Vorhaben
kannst du mit dieser Form sprechen.
Tip: Look at page 115, too.

EXERCISE 4 ■■ Put in the right form – simple present
or present progressive. Tip: Look at page 115.

TV 4 *L.L.Bean* is a big store in Freeport, Maine, that (sell)
clothes and sports equipment. It never (close). Yes, it's
open 24 hours a day, 365 days a year. Every day people
(come) here from all over the world. Today I (talk) to
Jim Olsen. He usually (work) in the restaurant. Hi, Jim.

JIM Hi. I (help out) in the restaurant now, but next week I
(sell) clothes in "Wintersports". Everybody (buy) winter clothes now.

TV 4 Christmas (come) soon. You can have a break.

JIM You must be joking. People (love) shopping in the Christmas holiday.
It's our busiest time!

EXERCISE 5 ■■ **A week in New York: *each other* or *themselves*?**

Tina and Sal enjoyed … in New York. "Teenagers can look after …," they told their parents. "And we're friends, so we'll look after …, too." They stayed at a cheap bed and breakfast. Every morning they found their breakfast – cake! – outside their room and helped … to lots of it. They soon stopped talking to … about their untidy room. And after the week they liked … even more!

✔ **CHECKPOINT**

> ***themselves – each other***
> ***themselves*** = "sich" im Sinne von "**sich selbst**": Most people like to see themselves on TV.
> ***each other*** = "sich" im Sinne von "**einander**": Tim and Pat haven't seen each other for years.

WORDPOWER

WORDPOWER 1 ☐ Colours

The colours of this Indian badge – red, white, black, yellow – stand for all the people in the world.

Colours – what do you think of?

red – stop signs, …   **black** – coal, …
white – snow, …   **yellow** – sun, …

WORDPOWER 2 ■ One word is wrong.

1 immigrant, equipment, viewer, dentist
2 reason, tip, money, dollar
3 friendly, blond, tall, describe
4 eye, smell, arm, leg
5 dance, swim, sing, translate
6 church, police station, motel, lift

WORDPOWER 3 ■ Find another word

for: Tip: Look at pages 22–29.
1 with no home – homeless
2 with very little money – …
3 Native American
4 Spanish-speaking people in the USA
5 people who live in a country, but come from another country
6 interesting places for tourists

WORDPOWER 4 ■■ What is it?

Tip: All the words finish with *-ation(s)*.
1 Where some Indians live.
2 Something that asks you to come to a party.
3 Nice things in a room for a party.
4 Where you can stay or live.
5 Being unfair to somebody who's different.

WRITING

EXERCISE ■■ An officer's day

Tim Woods from *US Immigration* had a terrible day last Saturday. Write about it.

- last Saturday – terrible day – lots of travellers
- planes late – people tired and angry
- ask questions – all day
- drive – home – evening – lots of traffic
- drive too fast – police car – stop
- ask lots of questions
- arrive home – very late – family not there
- all at cinema – new film: "Life is fun"

Last Saturday Tim Woods had a terrible day, because …

PRACTICE PAGES

READING The woman on the bus

BEFORE YOU READ ■ When should you give your seat on a bus to another passenger?

Many Blacks still belong to the poorest parts of American society. But things were much worse for Blacks fifty years ago, especially in the south of the USA.

At that time Blacks and Whites were still kept separate in the southern states. For example, there were separate doors at the cinema for Whites and "Coloreds", separate queues in shops – and separate seats on buses ...

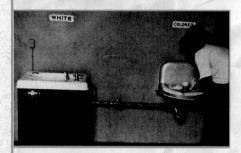

When Rosa Parks got on a city bus in Montgomery, Alabama, on December 1st, 1955, she didn't plan to start a protest movement. She was just tired after a long day at work. As usual she sat down on the "Black seats", behind the white passengers.

More and more people got on the bus. Soon the "White seats" were full, and a white man was standing. The bus driver said that Parks had to give the man her seat. She said "no". She was tired – and she was fed up. She didn't want to stand just because she was black. The driver called the police, and two police officers took Parks to jail.

Blacks in Montgomery were very angry about this. They picked a leader and organised a boycott of Montgomery's buses. For 381 days almost no Blacks travelled on the city buses. So the bus company lost a lot of money. And all over the country Blacks organised other protests. The Civil Rights movement in the USA was born.

The leader of the Montgomery bus boycott became famous across America. His name? – Martin Luther King, Jr.

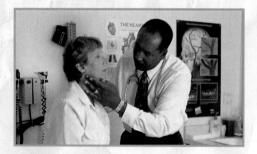

And what about Rosa Parks? She worked for the Civil Rights movement, started *The Rosa Parks Institute* for young people and an information service about the Civil Rights movement, *The Parks Legacy*. She wrote books, too. In *Dear Mrs. Parks* (1996) she writes:
"I am 83 years old and there is always more in life to learn. I started taking swimming lessons last year. I ask a lot of questions. You can drown yourself with problems if you don't ask questions."

Today the third Monday in January is Martin Luther King, Jr. Day in the USA. Many people think there should be a Rosa Parks Day, too.

Many African-Americans, like the ones in these photos, have become respected and successful members of American society – because of the woman on the bus.

Tip: You can find new words in the *Dictionary* (page 138).

EXERCISE 1 ☐ Basic reading: What's right?

1 Life *was/wasn't* better for Blacks fifty years ago.
2 Blacks organised protests *only in Montgomery / all over the USA*.
3 Parks *had / didn't have* a seat on the bus.
4 Parks' protest *helped / didn't really help* Blacks in the USA.

EXERCISE 2 ■ Reading for details: Answer the questions.

1 Where were Blacks kept separate?
2 When was the famous bus journey?
3 Who said that Parks had to stand?
4 Who was the leader of the boycott?
5 How old was Parks in 1955?
6 When's Martin Luther King, Jr. Day?

EXERCISE 3 ■ Language tasks   Tip: All the words are on page 32.

1 Find the opposites: a) richest; b) better; c) northern; d) empty; e) sit; f) won.
2 Find the words in the text for: a) Fahrer, Passagier, Anführer;
                               b) getrennt, berühmt, erfolgreich.

EXERCISE 4 ■■ Writing

Dear Mrs Parks is a book with letters from young people to Rosa Parks. Write a letter to
The Parks Legacy with questions you'd like to ask about this famous woman.
Begin with *Dear Sir or Madam,* … Finish with *Yours faithfully,* …

LISTENING 🎧 The Museum of the American Indian

You're going to hear part of a radio programme. Listen.

EXERCISE 1 ■ Which photo (A-D) comes first? Which photo comes next?

EXERCISE 2 ■ Listen again. Right or wrong?

1 The museum is near Battery Park.
2 The museum isn't free.
3 Laura Blackburn is visiting the museum.
4 Laura came to New York three years ago.
5 Laura only speaks English.
6 Laura is interested in Indian things.

EXERCISE 3 ■■ Read Dan's report. Listen again. What are the missing words?

The Museum of the American Indian is in …, near Battery Park. The museum is open
every day from 10 am to … Laura Blackburn works in the … there. She's a Delaware …
She has always lived in … She never wears Indian … but she wears her grandmother's …
She's … to be an Indian.

Tip: Listen to the cassette/CD again and check your answers.   Weitere Fragen: W 52-53

*SERIAL
Point of no return (2)

Tip: You can find new words in the *Dictionary* (page 138).

The story so far:

Dave Kelly from Chester, England, is looking for his ex-girlfriend Sharon Glenn in the USA. She moved to America with her new boyfriend Wayne. But then Wayne left Sharon. Dave is a guest on the famous breakfast TV show *Today*. He has a photo of Sharon and hopes that the viewers can help him to find her …

San Diego beach

The place was really full again this morning. Americans loved having breakfast in a restaurant. Sharon was sure some people got up extra early to
5 have time for breakfast here on their way to work. The men at table 3 were leaving. "*Adios*. Goodbye." You heard a lot of Spanish in California, especially here in San Diego, near the border
10 with Mexico.

Sharon saw that the customer on table 4 didn't have any coffee. *OK, OK. I can see you over there on table 4. You need some more coffee. Here I come*
15 *with the free refill. … He didn't even see me. He's too interested in the TV over there.*

She was tired, really tired. Well, at least she was near the ocean. She
20 could spend the afternoon on the beach. Work and beach, work and beach. Was that all she had now? She didn't really know anybody here. José, the owner of the
25 restaurant, was nice enough to her. He had given her the job six months ago. And then he had said, "Can I see your papers, please?" And she had given the answer she
30 had practised again and again.

"I don't have any papers. I live in a caravan near the beach. Last week somebody broke into it and stole all my money and papers. But I'll have new papers soon." As she cleared
35 table 5, she remembered José's answer. "I'm from Mexico, but I've been here long enough to know you aren't American. But you can have the job. I know what it's like to be an illegal
40 immigrant. But try to learn the language. Here in the States, you live in a *trailer* not a *caravan*. See you tomorrow – at 6 am."

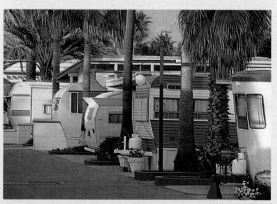

Trailers near the beach

45 A woman had just sat down at table 5.
"Coffee?"
"Yes, please."
"And what would you like to eat?"
"Ham and eggs, please."
50 "How would you like your eggs?"
"Sunny-side up, please."
"And what sort of toast – white or
whole wheat?"
"Whole wheat, please."
55 "OK. Five minutes."

She was getting used to the dialogues
now. And it was easy to do the
American accent. When she had first
come to the USA, she hadn't wanted
60 to change the way she spoke. But at
that time she had thought she'd soon
have a Green Card – a work permit.
That was when she and Wayne had
still been together …

65 The breakfast for table 5 was ready.
She carried the big plate over.
"Enjoy your breakfast. Let me know if
you want some more brown toast,"
said Sharon.

Eggs – sunny-side up

"Brown toast? That's what English 70
people say for 'whole wheat toast'.
Are you from England?"
"Me?" What could she say? She looked
out of the window and saw a big truck
in the car park: *Burtons of Toronto.* 75
Drivers from that company often came
into *José's.*
"No. I – er – come from the north,
from a small town near the Canadian
border. I must have heard the word 80
there."
"Really? I once worked on the
Canadian border. What town are
you from?"
"Er, Burton. Don't let your breakfast 85
get cold."

The woman started eating, but she looked at Sharon again and again. Another woman sat down at her table.

90
"Hi, Donna. How was New York?" she said.

"Hi, Teresa. It was great."

"Why aren't you in uniform today, Donna?"

95
"I don't start work again till tomorrow morning."

"Lucky you," said Teresa.

"Now let's see if we can get you some coffee," said Donna. "Where's the waitress? Oh, she's over there. Say, have you seen her here before?"

"Sure. She started when you were away. She's friendly, but she doesn't say much."

105
"Where's she from?"

"I don't know. But she lives in a trailer near the beach."

"I've just spoken to her. She sounds as if she doesn't come from here."

110
"Oh, Donna. You aren't on duty at *US Immigration* now."

"Yeah, I know. Sorry. I have to go now. I have to be at the bank in ten minutes. Bye now."

115
Donna got up and paid.

A Green Card

After she had left the restaurant, the waitress came over to Teresa.

"Sorry you had to wait. I didn't see you. What would you like?"

120
Teresa ordered her breakfast. Donna was right. The young woman sounded different.

Teresa looked at the TV screen. Katie, from the *Today* show, was talking to somebody. But who was it? Teresa didn't know the young man in the studio.

125
… If you have news about her, please phone NBC.

130
That photo! Who was it? Teresa knew she had seen the young woman before.

The waitress brought her meal over.

"Enjoy your meal. Is everything OK?"

135
"Er, yes, thanks."

The TV was too loud. Sharon walked over to it. *What? Dave? On the* Today *show? Here in America!* She ran into the kitchen. José was watching TV, too.

140

145

"Do you want to see him again?"
"No, I don't."
"Well, you have to decide," said José.
150 "We all make mistakes sometimes. It doesn't always mean that you can't go back to your old life."
"I can't go back. It was terrible what I did to Dave. And I'm not really sure
155 if I want to go back to my old life."
"But what about your poor family?"
She didn't answer.
"I don't want to lose you. You've worked really
160 hard. But look!"

She looked through the kitchen window. Teresa was talking excitedly to the people at the tables
165 next to her. She knew!

"Tomorrow morning – if not earlier – the cameras will be here," said José.
170 "I'm sorry, José. You've been so nice to me."

"Where will you go?"
"I don't know. Just away from here."
"I have an idea," said José.

Two hours later a big truck left the car 175 park. It was going to Toronto, Canada – 2,400 miles away. But would that be far enough? And wasn't it just stupid to run away?

(To be continued)

W 19, 19-22

UNIT THREE
Northern neighbours

The Canadian Rocky Mountains

Vancouver

The Canadians are the northern neighbours of the Americans. But many Americans don't know much about their neighbours in the north.

■ **Quiz: How much do you know about Canada and the Canadians? Look at these sentences. What's right?**
1 Most Canadians speak *French/English*.
2 Most Canadians live *in/outside* cities and towns.
3 Canadians use the Canadian *dollar/pound*.
4 Canadians have *warm/cold* winters.
5 Their country is *smaller/bigger* than the USA.
6 There are *fewer/more* Americans than Canadians.

The USA-Canada border – 8,890 kilometres long!

■ **Two different countries: Look at the photos and say how Canada is different from the USA.**

some Canadians – French

guns – not allowed in Canada

use kilometres – not miles

Canadian dollars

ℹ️ CANADA

● Canada (capital: Ottawa) is the second biggest country in the world. The USA is the third biggest. But Canada has only 30 million people (USA: 268 million). And most of them live in cities and towns in the south of the country.

● The first people in Canada were North American Indians and Inuit (Eskimos).

● Then people from France and Britain came to Canada. After a war between Britain and France, all Canada belonged to the British.

● Canada has been independent from Britain for over 100 years. But the Queen is still the queen of Canada, too. Her picture is on Canadian money and stamps.

● About 69% of Canadians speak English at home and 23% speak French. Most of the French-speaking people live in Quebec, one of Canada's ten provinces. About 8% of Canadians speak other languages at home: Chinese, Italian and German, for example.

● About 16% of the people who live in Canada are new immigrants (USA: 8%). Most immigrants today come from Asian countries.

What about Germany?

● How many people live in Germany (number 61 on the list of biggest countries)?

● Lots of Germans still go to live in Canada. Why do you think they leave Germany?

W 22, 1

* SONG 🎧 Miss Chatelaine

Just a kiss, just a kiss,
I have lived just for this.
I can't explain,
Why I've become Miss Chatelaine.

Just a smile, just a smile,
Hold me captive just a while.
I can't explain,
Why I've become Miss Chatelaine.

Every time your eyes meet mine,
Clouds of qualm burst into sunshine.

Miss Chatelaine is sung by k.d. lang. k.d. lang stands for Kathryn Dawn Lang. She comes from the Canadian province of Alberta. Her CDs have been big hits, and she has done a lot of work for animal rights and AIDS charities. You can find out more about her on her fan club's web site: www.kdlang.com. *Chatelaine* is the most popular Canadian women's magazine.

* CLASS PROJECT Pictures of Canada

Photos in tourist brochures about Canada show "typically Canadian" things. Here are some examples:

beavers, caribou, Indians, Inuit, maple syrup, Montreal, moose, "Mounties", national parks, Niagara Falls, Ottawa, polar bears, Quebec City, rafting, Rocky Mountains, salmon, snow, Toronto, totem poles, trains, trees, Vancouver, whales

Tip: You can find new words in the *Dictionary* (page 138).

Make a class poster, "Pictures of Canada – what the tourists come to see".

MOOSE

Moose are big, brown animals. They're very shy. Don't go too near them. There are moose in the USA, too.

A Toronto, with almost five million people, is the largest city in Canada.

Hi from Toronto!

"Hi! My name is Anne Watson and I've lived in Toronto for 14 years. I was a baby when my parents arrived here from Kingston, Jamaica. They have a restaurant on Baldwin Street. This is one of the streets where the Kensington Market takes place every day. If you want to see
5 how many different groups live in this city, just come to the market!

Toronto is a really exciting place, with the famous CN Tower and skyscrapers. There are lots of film studios here. And American film companies often come here when their films really take place in New York. They've done this for years. Downtown Toronto looks
10 like New York, but making films here is easier and cheaper.

People always ask about the long, cold winters here, but they aren't really a problem. We have fantastic malls, where you can spend all day. I love ice-skating in front of City Hall, skiing in the zoo and watching hockey – that's ice hockey here, of course. I've been a
15 Toronto Maple Leafs fan since my tenth birthday, when I saw my first game. And don't forget. We have long, hot summers in Toronto, too."

Anne Watson

Fifty years ago Toronto was like a British city with an American "flavour". Eighty per cent of the people came from Britain or Ireland. It was called "Toronto the Good", because most people had a quiet life and followed the rules. For example, department stores covered their windows on Sundays so people couldn't go window-shopping. All cinemas were closed on Sunday, too. But things are different now.

Toronto – with the famous CN Tower

Kensington Market

Now Toronto is a city with lots of different "flavours". Immigrants from all over the world have come to the city. Toronto's Chinatown is one of the largest in North America. Italians are now the largest European group. Many of them live in Little Italy. And there are over 240,000 Blacks, from Jamaica and other parts of the Caribbean. The city is very popular with new Canadians. Today about 30% of all immigrants come to Toronto and the city has grown. The place has become busy and exciting, but it's still the safest city in North America.

EXERCISE 1 ■ Which information about Toronto is right?

1 People often call Toronto "*Hollywood/Denver* of the North".
2 In winter people go *skiing/ice-skating* in front of City Hall.
3 The Maple Leafs are Toronto's *ice hockey/baseball* team.
4 Many years ago there *was/wasn't* a lot to do in Toronto on Sundays.
5 Modern Toronto has *few/many* "flavours".
6 *Most/Some* immigrants who come to Canada live in Toronto.

EXERCISE 2 ■ Tips for Toronto

1 Why should you go to Baldwin Street?
2 Where can you get a good view of Toronto?
3 It's cold. You're in Toronto. Where can you spend the day?
4 Where in Toronto can you see animals and ski?
5 Somebody in Toronto has invited you to a hockey game.
  Of course, you don't ask where the field is. Why not?
6 You're going to Toronto in summer. What clothes do you need?

EXERCISE 3 ■■ What do you think of Toronto?

Make notes about Toronto. For example: exciting place, skyscrapers, …
Then say if you'd like to live in the city. Why / Why not?   W 23, 2; W 24, 3

B **LISTENING 🎧 Hyder and Stewart: good neighbours**

Listen to this interview from the USA-Canada border.

EXERCISE 4 ■ What's right?

1 Hyder is in the *USA/~~Canada~~*.
2 Stewart *is/~~isn't~~* bigger than Hyder.
3 *~~Hyder~~/Stewart* is better for shopping.
4 Children *can/~~can't~~* go to school in Hyder.
5 You *can/~~can't~~* use Canadian money in Hyder.
6 Tourists *sometimes/~~never~~* come to Hyder.
7 There *are/~~aren't~~* bears in this part of Alaska.

Welcome to Hyder

EXERCISE 5 ■■ Listen again. What could somebody from Stewart say about Hyder?

Stewart and Hyder are good neighbours.
People in Hyder need us because …
They use …
Their children …

Tip: Listen to the cassette/CD again and check your answers.

STORY 🎧

What people say is often different from what they think. Why?

Just be yourself

Canada and the USA: each country has its own picture of the other. Some Canadians think all Americans are noisy and boastful. And some Americans think all Canadians are quiet people who always say sorry.

March 15th, Toronto Airport, 10.00 am. "So this is Canada. Toronto Airport looks really nice. Not as nice as the airport in Phoenix," he thought, "but I won't tell the
5 Mace family that."
It was Chuck Henley's first visit to Canada. He quickly looked at the photo of his stepfather's relatives again. Ah, that looked like Simon and his mother
10 over there.
"Hi, you must be Chuck," said the woman. "Welcome to Canada, Chuck."
"Hallo, Mrs Mace. Hi, Simon. It's great to be here. I've always wanted to see
15 Canada," said Chuck. But he thought: *My mom thought I should come here. I really wanted to spend the week in Florida.*
"Of course. Canada is so special," said Simon. But he thought: *It's so cold. I'd*
20 *rather be in a warm place like Florida.*
"Give me one of your bags. And let's go home. Dad is making a fantastic Canadian breakfast: famous Canadian bacon, eggs, pancakes and – maple syrup!" *(I'd rather*
25 *have those American "Chocpops" we bought yesterday.)*
"That sounds great," said Chuck. *(We have bacon, pancakes and maple syrup in the USA, too.)*

On the trip from the airport to the Maces' home, 30 Simon told Chuck all about the famous CN Tower, the tallest building in the world. Chuck found out, too, that Canada had the biggest mall in the world – in Edmonton, Alberta – and the longest street in the world. 35
"Very interesting," said Chuck. *(Is somebody paying this guy to give me all this boring information?)* "And the weather here in March is much better than I thought. It's almost as warm as in Phoenix." *(... in December!)* 40
"Yeah, we have weather in Canada, too," said Simon.
"What do you mean?" asked Chuck.
"Well, the weather on your stupid American TV stations seems to stop at the border!" said Simon. 45 *(Was that too tough? It was very unfriendly.)*
"I'm sorry about that," said Chuck. *(But it isn't my fault if Canada isn't on American weather maps.)*
"We get too many American TV stations here," 50 said Simon. "The Canadian ones are so much better." *(A lie. They're often so boring.)* "Some are in French, too." *(But I never watch them.)*
"In French? That's interesting," Chuck said. *(Boring.)* Do you watch the French stations, 55 Simon?"
"Often." *(Another lie.)*
"Do you understand them?"
"Of course." *(Enough lies! French is my worst subject at school.)* 60

The Maces' home, 11.30 am.
After breakfast Chuck asked if he could phone his parents. While Chuck was phoning, Simon's parents spoke to him. "Chuck is very
65 nice – and so polite," said Mr Mace.
"And so boring," said Simon.
"Please stop being *Mr Proud Canadian*," said his mother.
"Yes, just be yourself," added Mr Mace.
70 Upstairs Chuck was phoning his mum. He told her how difficult it was to stay polite when Simon was boastful.
"You're the guest, but don't try to be *Mr Nice Guy USA* all the time," she said. "Be polite,
75 but be yourself."
After that things got much better between the boys. They talked a lot and went to interesting places in the city. They became friends.

A week later it was time for Chuck to go home to Phoenix. Mr Mace and Simon took 80 him to the airport.
"We've had a great week together," said Simon. "Even if we didn't agree on so many things."
"Yeah," said Chuck. "But that's OK. And 85 Toronto isn't a bad place." *(It's fantastic!)*
"You know," said Simon. "If I have time, I might visit you in Phoenix." *(I can't wait.)*

TASK A ☐ **Find ...**

1 a warm place.
2 famous Canadian breakfast food.
3 the tallest building in the world.
4 where weather "stops" on American TV.
5 the language Simon learns at school.
6 where Chuck and Simon had breakfast.
7 what Simon's mum called him.
8 what Chuck's mum called him.

TASK B ■ **Who thought this?**

1 "I think Chuck should go to Canada for a week."
2 "I'll drive to the airport with Simon."
3 "I'll stay at home and make breakfast."
4 "These Canadians are boastful."
5 "I'm going to show him how great Canada is."
6 "Why's he telling me all these things about Canada?"
7 "I think American TV is much better than Canadian TV."
8 "He's OK really. I'm sorry he's going back to Phoenix."

TASK C ■■ **Chuck and Simon were downtown together. Write the dialogue.**

I know. You told me yesterday – three times!
Hey, they have American ice-cream – the best in the world!
Sorry. Let's have an ice-cream with maple syrup. The place isn't far from here.
And you Americans swim in cola. – Here it is.
This is the longest street in the world.
I think you Canadians *drink* maple syrup.

SIMON This is the longest street in the world.
CHUCK ...

W 25, 4-6

ACTIVE ENGLISH

Victoria, Canada, looks very British.

ACTIONS Being polite

Are Anna and John from the same city?

JOHN   You're new here, aren't you?

ANNA   Yes, I am. I'm Anna. Pleased to meet you.

JOHN   Hi, Anna. I'm John.

ANNA   Hi. Are you from here, John?

JOHN   No, I'm not. I'm from Toronto.

ANNA   Oh. I'm from Victoria.

EXERCISE 1 ■ Find out – politely – about your partner. Make dialogues.

YOU   You're new here, aren't you?

A PARTNER   Yes, I am. I'm …
Pleased to meet you.

YOU   Hi, … I'm …

A PARTNER   Hi. Are you from here, …?

YOU   No, I'm not. I'm from …

A PARTNER   Oh. I'm from …

YOU		A PARTNER	
Peter Brownsville	Jane Ottawa	Laura New York	Mike Vancouver
Shelly Toronto	Bobby Chicago	Adam Flagstaff	Tim Los Angeles

W 26, 7

Does James want a drink?

JAMES   I'd like a hamburger, please.

ASSISTANT   OK. Would you like anything else?

JAMES   Yes, I would. Large fries, please.

ASSISTANT   Thank you. Is that everything?

JAMES   Yes, it is. Thank you.

EXERCISE 2 ■ At a fast food place: Make dialogues.

YOU   I'd like …, please.

A PARTNER   Would you like anything else?

YOU   Yes, I would. …, please.

A PARTNER   Thank you. Is that everything?

YOU   Yes, it is. Thank you.

A hamburger	Small fries
A cheeseburger	Large fries
An Egg McQueen	A cola
A chickenburger	A salad
A veggieburger	An ice-cream

W 26, 8-9

ℹ POLITE PHRASES

● Saying *please* and *thank you* is very important in English-speaking countries.

● Don't ask too many direct questions. Using phrases like *isn't it?, aren't you?, don't you?* (= nicht wahr?, oder?) can make things less direct. And try not to just answer *Yes* or *No*. It doesn't sound polite. Say *Yes, it is, No, it isn't, Yes, I do,* for example.

● If you need help or information, say *Excuse me* (not *Hallo!*). Then start your question with *Could you tell me …?* or *Do you know…?*

● You should be polite in shops, too. Always say *please* and *thank you*. And don't forget: in Britain and North America people always queue.

● And if you still do something wrong, always say *Sorry!*

How does Amy want to travel?

AMY   Excuse me. Could you tell me the time, please?

WOMAN   It's 7 o'clock.

AMY   Thank you. And do you know where the station is?

WOMAN   It isn't far. One more block.

AMY   Thank you very much. You've been very helpful.

WOMAN   You're welcome.

Is Amy travelling alone?

AMY   Could you do me a favour and take my photo?

MAN   Sure. Say "cheese".

AMY   Thank you very much.

MAN   You're welcome.

EXERCISE 3 ■   Ask for help.

- Excuse me.
- Do you know what the time is / where the … is / …?
- Could you do me a favour and help me with this bag / open the door for me / wait outside with my dog / …, please?
- Thank you very much.

- Yes. / Sure. / Yes, can I help you?
- It's … / It's in … Street. / … blocks from here. / …
- You're welcome.

W 26, 9

EXERCISE 4 ☐   Meeting somebody at a party: Make a dialogue.

| Frage, ob er/sie vielleicht neu hier ist. |
▼
| Bejahe dies. Sage, wie du heißt. |
▼
| Sage, wie du heißt. Sage, du freust dich, ihn/sie kennen zu lernen. |
▼
| Frage, ob er/sie von hier ist. |
▼
| Verneine dies. Sage, du bist aus … |
▼
| Sage, du bist aus … |

Tip: Look at page 44.

EXERCISE 5 ■■   Problems at a station: Make a dialogue.

| Bitte um Hilfe. |
▼
| Frage, ob er/sie aus Deutschland kommt. |
▼
| Sage ja. Du kommst aus Hamm. Du verstehst den Fahrplan nicht. Wann fährt der Bus ab? |
▼
| Sage, dass er um 10.20 Uhr abfährt. Frage, ob er/sie zum Flughafen will. |
▼
| Sage ja. Frage (höflich), ob der Bus billiger ist als der Zug. |
▼
| Sage ja. Die Fahrkarte kostet $10. |
▼
| Bedanke dich für die Hilfe. |
▼
| Sage „Bitte schön". |

PRACTICE PAGES

STRUCTURES

EXERCISE 1 □ A trip to the mountains

| bought ▪ camped ▪ enjoyed ▪ met ▪ saw ▪ went |

Banff National Park, Canada

1 I … to Banff National Park last July.
2 I … my visit a lot.
3 I … lots of animals.

4 I … near a lake.
5 I … some nice Canadians.
6 Here's a postcard I … on my trip.

EXERCISE 2 ■ *For* or *since*?

1 Tourists have spent holidays in this hotel *for*/*since* 1929.
2 The CN Tower has been here *for*/*since* many years.
3 Thousands of people have visited this museum *for*/*since* 1914.
4 "Caribana" has taken place every year *for*/*since* 1966.
5 The Skydome has been open *for*/*since* 1989.
6 People have visited the Canadian National Exhibition every summer *for*/*since* over 100 years.

> ✔ **REVISION**
>
> **for, since** = seit
> **for** = Zeitdauer (z. B. seit zwei Tagen)
> I've been in Toronto for two days.
> **since** = Zeitpunkt (z. B. seit Dienstag)
> Jim has been here since Tuesday.

EXERCISE 3 ■ Traffic problems in downtown Toronto: What are the drivers saying?

1 "I (be) here for 20 minutes." – "I *'ve been* here for 20 minutes."
2 "I (live) in Toronto since 1996. This is the worst traffic I've seen."
3 "Oh no! I (arrive) late at the office every day for a week."
4 "I (try) to phone my boss five times since 8 o'clock."
5 "I (listen) to all the traffic reports for the last half hour. There's no news. What's happening?"
6 "Stay cool, you guys! I'm from New York. I (drive) in traffic like this for years!"

EXERCISE 4 ■■ A tourist bus has just arrived: *Simple past* or *present perfect*?

1 "Welcome everybody! You (arrive) at Fort Louisbourg.
2 First the history: This place (belong) to the French till 1758.
3 They (want) to protect Quebec from the British.
4 But the British (attack) and Louisbourg (become) theirs.
5 OK, enough history. Who (not have) lunch yet?
6 I'll wait outside the restaurant. I (have) my lunch."

Fort Louisbourg – a living museum

EXERCISE 5 ■■ **Problems at the cinema: What are the right forms of the verbs?**

Tip: One form is simple past and one form is past progressive in each sentence.

1 It (rain) when Kim and Sal (leave) home to go to the cinema.
2 While the girls (wait) in the queue for tickets, they (meet) Martin, a friend from school.
3 Half an hour later, while the film stars (fight) monsters from Mars, the film suddenly (stop).
4 But that wasn't a problem for Kim. When it (happen), she (sleep).
5 And Sal? When the film (break), she (talk) to Martin!

 **CHECKPOINT**

> **Die Verlaufsform der Vergangenheit (*past progressive*-Form) zeigt an, was zu einem bestimmten Zeitpunkt gerade im Gange war.**
> The children were watching a very exciting programme when their parents came home.
> It started to rain while Pam was playing football.

WORDPOWER

WORDPOWER 1 □ **What's right?**

1 You can't bring *guns/guys* into Canada.
2 *Malls/Miles* in Canada are warm in winter.
3 Today Canada is *independent/immigrant*.
4 It has a long *border/borrow* with the USA.
5 *Hockey/History* is a very popular sport.
6 Canadians are usually *police/polite*.
7 They're often *pound/proud* of their country.
8 There's a *queen/queue* on their stamps.

WORDPOWER 2 ■ **One word is wrong.**

1 pound, money, cent, dollar
2 ice-skating, swimming, skiing, exciting
3 bacon, flavour, pancakes, maple syrup
4 Italian, Canadian, Jamaica, Chinese
5 musician, favour, relative, waiter
6 boastful, unfriendly, helpful, noisy

WORDPOWER 3 ■■ **What are the words?**

> at (2x) ▪ in (2x) ▪ into ▪ for ▪ from
> off ▪ to (2x) ▪ with (2x)

Uwe arrived … the airport … Toronto. He got … the plane … Germany and waited … his bags … the other people. The woman next … him had a bag … her. Suddenly a small dog came near her bag. The woman shouted … the dog. An officer came and spoke … her. "My dog is only doing his job," he said. "Open the bag, please." … the bag there was a big sausage – but you can't bring food … Canada!

WRITING

EXERCISE ■■ **An e-mail from Canada**

Write an e-mail from the Trans-Canada Highway to a friend in Texas. These notes will help you:

- Hi …, – have – great time – Canada
- yesterday – fly – Toronto to Calgary
- travel part of – Trans-Canada Highway
- one of – longest roads – in world – 7,699 km
- drive – Banff National Park – see – bears
- stop – café – Kamloops – have – great fries
- tomorrow – arrive – Vancouver – on ocean
- stay – hotel – look forward to – Chinatown

PRACTICE PAGES

READING The frozen north

BEFORE YOU READ ■ What do people usually tell pen-friends in their first letter?

Iqaluit
Nunavut
Canada

Hi,

Would somebody in your school like to be my pen-friend? My name is Ella and I'm 16 years old. I'm an Inuit, one of the "first Canadians". We prefer to say "Inuit" and not "Eskimo". I live in Iqaluit, the biggest town (4,500 people!) in Nunavut, in the north of Canada. There's me, my two brothers, my parents and my mother's father.

Perhaps you think Inuit live in igloos? Well, think again! We live in a wooden house on stilts. That's because the ground is frozen most of the year. It's very cold here. But we have central heating in the house. We have a TV and a video-recorder, too.

Sometimes I go ice-skating. I go fishing on a lake, too. I sometimes take my two brothers with me. They're younger than me. In summer we travel by boat. In winter we use a snowmobile.

I speak English and I speak the Inuit language. There's a school here in Iqaluit. My favourite subject is computers. And I love playing the guitar. There's a shop here, too, so we can buy fruit and vegetables. They're expensive because they've come all the way from the south of Canada or the USA.

My mother makes clothes. My father sometimes works as a tourist guide and sometimes he hunts. It's good that he has the job as a guide because he gets some money. Once lots of people here hunted seals and then sold the furs, but people don't want furs now.

I don't want to stay in the village all my life. I'd like to go to college in a big city like Toronto. And then I'd like to get a job there. My parents and my grandfather aren't so sure about this. They think I'll forget the Inuit life. But I've already decided to leave.

Are you going to write back to me?

Ella

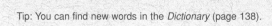

Tip: You can find new words in the *Dictionary* (page 138).

EXERCISE 1 ☐ **Basic reading: Right or wrong?**

1 Ella is looking for a pen-friend.
2 Ella lives in an igloo.
3 Ella is her parents' only child.
4 Ella goes to school.
5 Ella's parents work in a city.
6 Ella wants to leave Iqaluit later.

EXERCISE 2 ■ **Reading for details: Answer the questions.**

1 What's another word for "Inuit"?
2 How many brothers does Ella have?
3 What modern things are in the houses?
4 How does Ella travel in winter?
5 Why are fruit and vegetables expensive?
6 How does Ella's father get money?

EXERCISE 3 ■ **Language tasks**   Tip: All the words are on page 48.

1 Find: a) 10 words for people; b) 5 words and phrases for actions outside the house;
   c) 4 words for buildings.
2 Find the words: a) when the ground is very hard because it's cold; b) food that's good for you;
   c) an animal; d) something people make clothes from.

EXERCISE 4 ■■ **Write an answer to Ella's letter.**

Tell her about yourself. Say what you think about her life and her plans for the future.

LISTENING 🎧 Ben's cassette

You're going to hear Ben Burton, a Canadian teenager. He's talking about himself. Listen.

EXERCISE 1 ■ **These sentences are wrong. What's right?**

1 Ben has a sister. That's wrong. He …
2 Ben goes to school by tram.
3 Ben lives in a small flat.
4 Ben goes ice-skating with his friends at weekends.
5 Ben learned French from his father.
6 Ben would like a job as a teacher.
7 Ben's favourite subject at school is French.

Ottawa – the capital of Canada

EXERCISE 2 ■■ **Listen again. Find out why Ben …**

1 leaves the house with his mum every day.
2 doesn't see his neighbours every day.
3 can speak French.
4 sometimes goes to Ottawa.
5 has been in two musicals at school.
6 doesn't like maths lessons.

Tip: Listen to the cassette/CD again and check your answers.

Ice-skating in Ottawa

Weitere Fragen: W 53

*SERIAL

Point of no return (3)

Tip: You can find new words in the *Dictionary* (page 138).

The story so far:

Sharon Glenn is working as a waitress in a restaurant in San Diego. When she sees her ex-boyfriend Dave Kelly with her photo on TV, she leaves the restaurant in a truck that's going to Canada …

"So why do you want to go to Canada?"
Sharon looked at Maggie O'Neill, the Canadian trucker who was taking
5   her to Toronto. But Sharon didn't want to talk.
"José told me to look after you, Sharon. And I'm going to do that. But tell me something about yourself.
10   I mean, we're going to be together for the next five days. That's your bed behind you."
Sharon laughed. "I'm sorry," she said. "It's just that I'm so worried. OK, I'll
15   start at the beginning."
And so Sharon told her story, about the two men in her life, Dave and Wayne.

Crossing America by truck

"What's this Dave like? Is he good-looking?"
"Well, *I* think he is. But that isn't the   20
most important thing. He has a great sense of humour, he's interested in animals and water sports, like me, and we like the same music. We often go – er, went – to the disco together."   25
"How long have you known him?"
"All my life. We lived in the same street. We were children together, went to school together, played together.
Then, you know how   30
it is. When you're about twelve, boys in your class seem so silly, so young, just interested in sport.   35
I started to spend more time with my best friend, Claire. I saw Dave at school every day, of course,   40
but he was just one of the silly boys in my class. Most girls sat together and most boys sat   45
together. Two different worlds."

"And what changed everything?" asked Maggie.

"The big party on our last day at school. I looked at Dave during the evening and suddenly he looked different, older. I went over to him and we just started again where we had stopped five years earlier. We danced and talked all evening. Later we kissed."

"And that was a very special kiss," said Maggie.

"Oh yes," said Sharon and was quiet.

Maggie didn't ask her any more questions for the next few miles. Sharon was looking out of the truck window at the desert around her and thinking about the emptiness in her life.

"Maggie! What's that? A castle in the desert?"

"Yes," said Maggie. "We're in Nevada now, where dreams can come true."

"What do you mean?" asked Sharon.

"That castle isn't a real castle, of course. It's a casino. Nevada is one of the few places in the USA where there are casinos. Wait till you see Las Vegas."

A casino in Las Vegas

Maggie was right. Las Vegas, this city in the middle of the desert, was like no other city Sharon had seen. Everything was unreal: the "Statue of Liberty", the "Empire State Building", the "Eiffel Tower", the pyramid …

Then Maggie wanted to hear about Wayne.

"He was a bit like Las Vegas," said Sharon, " – exciting, but unreal. And he was American!"

"And do you like the States?"

"Yes, I do. But I miss England, too – English food, English TV, even English weather."

"And Dave? Do you miss him?"

Sharon looked at her. "I don't know."

A week later in another truck …

95 "So why do you want to go to Toronto, Dave?"

Dave looked at the big Canadian trucker as he drove his truck onto the interstate, 2,400 miles of superhighway
100 from Mexico to the Canadian border at Detroit.

"I'm looking for a girl."

"Aren't there girls in England?"

"It's a long story."

105 "It's a long trip."

"Sorry, Pete," said Dave. "OK. I came to José's restaurant with a TV team after one of his customers had phoned NBC. She had seen a photo of my girlfriend
110 Sharon on the *Today* programme. José told me about the Canadian truck that was taking Sharon to Toronto. But he didn't tell me till he thought Sharon was
115 far enough from San Diego."

"Why do you think he told you?"

"He said he liked me. He said he hated to see me sitting
120 outside the restaurant and waiting for a girl who would never come. He told me because he had given Sharon a chance, and he wanted to give me a chance, too. Everything started last 125 spring. I was away from Chester at Midland College in Birmingham. Sharon met Wayne at the sports centre. Wayne's parents are rich. They have a very big truck company in San Diego." 130

"Is his name McAllister?"

"Yes, it is. How do you know?"

"*McAllister Trucking* is the biggest truck company in the west. What was McAllister Junior doing in Chester?" 135

"Having a long holiday. His sister lives in Chester. She was a TV producer in LA. Now she's with *Granada Television* in Manchester."

Dave's and Sharon's trip across America

140 "So Sharon liked all the glamour?"
"I don't know," said Dave. "I just don't know."
"Go on," said Pete.
145 "My course had finished and I came home to Chester – and to my first job, in a big garage. I phoned Sharon and asked 150 her if we could go to the cinema. I thought she'd say "no". The last four weekends that I had been back in Chester she had 155 always been busy. So I was surprised when she said she'd meet me. But she didn't want to see a film, she said she just wanted to talk."
"And she told you the news?"
160 "Yeah. She told me she loved Wayne and that she was going to California with him after her course. His parents had already said she could work in the offices of their truck company 165 and they would organise her work permit, her Green Card. She went to California last August."

The "castle" in the desert in Nevada

"And you didn't try to stop her?"
"How? Sharon is a free person."
"You can talk, can't you? You have 170 to sell yourself in this world, man."

Dave was quiet for a long time. He didn't even mention the "castle" in the desert as they drove into Nevada.

Four days later, as they were leaving 175 Detroit, Pete said, "Only another mile now, and then we'll be in good old Canada. Where's your passport?"
Dave looked in his bag. Then he saw the sign: *Welcome to* 180 *Canada*.

What was he doing? Would he find Sharon? And where would he start looking? Canada was the second biggest country in 185 the world. And if he found her, how could he persuade her to come home with him?

(To be continued)

Detroit

W 30, 16-19

53

UNIT FOUR

Young in the UK

Teenagers in Britain and Germany – they often like the
same music, go to the same films and do the same things.
But there are some differences, of course.

■ Quiz: Teenagers in Britain

1 What sports are popular? – Cricket, …
2 What snacks are popular? – Hamburgers, …
3 What magazines are popular? – Fashion magazines, …
4 What evening activities are popular? – Going to
   discos, …
5 What music is popular? – Hip hop, …

Now answer the same questions about teenagers in Germany.

■ Many young people in the UK help others and try to improve things in the world. Look at the photos. Put the phrases and photos together.

1 Helping old people
2 Working on projects for the environment

3 Going to demonstrations
4 Collecting money for charity

What do young people in Germany do to help?

■ Word pool: Teenagers

boyfriends · cafés · CDs · clothes · clubs · computer games · concerts · discos · drugs
fashion · friends · getting a job · girlfriends · magazines · make-up · money · parties
problems with parents · snacks · tests · the cinema · videos

Tip: You can find new words in the *Dictionary* (page 138).

Find words that tell you …
– where teenagers like to go: cafés, …
– what they buy: CDs, …
– what they worry about: boyfriends, …

And you?
I love buying CDs / …
I hate doing homework / …
I'm interested in music/…
I worry / don't worry about tests/…

W 33, 1

ℹ TEENAGERS' RIGHTS

● When you're 13, you can have a part-time job. A lot of young people deliver newspapers.
● When you're 16, you can leave school. You can have a job, ride a moped and buy cigarettes and lottery tickets. And you can get married – if your parents say yes.
● When you're 17, you can ride a motor bike and drive a car.
● When you're 18, you can have a credit card and vote. You can go to all films at the cinema, and you can drink alcohol in a pub.

And you?
● When can you do these things in Germany?
● What do you think is the right age for each of these things? Why?

* SONG 🎧 I want to be free

I'm bored.
I don't want to go to school.
I don't want to be nobody's fool.
I want to be me. I want to be me.
I don't want to be sweet and neat.
I don't want someone living my life for me,
I want to be free.

I'm going to turn this world – inside out,
I'm going to turn suburbia – upside down.
I'm going to walk the streets – scream and shout,
I'm going to crawl through the alley-ways – be very loud.

* CLASS PROJECT Are these things important for you?

This is what British teenagers answered in a survey:

Buying your own home	59 %
Having your own company	48 %
Having children	46 %
Being a millionaire when you're 35	43 %
Playing sport for your country	21 %
Being famous	18 %

For how many people in your class are these things important? Make a survey.
Do people in your class and young people in Britain think that the same things are important?

Whatever you do, do something for Red Nose Day

"It's Red Nose Day <u>soon</u>. Collect money for <u>charity</u> and have fun at the same time. <u>Whatever</u> you do, do something!" That's a message you often hear on radio and TV in Britain before Red Nose Day.

Red Nose Day comes every two years in spring. On that day you see
5 red noses everywhere – on the street, in shops, at work, in schools and on TV. People wear them and they even buy red noses for their cars. There are Red Nose T-shirts and there's a Red Nose single that's usually very popular. Most of the money for these things goes to charity.

On Red Nose Day and in the weeks before the day, thousands of
10 people, young and old, are busy. They sell cakes or organise discos, fashion shows and sponsored walks, for example. One way of getting money is to look for sponsors who will pay you to do crazy things. Here are some examples for Red Nose Day activities from a school notice-board:

FIND SPONSORS WHO WILL PAY YOU TO
- Say nothing all day.
- Wear silly clothes.
- Wear funny make-up.

SPONSOR A TEACHER TO WEAR SPORTS CLOTHES.

Teachers must say "Mr" and "Miss" to students on Red Nose Day. They pay £1 for every mistake.

Pay £1 and come to school in jeans.

15 On Red Nose Day there's a special TV programme. It's six hours long, with lots of stars. They do the show for nothing. They ask viewers to phone the programme and give money. People in Britain collected £27 million, over £3 million from schools, on the last Red Nose Day. All the money goes to charity – in Britain and other countries.
20 So remember: Whatever you do, do something.

EXERCISE 1 ☐ What should or shouldn't you do?

TIPS FOR RED NOSE DAY
- Find a way of getting money.
- Don't do dangerous things.
- Find as many sponsors as you can.
- Collect as much money as you can.
- Don't forget to wear a red nose.
- And have fun!

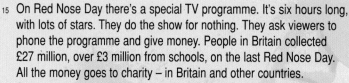

1 You should find a way of getting money.
2 You shouldn't …

EXERCISE 2 ■ Find the words.
1 A small CD. – A …
2 Where people can see modern clothes.
3 Somebody who pays you to do crazy things.
4 Something on a wall where you can get information.
5 Somebody who watches TV.

EXERCISE 3 ■■ What could you do?
Make a list of things you could do to collect money for charity and have fun. Use all the ideas in the text, then find your own ideas.

W 34, 2-3

B

Whatever you do, do something for the environment

Young people often take part in demonstrations and protests. In 1997 work was starting on a new road in the south-west of England. "Swampy" (Daniel Hooper, 23) and his friends believed that it would destroy the local environment. They decided to protest. They made tunnels under the ground and lived in them so that work on the new road couldn't start. Nobody could get them out – and Swampy became famous.

SWAMPY'S PROTEST

LAST NIGHT a happy Swampy came out from the underground tunnel that has been his home for a week. First he phoned his mother to tell her he was OK. "We weren't cold," he said. "And we had lots to eat. But it's time to finish the protest now because it's safer for everybody."

Thank you!

You often hear that young people only think of themselves. So let's say thank you to this young man and his friends who, in one week, have shown the country what's happening to our environment.

A successful protest

Was it worth it? "Well," said Swampy, and looked at all the reporters from the serious and the popular newspapers, "at least everybody knows about the problem now."

EXERCISE 4 ☐ Right or wrong?
1 Swampy wasn't really the man's name.
2 Swampy made the tunnels alone.
3 Swampy stayed in the tunnel for a week.
4 The police got Swampy out of his tunnel.
5 This reporter is against Swampy.

EXERCISE 5 ■ Find the words.
1 Swampy became … because of his protest.
2 Swampy felt … after the week.
3 They weren't … in the tunnels.
4 Swampy finished the protest because it was …
5 Swampy thought his protest was …

EXERCISE 6 ■■ Write a report for a newspaper that's against Swampy's protest.
last night – Swampy – underground tunnel – look terrible – not very clean – finish protest – dangerous – lots of police – very expensive – not worth it – workers will build road

W 35, 4-5

C

LISTENING 🎧 At an international newspaper shop

Here are some tourists at an international newspaper shop in Germany. Listen.

EXERCISE 7 ■ Which newspapers were bought? Which photo (A-C) is right?

EXERCISE 8 ■■ Listen again. Find two serious and two popular newspapers.

Tip: Listen to the cassette/CD again and check your answers.

Alex changed his mind about the demonstration. Why?

The demonstration

There were plans to build a new airport in Sheffield. Some people organised demonstrations against the new airport. But demonstrations don't always help. The new airport opened in 1998.

"Hi, Alex. When are we going to meet this afternoon?" It was Marian Kennedy on the phone.

"Meet? I have to work on my Red Nose Day
5 poster," said Alex Barker. "I'm already late with it and …"

"But, Alex," said Marian. "It's the day of the demonstration. You know, the demonstration against the new airport."

10 "Yes, I know," answered Alex. "But … Well, demonstrations are a waste of time. Red Nose Day is more important, isn't it?"

"But, Alex," said Marian. "If we don't protest now, new projects will destroy more of our
15 environment."

"Don't be silly," said Alex. "And the new airport isn't near my house. I won't hear the planes. So it isn't my problem."

20 "Your problem is that you only think of yourself!" said Marian. "I think the demonstration is important and I'm going. Goodbye."

25 When Marian arrived in the city centre, there were hundreds of people there. There were a lot of police officers, too.

30 At two o'clock a man with a megaphone started talking about the airport.

"The city wants to build an airport," he said. "Our answer is: People, not planes!"

Then everybody started walking towards the
35 town hall. When somebody in front of the crowd shouted "What do we want?", the crowd answered "People, not planes!". Marian walked in the crowd and soon she was shouting, too.

40 When the crowd stopped in front of the town hall, the shouting became louder. People got angry. Suddenly a bottle was thrown at the wall of the town hall.

Two police officers ran into the crowd.
45 "Did you throw that bottle?" one of them
asked. "No, I didn't," a boy answered. "It was
a man over there."
Marian looked at the boy. It was Alex. "Alex!"
said Marian. "What are you doing here?"
50 Alex smiled. "Hi, Marian," he said. "You're
surprised, aren't you?"
"Yes, I am. Why did you change your mind
about the demonstration?" she asked.
"Well," answered Alex. "I listened to the
55 news on the radio this morning. And do you
know what I heard? The city is planning a
new road to the airport – behind our house!
And I thought: Marian is right. The
demonstration *is* important. I should go to
60 the demonstration, too. And here I am!"
"So you heard about the new road behind
your house. Then you changed your mind.
You aren't really interested in the
environment," she said.

"OK. OK. I was only thinking of myself when 65
I decided to come to the demonstration," Alex
said.
"Typical!" said Marian.
"Wait a minute," said Alex. "What about my
poster and all the other things I'm doing for 70
Red Nose Day?"
"You're right," said Marian. "Demonstrations
aren't the only way of improving things in
the world."

TASK A ☐ **Find the lines that show …**

1 why Alex changed his mind about the
   demonstration.
2 that Marian understood why the poster
   was important for Alex.
3 why Marian believed the
   demonstration was important.
4 that Marian didn't believe Alex was
   really interested in the environment.
5 why the crowd shouted "People, not
   planes!".
6 why Alex didn't believe the
   demonstration was important.

▪ Lines 16–19	▪ Lines 35–37
▪ Lines 54–60	▪ Lines 72–74
▪ Lines 13–15	▪ Lines 61–64

TASK B ■ **Tell their stories.**

5 I told Alex he wasn't really interested in
   the environment.
7 I met Marian in the crowd at the town hall.
2 I heard about the new road on the radio.
4 I walked to the town hall with the crowd.
1 I didn't want to go to the demonstration.
3 I wanted to go to the demonstration.
9 Then Alex answered the police officer.
8 A police officer asked somebody about a
   bottle.
6 I changed my mind about the
   demonstration.

1 **ALEX** I didn't want to go to the
   demonstration. I heard …
2 **MARIAN** I wanted to go to the
   demonstration. I walked …

TASK C ■■ **You're Marian.**
Write something for the school notice-board about the demonstration next week.

W 36, 6-8

ACTIVE ENGLISH

ACTIONS Being a good friend

Can David cheer Molly up?

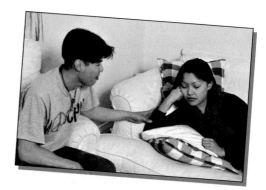

DAVID Cheer up, Molly. You look down.

MOLLY I don't feel great.

DAVID What about going to the cinema?
That'll cheer you up.

MOLLY No, I'm fed up with going to the cinema.

DAVID I know – let's go to the youth club.

MOLLY OK. That isn't a bad idea.

EXERCISE 1 ■ **Make dialogues with a partner.
Cheer him/her up.**

YOU Cheer up, *(name)*. You look …

> ill ▪ down ▪ sad ▪ tired ▪ …

A PARTNER I don't feel …

> great ▪ very happy

YOU What about …?

> going to: my/your/…'s house ▪ the cinema
> the youth club ▪ a match
>
> playing: cards ▪ computer games ▪ football
>
> listening to: CDs ▪ cassettes ▪ the radio
>
> going: ice-skating ▪ swimming ▪ shopping
> inline-skating ▪ dancing

A PARTNER No, I'm fed up with …

YOU I know – let's …

> phone … ▪ surf the Internet ▪ tell jokes
> go for a walk ▪ …

A PARTNER OK. … / Oh no! …

> That's a good/great/bad/boring/silly idea.
> That isn't a bad idea.

ℹ️ HELP FOR YOUNG PEOPLE WITH PROBLEMS

● Students at British schools can talk to their teachers if they
have problems at home or at school.

● Teenagers can write about their problems to magazines like
Just Seventeen, Sugar or *TV Hits.*

● Some young people can't talk about their problems with their
parents. Perhaps they even want to leave home. They can
phone *Childline* or the *Samaritans* to get help – even at night.

● If you have a problem, who can you tell?

● Do you like reading problem pages in magazines?

Has David cheered Molly up?

DAVID   How do you feel today, Molly?
MOLLY   Much better, thanks, David.
            I'm sorry that I was so grumpy yesterday.
DAVID   That's OK. We all feel down sometimes.
MOLLY   Well, you cheered me up. Thanks again, David.
DAVID   That's OK. That's what friends are for.
MOLLY   Well, you're a great friend, David.

EXERCISE 2 ■ **Make a dialogue between Tom and Diana.
Put the sentences in the right order.**

That's what friends are for.

Yes, much better, thanks, Diana.
Sorry I was so grumpy yesterday.

Thanks, Diana.

That's OK. I'm sometimes grumpy, too.

Do you feel better today, Tom?

Well, you cheered me up.
You're a great friend, Diana.

EXERCISE 3 ☐ **Make a dialogue: Your
partner feels down. Cheer him/her up.**

Sage ihm/ihr, dass er/sie bedrückt aussieht.

Sage, dass du dich nicht grossartig fühlst.

Schlage vor in den Jugendclub zu gehen.

Sage, dass du es satt hast in den Jugendclub
zu gehen.

Schlage vor schwimmen zu gehen.

Sage, dass das keine schlechte Idee ist.

Tip: Look at page 60.

EXERCISE 4 ■■ **Make a dialogue.**

Schlage vor zusammen im Internet zu surfen.

Lehne den Vorschlag ab.

Mache den Vorschlag auszugehen.
(Wohin? Das kannst du entscheiden.)

Lehne diesen Vorschlag auch ab. Füge
hinzu, dass es dir Leid tut, dass du so
schlecht gelaunt bist.

Sage, dass das in Ordnung ist. Mach einen
zweiten Vorschlag auszugehen.

Nimm den Vorschlag an. Schlage ein Treffen
vor. *(Wo? Wann? Das kannst du entscheiden).*

PRACTICE PAGES

STRUCTURES

EXERCISE 1 ■ **What parents often say: Put the right sentences together.**

1 Trainers aren't good for your feet.	You shouldn't be so untidy.
2 You look tired.	You should find a Saturday job.
3 You never have enough money.	You should work harder.
4 Your room always looks terrible.	You should go out more often.
5 Your teachers aren't happy with you.	You shouldn't go to bed so late.
6 You sit in your room too much.	You should wear shoes sometimes.

EXERCISE 2 ■■ **What are your five most important rules for parents?**

Parents should/shouldn't …

EXERCISE 3 ■■ **And what five rules should parents have for teenagers?**

Teenagers should/shouldn't …

EXERCISE 4 □ **What might they do when they're eighteen?**

travel to the USA ▪ work for charity ▪ look for a job ▪ buy a motor bike ▪ get married

1 DAVE   2 JULIE   3 VANESSA   4 TARA   5 MIKE

EXERCISE 5 ■■ *Mustn't* or *don't have to*? **Sue and her brother are going to a demonstration against a new road. What's she telling him?**

1 You … miss the demonstration. It's very important. It starts at 9.00.
2 You … be there at 9.00. You can come later.
3 You … get angry. The police don't like it.
4 You … carry a sign, but you can if you want to.
5 And you … throw things. It's very dangerous.

✔ **REVISION**

Mit *mustn't* sagst du, was jemand nicht tun darf:
You mustn't go into this tunnel. It isn't safe.
Mit *don't/doesn't have to* sagst du, was jemand nicht zu tun braucht:
You don't have to go into that tunnel if you're frightened.

Tip: Look at page 116, too.

EXERCISE 6 ■ ■ Here are some German signs. Tell your English friend what they mean.

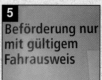

WORDPOWER

WORDPOWER 1 ☐ Find things you can do when you're older.

buy ▪ drink ▪ drive ▪ get ▪ go to ▪ have leave ▪ ride

➕

all films ▪ married ▪ cigarettes ▪ a moped a motor bike ▪ a credit card ▪ school ▪ lottery tickets ▪ a car ▪ alcohol in a pub

Tip: Look at the box on page 55.

WORDPOWER 2 ■ *For* and *against*

Make two lists: People go to demonstrations *for …* and *against …* ~~pollution / new airports~~

~~more money~~
~~better~~
~~hospital~~

animal rights ▪ better hospitals faster trains ▪ jobs ▪ more money more roads ▪ new airports ▪ pollution

~~faster trains~~
~~more roads~~

WORDPOWER 3 ■ ■ Make a word web about *your* life as a teenager.

go out on Saturdays — help at home — I can … — I have to … — My life as a teenager — I shouldn't … — I don't have to … — stay out after 11 pm — do the shopping

WRITING

EXERCISE ■ ■ Read this interview and write a newspaper report.

When Gemma King went to a pop concert, something happened to her. A newspaper reporter talked to her in hospital.

REPORTER What happened, Gemma?

GEMMA Well, there was a big crowd at the concert. When the car arrived with Robbie in it, I had a really good view.

REPORTER So how did you hurt yourself?

GEMMA When Robbie got out of his car, we all pushed to get nearer. Everybody wanted to see him. I fell and broke my leg.

REPORTER Did Robbie visit you in hospital?

GEMMA Yes, but he had to sing in the concert first, of course. So he came this morning.

REPORTER What was it like to meet him?

GEMMA Brilliant! He brought me some flowers and gave me his latest single. Now I'm almost pleased that I broke my leg.

STAR VISITS FAN IN HOSPITAL

Yesterday hundreds of fans waited to say hallo to famous pop star Robbie

PRACTICE PAGES

READING From a magazine for teenagers

BEFORE YOU READ ■ What do you like about your best friend?

ANDY'S QUESTION PAGE

MOST OF YOU have a best friend: a girl or boy at school perhaps or your brother or sister. But what are the most important qualities of a really good friend? That's my question for you today.

I asked some teenagers in Birmingham about this. Here are some of their ideas. Which six ideas are the most important in your opinion?

A best friend is somebody ...

■ ... who's always there when you need help.

■ ... who spends a lot of free time with you.

■ ... who tells you when you're wrong.

■ ... who shares your secrets – but only with you.

■ ... who likes the same music, hobbies and other things.

■ ... who you can always trust.

■ ... who sends postcards when he's/she's on holiday.

■ ... who feeds your pets when you're on holiday.

■ ... who lends you money if you need some.

■ ... who understands your problems.

■ ... who lends you magazines or CDs.

■ ... who laughs at your jokes.

■ ... who visits you when you're ill.

■ ... who never forgets your birthday.

I talked to two TV stars about their idea of a perfect friend ...

Jill Patrick, the star of the show *West London,* said, "In my opinion, a best friend should live near you and can help you night or day. At the moment my best friend is working far away, in Australia. I miss her."

Dan Collins, from *The 9 o'clock News,* said, "If you ask me, the perfect friend is somebody who knows that you aren't perfect – but still likes you. Your best friend takes you as you are. You can be yourself."

What do YOU think? Write to Andy and tell him. We'll print the best letters in our magazine next month.

Tip: You can find new words in the *Dictionary* (page 138).

EXERCISE 1 □ Basic reading: What's right?

1 Andy wants to hear about *families / best friends*.
2 The teenagers told Andy what friends *should/mustn't* do.
3 Jill Patrick and Dan Collins are *friends / TV stars*.

EXERCISE 2 ■ Reading for details: Who says this?

1 My best friend is in another country.
2 I talked to some young people in an English city.
3 A best friend lends you things.
4 A perfect friend understands that you aren't perfect.
5 A member of your family can be your best friend.
6 A best friend thinks about you when he's / she's on holiday.

> Andy ▪ a teenager
> Jill Patrick ▪ Dan Collins

EXERCISE 3 ■ Language tasks   Tip: All the words are on page 64.

1 Put the words together   spend + ?   trust + ?   send + ?
                         feed + ?   lend + ?
2 Find the missing words: a) A friend shares secrets … you.   b) You laugh … jokes.
                        c) Somebody takes you … you are.   d) Please write … Andy.

> CDs ▪ pets ▪ postcards
> somebody ▪ time

EXERCISE 4 ■■ Writing

What's *your* idea of a perfect friend? Write five sentences.

LISTENING 🎧 Best friends

The *Radio Sheffield Show*, with Chris Campbell. Six teenagers are talking about their best friends. Listen.

EXERCISE 1 ■ Find their best friends.

1 Katie: Picture …   4 Amy: …
2 Steve: Picture …   5 Barry: …
3 Jack: …   6 Liz: …

EXERCISE 2 ■■ Listen again. Right or wrong?

1 Katie's best friend is her brother.
2 Steve's best friend doesn't go to school.
3 Jack's girlfriend is 27.
4 Amy's best friend can cook.
5 Barry's best friend is older than him.
6 Mike is Liz's boyfriend.

Tip: Listen to the cassette/CD again and check your answers.

Weitere Fragen: W 54

*SERIAL
Point of no return (4)

Tip: You can find new words in the *Dictionary* (page 138).

The story so far:

When Dave comes to the restaurant in San Diego where Sharon works, she's already on her way to Canada in a truck. She doesn't want to meet Dave, but she isn't sure if she misses him or not. A week later Dave follows her in another truck. He hopes to find her in Canada …

Toronto, Canada

"Here we are, Dave. Toronto."
Dave looked at the *Welcome to Toronto* sign.
"You're a nice guy, Dave. I just wish
5 you could forget Sharon. You won't
find her in this city of over 4 million
people. And you only have a week
before you have to go back to New
York and get your flight home."
10 "I might be lucky," said Dave.

The big truck drove through the streets
of Toronto. First the buildings were
small. But when they got nearer to the
centre of the city, there were lots of
15 skyscrapers. Downtown Toronto looked
just like New York. Dave remembered
that he had read that a lot of American
film companies came to Toronto. It
looked like an American city, but it was
20 a lot easier and cheaper to work here.
Dave saw that they were now really
near the CN Tower, the world's tallest
tower and Toronto's most popular
tourist attraction. But Dave wasn't
25 here as a tourist.

When they arrived at *Burton
Trucking*, Pete asked some of the
other drivers about Sharon. Dave
waited at the truck. Ten minutes
30 later Pete came back with the news.

"One of our drivers took Sharon all
the way from *José's* to Toronto. But
she didn't say where she was going
to stay here."
"That's OK, Pete," said Dave. "Sharon is 35
here somewhere. So coming to Toronto
was the right thing."
"Oh, Dave! Toronto is enormous.
Look, here's the key to my apartment.
You can stay there till you go back to 40
New York. I'm going to stay at my
girlfriend's apartment. I'll see you
next Sunday."

High Park in Toronto

enjoying the summer weather. Then he took out the letter that Sharon had written to him from the USA, the letter he had read out on the *Today* programme. He read the letter, then slowly, very slowly, tore it into pieces. He had to forget that girl here and now. It was time to go home. Now, how would he get to New York next week for his flight back to England?

Dave travelled by subway to Pete's apartment on Bloor Street. It was near High Park, a fantastic place for cycling, jogging and having fun. Dave went there for a walk after the long journey. He wanted to think.

He thought about what had happened since he had come to North America two weeks ago. He had flown to New York, then to San Diego and now he was in Toronto, Canada. And what had he done? He had seen a lot of North America, but he hadn't found Sharon. She was running away from him. And now she was somewhere in this big city. He sat on a bench and looked around the park. There seemed to be only couples here. They were

He stood up and walked through the park. The bus would be cheapest, of course, but … It was her! At the stand! She was buying an ice-cream. He ran and shouted.
"Sharon! It's me! Hey!"
The girl looked at him. "Sharon? My name is Tina."
"I'm sorry. I'm so sorry. I thought you were another girl."
Dave walked away, sat on the grass – and cried. Forget Sharon? Never!

High Park subway station

He was outside the park now, in Bloor
100 Street. What was he going to do?
Everything was terrible. He went down
into the subway. For a long time he
stood on the platform and watched the
trains. It would be quick. He wouldn't
105 feel anything. He only had to move a
bit farther and he would just fall off
the platform. He didn't even have to
jump. He could hear it. The next train
downtown. He could see its lights now.
110 It was coming into the station, but it
was still moving very fast. Now, now,
NOW! – NO! That wasn't the answer.
He moved away from the edge of
the platform. Then, like a robot,
115 he walked along the platform, up
the stairs and out of the station. He
was suddenly very tired. He had to
sit down.

"Start, you stupid bike! Start!"
120 A young man was having problems
with his motor bike. Dave walked
over to him.
"Hi! Perhaps I can help. I'm a
mechanic."
125 "Thanks. I've had problems with
this bike all week. And I have so
much to deliver."

Dave looked at the bags on the
side of the motor bike – *Canada
Courier*. He soon found the
problem. It was easy. The young
man had a few tools on the bike,
so Dave did an emergency repair.
"But you should go to a garage as
soon as you've finished work today,"
he said.
"As soon as I've finished work today,
I'm going to buy you a meal," the
Canadian said. "Meet me here at 6.30.
OK?"

Dave and Harry Porter, the motor bike
courier, had a great evening at *The
Sports Potato* bar. And Dave had a new
friend (Harry), a place where he could
stay as long as he wanted (Harry's
apartment) and a job, half of Harry's
job. (Harry was starting college soon
and couldn't work as much). But Dave
had to do three things before the job
started a week later:
– He had to explain to Pete why he
didn't need his apartment.
– He had to be very careful with
his money.
– And he had to get to know Toronto!

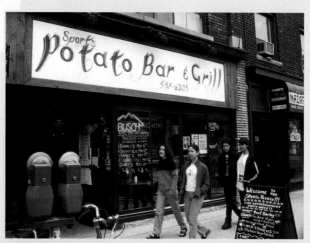

The Sports Potato bar

68

Dave had just come home from work when there was a ring at the door of the apartment. Dave opened it. "Hallo."

160 "Hi! Can I come in?" said the girl at the door. "You must be Dave. Harry told me all about you. You're the crazy English guy who threw away a ticket back to Europe. You left a

165 good job in Britain to stay in Toronto and look for a girl."

"Yeah. That sounds like me," said Dave. "But you haven't told me who you are yet."

170 "I'm Jill, Harry's sister. *Now* can I come in?"

Jill was great fun. They sat around Harry's kitchen table and talked a lot. Well, Jill and Dave talked. Harry was

175 watching ice hockey on TV. The Toronto Maple Leafs were winning.

Dave liked Jill. She was great. In the weeks that followed they often went out together. One evening they

180 went to the cinema and saw a sad romance, *The Canadian Dream*. Jill

Toronto Maple Leafs

started crying, so Dave put his arm around her. When the film had finished and the lights went on, Dave took his arm away. 185

"You can put your arm around me again, Dave," she said. "I think we could have a lot of fun together."

Dave looked at the young woman next to him. Oh yes. He was sure they could 190 have a lot of fun together. But what about Sharon?

(To be continued)

W 41, 16-19

UNIT FIVE

Jobs

Have you thought about a job? Do you know what you want to do?
Perhaps you've done work experience.

■ Look at the photos. What are the jobs?

Tip: All the jobs are in the "Work" box on this page.

What's each job like? What do you think?

■ Job adverts: Read these job adverts from the local newspaper.

JOB MARKET

DO YOU RIDE A MOTOR BIKE?
Do you want to earn £250 a week?
We need couriers.
3 weeks holiday –
some weekend work
Tel.: *Pronto* 469 2583

CARMAN'S GARAGE
We're looking for an APPRENTICE CAR MECHANIC
• £60 a week
• 1 day a week at college
• 4 weeks holiday a year
Good job for a hard worker who wants to learn.
Tel.: 698 4372 for more information

CASHIERS NEEDED
for *QUICKSERVE SUPERMARKET*
Now open all night.
Your hours: 8 – 4, 4 – 12, 12 – 8
£4.20 an hour, night work extra
Tel.: 298 3652

In which job …
1 … do you earn most money?
2 … do you have the most holiday?
3 … do you spend time at college?

4 … do you work at night?
5 … do you work at weekends?
Which job would/wouldn't you like? Why?

■ Word pool: Work

answer the phone · bank clerk · bricklayer · café · car mechanic · cashier
cook/serve meals · courier · department store · factory · garage · hotel
make/repair things · nurse · office · plumber · shop assistant · supermarket
take money · taxi driver · travel agency · waiter/waitress
work at a computer / alone / in a team / outside / with animals

Tip: You can find new words in the *Dictionary* (page 138).

Find words that tell you …
– what somebody's job is: bank clerk, …
– where people work: café, …
– what people do: answer the phone, …

And you?
I've done work experience in/at/with …
I enjoyed / didn't enjoy it because …
I'd like to be a / work in a …

- Most students in Britain do work experience in Year 10, when they're 14 or 15.
- Work experience is usually in spring or summer.
- Schools find jobs for students in factories, offices, hospitals, shops or other places.
- Students usually do two weeks work experience.
- They don't earn any money.
- A teacher visits the students at work.
- Students write a diary about their work experience.

And you?
- Where did you do your work experience? What was it like?
- What tips can you give other people about work experience?

W 44, 2

* SONG 🎧 Manic Monday

Six o'clock already,
I was just in the middle of a dream.
I was kissin' Valentino,
By a crystal blue Italian stream.

But I can't be late
'Cause then I guess I just won't get paid.
These are the days,
When you wish your bed was already made.

It's just another manic Monday.
Wish it was Sunday,
That's my fun day,
My "I don't have to run" day.
It's just another manic Monday.

* GAME What's my job?

Pick a job. Then write eight sentences about
your job. These questions can help you:
Is it a hard/easy/clean/dirty/popular job?
Where do you work? What do you do? Do you
have to wear special clothes? Do you work
alone / in a team / at a computer / outside?
Read your sentences to the other students.
Who can guess your job first?

What's my job?

I meet a lot of people.
Sometimes I work at night.
I don't work in a building.
I know my town very well.
People often phone and ask me to come.
Sometimes people stop me in the street.
I drive a car.
I take people where they want to go.

Work experience

It was the first day of work experience for the pupils in Year 10 at Clifton School in Bristol.

Emma Walker was looking forward to
5 working in a travel agency, but her first day was terrible. Most of the time Emma had to work alone. First she had to open all the letters – that was really boring. Then she had to make coffee for
10 everybody – she hated that. After that she had to answer the phone – and that was difficult because nobody told her what to say! In the afternoon she had to unpack the new brochures. They were
15 heavy and it was very hard work. Then she had to put the brochures into envelopes – another boring job. At five o'clock she went home. That was the best part of the day.

20 Daniel Green had a job at the Leopold Street Day Centre for old people. When he left home, he was a little nervous. Starting a job isn't easy and he didn't know anybody at the centre. But when
25 he arrived, everybody was very friendly and Daniel really enjoyed working there.

This is what Daniel wrote in his work experience diary:

MONDAY 9th

Working at the centre is great. My first job this morning was serving tea and then clearing the tables. Of course, I dropped a cup – and it broke! But the other helpers weren't angry. They just laughed. In the afternoon I enjoyed talking to some of the old people. They like chatting. I'm looking forward to playing cards with them tomorrow. I worked till 6 pm.

TUESDAY 10th

This morning I enjoyed working in the kitchen. At home I hate helping in the kitchen – but here it was great! All the helpers laughed a lot. Even washing up was fun. I didn't drop anything today! My job after lunch was tidying the bookshelves and the magazines. Then we played cards. Another good day.

EXERCISE 1 ☐ **Daniel's jobs**
Find seven jobs that Daniel did.
1 Serving tea
2 …

EXERCISE 3 ✗■ **What did Emma write in her diary?**
Use the *ing*-form of the verb and finish each sentence.
1 … was really boring.
   Opening all the letters was really boring.
2 I hated …
3 … was difficult.
4 … was very hard work.
5 … was another boring job.
6 … was the best part of the day.

EXERCISE 2 ✗ **What do old people enjoy doing at the day centre?**

Leopold Street Day Centre

- ◆ Talk to old friends.
- ◆ Meet new friends.
- ◆ Read newspapers and magazines.
- ◆ Play cards.
- ◆ Use the library.
- ◆ Have lunch or a snack.
- ◆ Drink tea or coffee.
- ◆ Chat with the helpers.
- ◆ Go on a trip every month.

1 They enjoy talking to old friends.
2 They …

W 45, 3a

Finding a job

This is what happened to two teenagers.

Gwen Morris, 17: I was lucky. Mrs Williams, our careers teacher at school, was great. She knew that I wanted to be a cook, so for my work experience she helped me to find work in a hotel kitchen.
5 I had to keep everything clean and help to prepare the vegetables. Most of the time I enjoyed it. After that Mrs Williams helped me to find a job. She helped me to fill in my application form and we practised my interview. Now I'm training to be a cook in a hotel in York. Sometimes I have to work very late but that doesn't worry
10 me. I love cooking, and working in the evenings isn't a problem for me. I live in the hotel so that I don't have to travel home late at night. I miss home a little but it's great to be independent. One day a week I go to college. Things are going well. I've just passed my first exam.

15 **Brian Murray, 17:** I haven't found a job yet. For three months I went to the job centre almost every day. I looked in the local newspaper and I applied to lots of local firms. I had two interviews, but I didn't get a job. I was very sad. But I didn't want to do nothing all day, so now I'm on a government training scheme at
20 *Briggs Plumbing*. I didn't think I wanted to be a plumber, but the work is sometimes very interesting and Mr Briggs says I'm good at it. I don't get much money on the scheme, but if I work hard, it might help me to get a job later.

EXERCISE 4 ■ Who thought it?

1 I'd love to get a job.
2 We'll practise her interview tomorrow.
3 I think he'd be a very good plumber.
4 I'll ask Mrs Williams to help me with my application form.
5 I don't want to do nothing all day.
6 It's so late. But at least I don't have to travel home.

EXERCISE 5 ■■ Gwen's interview

Here are some of the questions Gwen had to answer at her interview. What did she say?

1 Where did you do your work experience, Gwen?
2 What did you do on work experience?
3 What do you think about working late?
4 Why do you want to live in the hotel?
5 And why do you think you'd be a good cook?

W 45, 3b-4

C ## LISTENING 🎧 Job interviews

Ted Barker and Joyce Fairley are doing job interviews. They need a young man or woman for a summer job at the sports centre. Listen.

EXERCISE 6 ■ Tom or Simon?

Who should get the job? What do you think? Why?

EXERCISE 7 ■■ Listen again. Make notes.

What do Tom and Simon say about: their work experience; their hobbies; getting to work?

Tip: Listen to the cassette/CD again and check your answers.

STORY 🎧

Shellina has an idea. Will it work?

"The Coffee Pot"

The Internet is fun, but not everybody can go online from home. There's an easy answer in many towns now: Internet cafés.

Finding a place for work experience isn't always easy. Shellina Akbar was very unlucky. She wanted to work at *Cyber Computer Games*, but the company closed. Then she
5 tried to find a job in an office, but she wasn't successful. In the end she found a job as a waitress in a café. It was called *The Coffee Pot* and it belonged to Mr and Mrs Jones.

At 9 am on Wednesday Shellina arrived at *The Coffee Pot*. Mr Jones was in the kitchen. 10 Mrs Jones was at her computer in the office. Shellina started cleaning the tables and chairs. When some customers came in, she served them. There were never many customers, so the work was easy. But it was a little boring. 15

At 5.30 Emma Walker and Daniel Green from Shellina's class came into *The Coffee Pot*. They wanted two coffees. Shellina sat at their table.
"Do you enjoy working at the day centre, 20 Daniel?" asked Shellina.
"It's great," said Daniel, and he told Shellina all about the old people.
"I bet it's more fun than the travel agency," said Emma. "I can't stand the things I have 25 to do. But what's it like here, Shellina?"
"Well," answered Shellina, "Mr and Mrs Jones are very nice. The problem is … well, we don't have enough customers."
"I'm not surprised," said Emma, "It looks a 30 little dead, doesn't it? And I think we're the only people under fifty!"
"But I have an idea," Shellina smiled.
"Oh?" said Emma. "What is it?"
"Come back next week," said Shellina. 35
"You'll see."

Later Shellina talked to Mr and Mrs Jones and made
a suggestion.
"Why don't we make *The Coffee Pot* into an Internet
40 café?" Shellina asked. "We could use the computer
from your office, and I could bring my computer from
home. We could surf the Internet, and …"
"But that's expensive, isn't it?" asked Mr Jones.
"No," said Shellina. "It doesn't cost so much. And
45 customers could pay for every 30 minutes on the
Internet. We could advertise in schools."
"Let's try it," said Mrs Jones.

When Emma and Daniel came into *The Coffee Pot*
a week later, they were surprised – the café was
full! Groups of people were in front of the two 50
computers. People, young and old, were at every
table. Shellina was very busy. Daniel and Emma
had to wait before they could talk to her.
"Brilliant idea!" Daniel told Shellina, when she
stopped at their table. 55
"It has been hard work," said Shellina. "We had to
advertise, we had to find out about the Internet, …
I've learned so much in the last week. Work
experience is a great idea."

TASK A ☐ Find the lines about …

1 Daniel and Emma's first visit to
   The Coffee Pot. Lines … to 36.
2 Wednesday morning at *The Coffee Pot.*
   Lines … to 15.
3 Shellina's suggestion.
   Lines … to 42.
4 What happened before Shellina
   started her work experience.
   Lines … to 8.
5 Daniel and Emma's second visit to
   The Coffee Pot. Lines … to 59.

TASK B ■ Answer the questions.

1 Shellina didn't work at *Cyber
   Computer Games.* Why not?
2 Why was Shellina's job boring?
3 How do you know that most of
   Shellina's customers were old?
4 Shellina needed two computers.
   Where did they come from?
5 How did the new customers find out
   about the Internet café?
6 What was different at *The Coffee Pot*
   when Daniel and Emma went back
   there again? Find three things.

TASK C ■■ Shellina's work experience

Later Shellina applied for a job. What did she write about her work experience?

W 46, 5-8

ACTIVE ENGLISH

ACTIONS Talking about work

Jenny is talking to Ann Fields from the job centre about a summer job. How many hours a week will Jenny work?

ANN FIELDS	I have a job for you – working at *Tesco's*.
JENNY	Oh great! When can I start?
ANN FIELDS	On Monday August 10th.
JENNY	What will my job be?
ANN FIELDS	Serving the customers and filling the shelves.
JENNY	What are my hours?
ANN FIELDS	From 10 am till 5 pm, Monday to Friday.

EXERCISE 1 ■ Make dialogues with a partner about summer jobs.

A PARTNER	I have a job for you – …
YOU	Oh great! When can I start?
A PARTNER	On …
YOU	What will my job be?
A PARTNER	…
YOU	What are my hours?
A PARTNER	From … till …

BRISTOL JOB CENTRE

Summer jobs for young people:

Where	When	Jobs	Hours
The Tea Shop	5.8. – 5.9.	helping in the kitchen cleaning the tables	10.30 am – 6 pm Saturdays and Sundays
Kids' World	4.8. – 20.8.	looking after children cleaning the kitchen cooking for children	9 am – 2 pm Mondays and Wednesdays
Trends clothes shop	3.8. – 7.9.	helping in the office cleaning	9 am – 6 pm Saturdays
Parr's supermarket	28.7. – 29.8.	filling the shelves tidying the shop	5 pm – 8 pm Monday – Friday
Brown's Bookshop	28.7. – 23.8.	tidying the shelves serving customers	9 am – 3 pm Monday – Saturday

EXERCISE 2 ■ More ideas for summer jobs: Make sentences.

I'd like to work	in a clothes shop, in a fitness centre, in a hotel kitchen, on a farm, in a garage,	because	I'm good at cooking. I like clothes. I'm interested in sport. I'm interested in working with cars. I like working with animals.

Sam is telling a teacher about his work experience.

TEACHER What work did you do, Sam?
SAM I worked in a flower shop.
TEACHER Did you enjoy it?
SAM Well, yes and no.
TEACHER What do you mean?
SAM I enjoyed working with flowers.
But I didn't enjoy serving customers.

EXERCISE 3 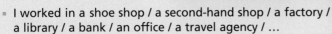 **Make dialogues about work experience.**

> What work did you do? ▪ Did you enjoy it?
> What do you mean? ▪ What did you enjoy?
> What didn't you enjoy?

> ▪ I worked in a shoe shop / a second-hand shop / a factory /
> a library / a bank / an office / a travel agency / …
> ▪ I worked with a bricklayer / car mechanic / plumber /
> TV engineer / …
> ▪ Yes, I did. / No, I didn't. / Well, yes and no.
> ▪ I enjoyed / didn't enjoy serving customers / cleaning/
> answering the phone / chatting with people /
> working hard / filling the shelves / …

EXERCISE 4 **Make a dialogue about work experience.**

Frage, was für Arbeit er/sie gemacht hat.
Sage, dass du in einem Blumenladen gearbeitet hast.
Frage, ob er/sie dies gern gemacht hat.
Sage ja.
Frage, was ihm/ihr Spaß gemacht hat.
Sage, dass du gern Kundinnen und Kunden bedient hast.

Tip: Look at the dialogues on this page.

EXERCISE 5 **Make a dialogue about your work experience.**

Sage, welches Berufspraktikum du gemacht hast.
Frage, wie es war.
Sage, ob es dir Spaß gemacht hat oder nicht.
Frage nach den Gründen.
Erkläre, was du gern bzw. nicht gern gemacht hast.
Frage nach den Arbeitszeiten.
Sage, von wann bis wann du gearbeitet hast.

W 47, 9-10

PRACTICE PAGES

STRUCTURES

EXERCISE 1 ☐ **A summer job: Put in the *ing*-forms.**

> applying ▪ being ▪ collecting ▪ finding
> going ▪ starting ▪ swimming ▪ working

… a summer job in our town is difficult. But I started …
for jobs early – and I was lucky. My job for this summer is … at the beach. That's great because I'm good at …, and I enjoy … outside. Of course, … other people's rubbish won't be much fun, and I won't like … to the beach on Saturdays. But I'm looking forward to … work on July 10th.

Finding a summer job in our town is difficult. But …

EXERCISE 2 ■ **Michael works in a music shop.**

😊 He listens to new CDs.

😃 He helps customers to pick their CDs and videos.

😖 He tidies the shelves.

🙂 He reads the latest music magazines.

🙁 He answers the phone.

😃 He looks for CDs in the computer.

🙁 He works two days a week till 9 pm.

😖 He asks customers to leave the shop when it closes.

> 😃 = jobs he enjoys   🙂 = jobs he loves
> 🙁 = jobs he doesn't like   😖 = jobs he hates

What does Michael think about the jobs he has to do?
1 He loves listening to new CDs.
2 He enjoys …

EXERCISE 3 ■ **Finding a job: Which sentences need the word *to*?**

Jenny is going **?** leave school in the summer. She hopes **?** get a job soon. She wrote to the garden centre but they couldn't **?** give her a job. She'd like **?** work outside. So her careers teacher said that she should **?** get a job in the park. She had **?** go for an interview, but she didn't get the job. Today she saw an advert for a job on a farm. The farm is near her home so she might **?** apply. She must **?** send an application before next week.

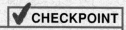

✔ **CHECKPOINT**

Der Infinitiv <u>ohne</u> *to* steht nach *can, could, will, would, must, needn't, might, should.*	**Der Infinitiv <u>mit</u> *to* steht nach bestimmten** Verben, z. B. *forget, help, hope, learn, teach, try, want, would like.*
Sally might apply for a job.	I hope to get a job soon.
	I want to work with animals.

⚠ **Beachte auch:** I'm going to leave school soon. We have to learn French.

EXERCISE 4 ■■ Du sprichst mit einem britischen Freund – auf Englisch natürlich!

Wie fragst du, …

1 … wann er sein Berufspraktikum gemacht hat?
2 … wo er gearbeitet hat?
3 … was er tun musste?
4 … was er gern getan hat?

Wie sagst du, …

5 … dass du im Juli die Schule verlässt?
6 … dass du Koch/Köchin werden willst?
7 … dass du schon eine Stelle hast?
8 … dass du in einem Hotel arbeiten wirst?
9 … dass du dich auf die Stelle freust?

WORDPOWER

WORDPOWER 1 ■ That isn't right!

What's right? Write it again.

APPLICATION FORM	
Job:	16
Name:	Bricklayer
Age:	271 43 62
Address:	Summer job at a sports centre
Telephone:	I like being outside
	I can carry heavy things
School:	19 Down Street, Bristol
Work experience:	football, cycling, fitness training
Hobbies:	English, maths, German, science, history, music
School subjects:	Matt Gregson
Why do you want this job?	King's Road School

WORDPOWER 2 ■ Jobs

What are the missing words?

Job	Place of work	What he/she does
?	?	serves meals
careers teacher	?	?
?	bank	?
?	garage	?
?	?	cooks meals
shop assistant	?	?
?	hospital	?

WORDPOWER 3 ■■ What are the words?

1 Somebody who builds houses
2 When a student finds out what a job is like
3 Something you fill in when you want a job
4 A school young workers go to
5 Somebody who helps students to find a job

WRITING

EXERCISE ■■ Lucky Pete: Tell the story.

Pete was driving along the road.
A man stopped his taxi.

a) nervous / late
b) wanted / the airport

c) bad / traffic
d) very nervous

e) arrived / paid
f) ran

g) sandwich and coffee
h) came back

i) wrong airport
j) Gatwick airport /not Heathrow

PRACTICE PAGES

READING Applying for a job

BEFORE YOU READ ■ How do you apply for a job?

CV

Family name	Mushtaq
First name	Mohammed
Age	16
Place of birth	Sheffield, England
Nationality	British
Address	23 Cherry Tree Road, Darnall, Sheffield S9 4TU
Telephone	0114 843 068
Languages	Urdu, some German
School subjects	Maths, English, physics, biology, history, German, design and technology, art
Hobbies	Computers, playing the guitar, cooking, gardening
Sports	Hockey, cricket, mountain biking, inline-skating
Evening and weekend jobs	Delivering newspapers (2 years) Working at a garden centre in Darnall (1 year)
Work experience	2 weeks in *Brightways* supermarket
Foreign travel	School trip to Germany Family holidays in Pakistan

23 Cherry Tree Road
Darnall
Sheffield S9 4TU

June 26th

The Manager
Highgate Garden Centre
Highgate Road
Sheffield

Dear Sir or Madam,

I saw the advert in the Sheffield News for a job in your garden centre this summer. I'm very interested in gardening and I'd like to apply for the job.

I worked at a garden centre in Darnall on Saturdays last year. That job has finished now because the centre had to close. I served customers and looked after the plants there. The manager, Mr Davis, was very pleased with my work and I was always punctual. I've had other jobs, too. I delivered newspapers for two years and I did my work experience in a supermarket in Sheffield.

When I leave school, I want to do gardening at college. I'm interested in learning as much as I can about plants and gardens. I'm sure that a summer job at your garden centre will be very useful.

I'm fit, I do a lot of sport and I can carry heavy things. I can start work from July 13th. I'm looking forward to hearing from you.

Yours faithfully,

Mohammed Mushtaq

Tip: You can find new words in the *Dictionary* (page 138).

EXERCISE 1 ☐ **Basic reading: Is it a) in the cv only, b) in the letter only, c) in the cv and in the letter or d) not in the texts?**

1 Mohammed wants a job at a garden centre.
2 He lives in Sheffield.
3 He has no sisters.
4 He has lots of hobbies.
5 He's interested in gardening.
6 He's British.
7 He wants to work in the summer.
8 He hates working in an office.

EXERCISE 2 ■ **Reading for details: One thing is wrong in each sentence. What is it? What's right?**

1 Mohammed can speak Urdu and French.
2 He doesn't learn history at school.
3 He has never been outside Europe.
4 He works at a garden centre in Darnall.
5 Mr Davis was the manager of a garden centre in Highgate.
6 Mohammed hasn't had other jobs.
7 When he leaves school, he wants to do German at college.
8 Mohammed can start work in June.

EXERCISE 3 ■ **Language tasks**   Tip: All the words are on page 80.

1 Which word is wrong here: *physics, biology, nationality, technology*?
2 And which word is wrong here: *advert, plant, garden centre, flower*?
3 Find the missing words: a) Mohammed would like to … for the job.
    b) He … customers.
    c) He … after plants.
    d) He … newspapers.
    e) He can … heavy things.
    f) He can … work soon.

EXERCISE 4 ■■ **Writing**
Write your own cv.

LISTENING 🎧 An interview for a summer job

Tracy Brown is in a shoe shop for an interview with Mrs Singh, the manager. Listen.

EXERCISE 1 ■ **Right or wrong?**

1 Tracy is still at school.
2 Her favourite subject is German.
3 She likes to get up early.
4 She worked at a flower shop last spring.
5 She still works there.
6 She doesn't like the old people at the day centre.
7 The job will finish soon.
8 That's a problem for Tracy.

EXERCISE 2 ■■ **The job advert**
Write Mrs Singh's advert for this summer job. Listen again and make notes that will help you.

Tip: Listen to the cassette/CD again and check your answers.   Weitere Fragen: W 54

*SERIAL
Point of no return (5)

Tip: You can find new words in the *Dictionary* (page 138).

The story so far:

Dave arrives in Toronto. He decides to stop looking for Sharon. Then he sees a girl who looks like her and becomes very sad. He thinks about killing himself, but he changes his mind. He meets Harry, a motor bike courier. He can live in Harry's apartment and share Harry's job. Dave enjoys going out with Harry's sister, Jill. But can he forget Sharon …?

Toronto in winter

Happy *Christmas from Dave.*
PS: I'll phone you on the 25th.

from all of us!

Dave put the card in its envelope and looked across the table at Harry.
5 "Don't look so sad," Harry said. "You could make things so much easier for yourself. My sister is crazy about you. But you're still looking for a girl who probably doesn't want to see you again
10 and who probably has a new boyfriend now. It's time to move on, Dave."
"You've said all that before," said Dave.
"I know. But you're making a big mistake. I'm happy you're doing half
15 my job for me and you're a great guy. But you should be back in Britain, with a real career."
"You sound like my parents," said Dave. – His parents! He read their last
20 letter again.

… Mrs Dunn at the garage says you can still have the job if you come back soon. Try not to get into trouble with the Canadian police on that motor bike. We're worried that you don't 25 *have a work permit. (– Me, too!) How long can you stay in Canada?*
(– Six months, but only as a tourist.)
And do you have enough money?
(– Not really.) We'll send you the 30 *money for the ticket back to England. Sharon's mum sends her love, too. She says you should forget about her daughter and come home.*
Dave put the letter down. He opened 35 the card to his parents again and wrote:
PS 2: If I haven't found Sharon before Valentine's Day, I'm coming home.

Ice-skating at Toronto City Hall

Happy *Christmas from Sharon.*
PS: I'll phone you on the 25th.
She put the Christmas card in the
envelope with the letter to her mum.
She wrote to her every month, but her
mother could never write back, because
she didn't know Sharon's address. And
Sharon would never tell her. Her mum
would tell Dave and he'd be on the
next plane to Toronto. It was good that
she had got out of *José's* before Dave
arrived there with the people from
NBC. She had seen the pictures on the
Today show. At that time she wasn't
sure if she wanted him to find her.
And she certainly didn't want him to
find her now. She was enjoying life
in the big city. There was so much to
see and do. And the people were really
friendly. She was even getting used to
the very cold winter. Her friends said
the winter hadn't really started yet. She
should see what January and February
were like. She told them that they
should see what Chester was like in the
winter – not as cold as Toronto, but
with lots of rain and everybody grumpy
as soon as Christmas was over. She was
looking forward to ice-skating at the
weekend. And after Christmas she was
going skiing near Montreal with her
new friend from the office, Christine
Kellerman. She wasn't ready for a
boyfriend yet, but that Richard Forrest
from the office seemed very interested
in her. He was friendly and very good-
looking. And surely all North American
men weren't like Wayne …

Eight o'clock. She didn't want to be late for the office. She was
80 looking forward to the lunch break today. It was Christine's birthday and they were all going to have a meal together at a restaurant on Yonge Street, near the office. She
85 wondered if Richard Forrest would be there, too.

She checked her bag – money, subway tokens, passport: Rachel Watts, born in Montreal, Canada.
90 She had spent her last cent on that passport – and it had been worth it. OK, she had been through a terrible time and she had hurt Dave. But it was over now and he probably had
95 another girlfriend.

Dave was on his motor bike near Lake Ontario when he got the message. "Pick up package from airport. Take to Cornison and Company, 6500 Yonge
100 Street."

Yonge Street, Toronto

Toronto airport

Dave liked going to Yonge Street, the street with all the CD shops – and offices. Every time he went to an office, he hoped to see Sharon at a computer
105 there. Crazy!

As Dave stood in the lift that was taking him up to the offices of Cornison and Company, he saw himself in the mirror – motor bike clothes and a red helmet with the words
110 *Canada Courier* on it. He didn't look like Dave Kelly from Elm Road in Chester, England. But with that helmet on, even his own parents wouldn't know who he was. He walked out of
115 the lift and over to the woman at the reception desk.

"Package for Barbara Madison," he said in an accent that sounded less British and more Canadian every
120 day. While the woman was signing for the package, the lift doors opened and about ten people came out. They were talking and laughing. The woman at the desk
125 said, "Rachel, there's a package here for Barbara Madison. Can you take it to her, please?"

Dave felt dizzy in the heavy helmet as the young woman
130 moved away from the good-looking man in the expensive suit and came over to the reception desk. Rachel? It was Sharon Glenn from Chester, England!
135

84

What was he going to do now? While he was trying to think, he saw that the good-looking young man was waiting for Sharon. No! He couldn't talk to her now. It wouldn't be fair. He turned away from her and walked over to the lift …

Four days later Dave was sitting at a small table in *The Sports Potato*. He was looking at the door. Then she arrived, walked over to his table and sat down.

"Hallo, Dave. Don't speak. Just listen. I've read your letter again and again. I'm pleased you've found me …"

"Oh, Sharon, …."

"I'm pleased you've found me because now I've had to make up my mind. And I've decided. I'm not running away any more."

"That's great, Sharon. I always knew …"

"No, Dave. Please listen. I like it here and I want to stay."

"That's OK. We don't have to go back to England, Sharon. We can stay here together."

"Sorry, Dave. What we had is in the past now. It's over. I'm not the same Sharon you knew in England. Goodbye, Dave."

"But, Sharon. It can't end like this."

"Please, Dave, try to understand me. I know so much more now."

"What do you know?"

"I know that I've moved on."

"Moved on?"

"Yes – and I'm past the point of no return."

The End

W 49, 13-16

85

A ▸ A LETTER FROM HOLLYWOOD

Dear Mum,

California is great and now I'm in Los Angeles, in the most famous part of
the city – Hollywood. You know, where they make all the films, where the
film stars live and where you see a famous face in every café and shop.
5 That's the picture most people have of the place. Well, Mum, the reality is
a little different.
I'm writing this in a café on Hollywood Boulevard. Outside the window
a homeless young man is asking for money. I read that there are about
5,000 homeless young people in Hollywood.
10 I can see groups of tourists from where I'm sitting. They're standing in
the rain (yes, rain in southern California, lots of it) on the corner of
Hollywood Boulevard and Vine Street. There's a story that in the great
years of Hollywood you only had to stand on that corner and the big film
bosses in the many cafés on the Boulevard would see you. That was in the
15 days when all the studios were near here. Most of the studios are in other
parts of LA – or the USA – now.
I'm going to finish this letter soon. This really isn't the world's nicest café
and I can't see anybody who looks even a little famous. I'm going to act
like a real tourist and walk along the Walk of Fame. It sounds great, but
20 it's just the pavement along Hollywood Boulevard, past the cheap cafés
and souvenir shops. You walk over metal stars with the names of film
stars on them. People thought they could make modern Hollywood more
interesting. What a joke! After the Walk of Fame, I'll go to look at the stars'
handprints in the cement outside the Chinese Theatre. That's all I'll see of
25 the stars in Hollywood!

Lots of love from,
                              Richard

PS A woman who's selling maps with
stars' homes has just arrived. Lots of
people have bought one. (Not one of the
30 homes is in Hollywood. And many aren't
even in LA! And all you see is the gate
and a big security guard.)
PS 2 Yesterday I tried to climb the
hills to the famous Hollywood sign.
35 It's impossible to get to it. My arms
and legs look terrible today.

EXERCISE 1 ■ Myth and reality
Make two lists: Hollywood – the myth,
Hollywood – the reality.

EXERCISE 2 ■ Hollywood reality
Write a few sentences about what tourists can
and can't do in Hollywood.

W 55, 1-2

ⓘ HOLLYWOOD

- The film industry started in the east of the USA, but bad weather made the work very difficult. California had good weather and lots of different places to make films.
- The first studios opened in 1911. Hollywood's best years were from 1930 to 1945.
- Then TV started and people stopped going to the cinema. Cameras got better and film-makers didn't always need good weather. Florida, Texas and New York became important centres of the film industry. Lots of Hollywood studios closed.
- They still make a few films – and many more TV programmes – in or near Hollywood. And then there are the "Oscars". This "night of the stars" is on TV. People all over the world watch the show. For these millions "Hollywood" means the exciting world of the American film industry. The real place, where it all started, is now a little shabby.

And you?
- What do you prefer to do – watch a film on TV or at the cinema? Why?

W 55, 3

LISTENING 🎧 Universal Studios

You're planning to visit Universal Studios, and you're phoning them to find out some information. You're going to hear a recorded message. Listen.

EXERCISE 3 ■ Look at the photos. What 3 things *can't* you see at the studio?

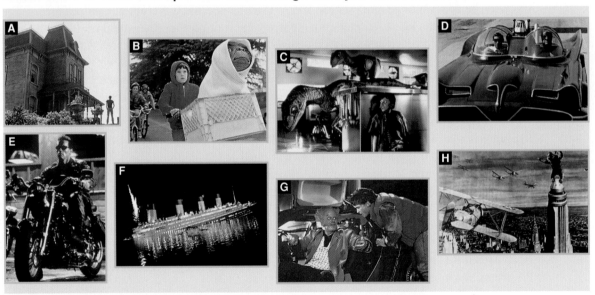

EXERCISE 4 ■ Listen again. Right or wrong?

1 The address is 1000 Universal City Plaza.
2 You can get there by bus.
3 The studios are only open in the summer.
4 Tickets for people over 11 cost $36.
5 There are special tickets for groups.

Tip: Listen to the cassette/CD again and check your answers.

EXERCISE 5 ■ Write an advert for Universal Studios.

What can people do there? Tell them where the studios are, how they can get there, when the studios are open and what the visit costs. Listen again and make notes.

W 56, 4

B WHERE'S THE REST OF ME?

Ronald Reagan was born in 1911 in Illinois. He went to school in Dixon, about 100 miles west of Chicago. At college he played football and acted in plays. When he finished college in 1932, he said he wanted to become an actor. The best job he could find was for a radio station in Iowa. He was a sports reporter there.

But then in 1937 Reagan went to Hollywood and asked if he could have a job as an actor at the Warner Brothers studio. He got the job. Over the next 27 years he was in more than 50 films. They weren't great films, and Reagan wasn't a great actor, but he was an attractive man, and people liked him. One of his best lines came in *King's Row*, a film about life in a small town in the USA. Reagan played a man called Drake McHugh. After a railway accident Drake's legs were amputated. When he woke, he asked, "Where's the rest of me?" This line later became the name of a book by Reagan about his life.

While he was in Hollywood, Reagan became interested in politics. When his job as an actor was over, he decided to go into politics, and in 1967 he became Governor of California. Before he started the job, a reporter asked him what sort of governor he would be. "I don't know," he answered. "I've never played a governor." Reagan believed that free enterprise was a good thing. He said that his government would give less money to poor people. He believed that poor people should stand on their own feet and not take too much money from the government. He believed that the country needed a strong military. In 1980 he became President. He was 69 and he stayed in the White House for eight years.

Reagan was a popular President, but he didn't do much for poor people or for minority groups. But people usually thought he was nice. He was good at talking to people – if somebody wrote the words for him first. Reagan gave a lot of work to his team in the White House. Some of them remarked that the President didn't spend enough time at his job. (He spent a lot of time watching films and telling funny stories.) Some people began to ask themselves if he was getting too old. Others thought he was a great President and that he was making America strong again. Some even thought his face should be on Mount Rushmore, next to the great Presidents Washington, Jefferson, Lincoln and Roosevelt.

After his time as President, Reagan got Alzheimer's disease. In 1994 he told the country about his disease in a letter. He wrote, "I now begin the journey that will lead me into the sunset of my life."

Mount Rushmore

W 56, 5

EXERCISE 6 ■ **Find the information.**

Name: Ronald Reagan

Born: First job: 1932, as …

School in: Next job: 1937, as …

Interests at college: Jobs in politics: …

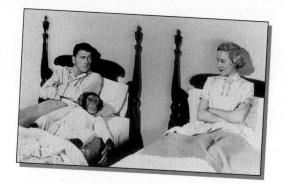

EXERCISE 7 ■ **Write a dialogue.**

Write a dialogue between somebody who wants Reagan's face on Mount Rushmore
and somebody who's against the idea. Say why he should/shouldn't be there.

Tip: The text on page 88 will help you.

EXERCISE 8 ■ **An interview with Ronald Reagan**

Look at lines 21–25 in the text on page 88. What did Ronald Reagan say to the reporter?

REPORTER What sort of governor will you be?

   REAGAN I don't know. I've never played a governor. I believe that … My government …

EXERCISE 9 ■ **Erica works at the Rock Museum. She's telling a friend what people asked her yesterday.**

They asked …

how much	the studios were on.
if famous stars	the tickets were.
where they could visit	would stay open.
which floor	visited the museum.
if she knew	the Beatles exhibition.
how long the museum	the words of *Dreams*.

1 They asked how much the tickets were.

EXERCISE 10 ■ **A reporter is talking about an interview she had in 1980 with Ronald Reagan. What were his words?**

1 He said free enterprise would work.
   "Free enterprise will work."
2 He said the country could be strong again.
3 He told me he was planning new things.
4 He mentioned that poor people got too much money.
5 He said he knew what the problems were.
6 He told me things would get better.
7 He said he was enjoying the interview.

W 56-57, 6

✔ **CHECKPOINT**

Direkte und indirekte Rede   Tip: Look at page 114 first.

Fragen

"What will the President do?"   ➜ The reporters asked what the President would do.

"Where's the rest of me?"   ➜ Drake wanted to know where the rest of him was.

Bei Fragen ohne Fragewörter benutzt du in der indirekten Rede *if*.

"Is Reagan in the TV room?"   ➜ They asked if Reagan was in the TV room.

"Does the President know?"   ➜ He asked if the President knew.

C | MEDIA JOB: MOBILE DISC JOCKEY

Here are some ideas for young DJs, from *The Mobile DJ Handbook* by Stacy Zemon.

Music is your life. You know all the latest hits and the old favourites. You're good at talking to people. Why not be a DJ?

- STOP! Ask yourself these important questions:
  1) Can I live on very little money?
5
  2) If I worked as a DJ, do I know who my customers would be?
  3) Am I good at organising things?
- So you answered "yes" to the questions? OK. Now find a name for your business. But think carefully. Maybe you think "Maria's Musical Madness" sounds great today. But in 2020? A DJ needs
10 a slogan, too. What would yours be?
- Mobile DJs aren't mobile all the time. They need an office, with lots of equipment (more money!) and, of course, an answering machine with an attractive message. What would your message be and would it get customers for you?
15
- Then it's time to go on the road. Great, you think. I just need my music equipment. Wrong! You need many more things, for example: first-aid kit, sewing kit, hairspray or hair gel, tools for your van, insect spray (for summer barbecues), … So much can go wrong!
- Find out about your customers *before* the show. If you took all the
20 latest CDs to the party and the guests were all over 50, it could be too late. Always plan, plan and plan again.

EXERCISE 11 ■ If …

1 If you were a mobile DJ,	you wouldn't have to do everything yourself.
2 If you only played German music,	you'd need lots of equipment.
3 If you didn't have a van,	you wouldn't be very popular in the USA.
4 If you had a business partner,	you couldn't move your equipment.
5 If your equipment didn't work,	you wouldn't get any money.
6 If you were late for a party,	you'd have to repair it.

1 If you were a mobile DJ, you'd need lots of equipment.

EXERCISE 12 ■ Ideas: If …

1 If I was a DJ, I'd …
2 If I went to the USA, I'd …
3 If I won lots of money, I'd …
4 If I wasn't at school today, I'd …
5 If I met my favourite star, I'd …

EXERCISE 13 ■ Answer the questions.

1 Would you like to be a DJ? Why / Why not?
2 What would you call yourself?
3 What would your answering machine message be?
4 What customers would be most difficult?
5 What customers would be easiest? Why?

 ✔ CHECKPOINT

Was unter bestimmten Bedingungen geschehen würde:
If I won some money, I'd (= I would) go to the USA. I wouldn't go to England.
If I went to Texas, I'd visit San Antonio.   Tip: Look at page 117, too.

D A POP GROUP

What's the group's name?

"Clef" and "Pras" met rapper "L-Boogie" (Lauryn Hill) and started a group. Their first CD came out in 1994. But it was their second CD, "The Score" (1996), that made them famous. It was the surprise hip hop hit of the year and got to Number One. The CD has two very different big hit singles: "No woman, no cry", Bob Marley's 1975 reggae hit, and "Killing me softly", Roberta Flack's 1973 romantic song. This shows the great talent of these hip hop musicians. Clef and Pras moved to the USA from Haiti. Because Haiti can be a dangerous place, many people try to leave the country and move to the USA. People who leave a country because it's dangerous there are called "refugees". So what's the group called? The answer is on page 137.

■ Quiz: What's the group?

Write about a music group. Tell your readers (= your class) their names, where they come from, the sort of music they play and some of their hits. Does the class know who they are?

W 57, 7-8

E ONE LAST THING

A | JOINING A CLUB

Why do teenagers join clubs? Some young people join clubs because they want to make new friends. Other teenagers want to practise a sport or hobby. They usually have to pay an annual membership fee (for example, £15 a year). Members pay less money than non-members per session at the club every week.

Jean Smart is a member of a swimming club. Jean's parents aren't always happy when she goes to her club. "When will you do your homework?" they ask.

But some parents are happy when their children go out. Jack Bolt's family moved to Sheffield six months ago, so he doesn't have many friends yet. Jack's parents hope he'll make some new friends at Abbeydale Youth Club.

> **Talk about a club.**
> **Are you a member?**
> **Would you like to join? Why?**
> **What does it cost?**
> **Do members pay less money per session?**

Last year Jean joined the swimming club.

JEAN   Hallo. I'd like to join the swimming club.
WOMAN Great! Can you fill in this form, please?
JEAN   OK. What does it cost?
WOMAN If you're under 16, it's £15 a year.
            And 40p per session.
JEAN   And when do we meet?
WOMAN Monday and Wednesday evenings from
            6.20 till 7.30.

EXERCISE 1 ■ **Jack is joining the photo club. What are the missing words?**

1 Hallo. I'd like to … the photo club.
2 Great! Can you … in this form, please?
3 OK. What does it …?
4 It's … per session.
5 And when do we …?
6 Saturday mornings … 10.00 … 12.00.

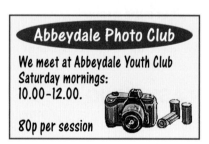

Abbeydale Photo Club

We meet at Abbeydale Youth Club
Saturday mornings:
10.00–12.00.

80p per session

EXERCISE 2 ■ **You want to join two clubs. Make dialogues with a partner.**

■ ABBEYDALE
■ AEROBICS
■ CLUB
We meet every
Wednesday evening
(7.30–8.30) at
Abbeydale Youth Club.
Membership: £10 a year
(if you're under 18: £3.50)

Sparkbrook Tennis Club

Saturdays: 2 pm–5 pm
Annual membership: £18

SHARKS! SKI CLUB

Saturday mornings
10.00–12.00
at
Sheffield Ski Village

Annual membership: £15
(Two hour card: £7.50)

W 58, 1-2

B A GROUP HOLIDAY

Abbeydale Youth Club organises short holidays for small groups of members. This year they want to go to the Peak District. The Peak District is a national park outside Sheffield.
Jack has written a letter to an outdoor centre for young people.

Abbeydale Youth Club | Your address
273 Abbeydale Road
Sheffield S2 9DL | This is the postcode.

Grindleford Outdoor Centre
Grindleford
Derbyshire DE4 2HH

September 21st — Date

You start a formal letter like this. — Dear Sir or Madam,

Seven members of our youth club in Sheffield are planning to spend three days in the Peak District at the end of October. Could you send us a brochure about the Outdoor Centre, please?

Is there accommodation for boys and girls? Can we have meals at the centre? What does it cost per night? Can we go potholing near the centre?

We're looking forward to hearing from you.

You finish a formal letter like this. — Yours faithfully,

Jack Bolt

You can have a PS at the end of your letter. — PS Could you send us a map of the national park, please? Thank you.

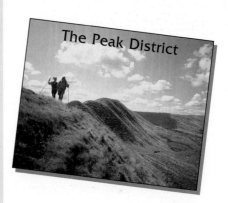

The Peak District

EXERCISE 3 ■ For each picture write a question from the letter.

1  2  3   4 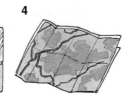 5

GIRLS   BOYS

1 Could you send us a brochure about the Outdoor Centre, please?
2 …   3 …   4 …   5 …

EXERCISE 4 ■ Write a letter to the Tourist Information Centre in Sheffield.

Your class is going to visit Sheffield for a week next year.
Ask for brochures and information about *your* interests.

The National Centre for Popular Music in Sheffield

C

AN ALTERNATIVE LIFESTYLE

It's two o'clock at the fair in Sligo, in the west of Ireland. Sally Proudfoot and Ross Langley are enjoying themselves. They aren't winning prizes or eating ice-cream. They're putting on a puppet show.

Sally and Ross left school in Liverpool a year ago. "We didn't want to go to college," said Sally. "And we didn't want a nine-to-five job. We wanted a different lifestyle."
Sally had an old van. Ross was good at making puppets. So they decided to travel in the van and put on puppet shows.

They came to Ireland last May. "Our first fair was in the capital, Dublin," said Ross. "We were a little nervous, of course, but our puppet show went very well. The children laughed and enjoyed the show. And now we travel from fair to fair. It's great. We love it."

They live and sleep in the van. "That's uncomfortable, isn't it?" I asked.
"Yes, but it's cheap. We needn't pay for accommodation," answered Sally.
"Living in a van is great. But cooking isn't easy," explained Ross. "It gets too hot.

We eat a lot of fruit and salad so we needn't cook every day."
"And we needn't cook tonight," said Sally. "We've made friends with some people in town. We can sleep in their house tonight. Now, that's luxury!"

And what do their parents think about their alternative lifestyle? "Oh, our parents needn't worry about us," said Ross. "We're safe, we're happy, and we earn a little money. Our parents should be happy."

I don't know if Ross and Sally's parents are happy. But I saw the children who watched the puppet show. And they looked very happy.

EXERCISE 5 ■ Write the sentences about Sally and Ross.

1 Sally/come from/Liverpool/Ross/and
2 go to/didn't/They/college/want to
3 decided to/puppet shows/put on/They
4 Ireland/travel/They/to fair/from fair/in

5 sleep/Sally/live/and/Ross/in a van/and
6 very happy/They're/their/with/lifestyle

1 Sally and Ross come from Liverpool.

EXERCISE 6 ■ Sally is telling a reporter about her lifestyle. Make the sentences.

1 We needn't cook tonight	so we needn't cook meals every day.
2 Our show never starts before 2 pm	because we live in the van.
3 We eat a lot of fruit and salad	so we needn't get nervous before the show.
4 We needn't stay in hotels	because we're staying with friends.
5 Our parents needn't worry about us	so we needn't work from nine to five.
6 We've done this show many times	because we're safe.

 **CHECKPOINT**

Was jemand nicht zu tun braucht: *needn't*
You needn't check the sports equipment. I've already checked it.
Cheer up. You needn't worry about the test. You've learned all the new words.

W 59, 3-4

D

THE STREETS OF LONDON

In the last few years the number of young homeless people has increased. How do they live? Where do they sleep? We met Lisa in a shop doorway near Victoria Station. We asked her a few questions.

Some homeless people sell *The Big Issue.*

REPORTER	When did you leave home?
LISA	A year ago. My parents argued a lot. My dad was often drunk. One day he hit me. So I left home.
REPORTER	Why did you come to London?
LISA	I have a few friends here. I knew there weren't any jobs. I wanted to earn some money.
REPORTER	How do you earn money?
LISA	I play my guitar in the street. And I sell *The Big Issue* at a station.
REPORTER	Where do you sleep?
LISA	Sometimes I spend a few nights with friends. But sometimes I sleep rough – in shop doorways. When it's too cold, I go to a hostel.
REPORTER	What's it like on the streets?
LISA	The streets are frightening at night. Sometimes I'm lonely. But I have my dog. He's my best friend.
REPORTER	Are people nice to you?
LISA	Some smile or talk to me. I've learned that there are a lot of good people in the world. But not everybody likes homeless people.

i THE BIG ISSUE

Some homeless people in Britain sell *The Big Issue* magazine. They buy the magazine for 40p and sell it for £1. Selling *The Big Issue* means that they can earn some money.

EXERCISE 7 ■ What's right?

1 Lisa *comes / doesn't come* from London.
2 She has *no / a few* friends in the capital.
3 Lisa *earns / doesn't earn* money.
4 She sleeps rough if *it's / it isn't* too cold.
5 The homeless girl *is/isn't* alone at night.
6 She *meets / doesn't meet* nice people.

EXERCISE 8 ■ Find the questions.

1 It's frightening at night.
2 I sell a magazine and I play the guitar.
3 Some are nice, some aren't.
4 A year ago.
5 With friends, in hostels or shop doorways.
6 I wanted to earn some money.

EXERCISE 9 ■ Work with a partner. Use the notes and write an interview with David.

REPORTER	When did you leave home?
DAVID	About nine months ago.
REPORTER	Why did you come to London?
DAVID	…

• left home about 9 months ago
• friends in London
• sell *The Big Issue*
• sleep rough – sometimes in a hostel
• streets are lonely and dangerous
• other homeless people are my friends

W 59, 5; W 60, 6

A PROJECT FOR YOUNG PEOPLE

WHEELS

What's joyriding?
Some young people enjoy driving cars – other people's cars! They drive too fast and there are a lot of accidents. Some joyriders die.

That's joyriding: **• Dangerous • Fast • Illegal**

What's Wheels?
Wheels is a project that gives young people an alternative. Young people learn to repair old cars in our garage. When they've repaired the cars, they can drive them – on our own track. They *don't* use roads.

That's Wheels: **• Safe • Exciting • Legal**

Who's Wheels for?
It's for all young people who are interested in cars and driving.

Why does Wheels need your help?
We have to buy equipment. We have to pay for our garage. We need money. Please support us. Give a donation. Become a Wheels supporter.

EXERCISE 10 ■ *Wheels:* Correct these sentences. Write them again.

1 Joyriders drive their own cars.
2 Joyriding is legal and dangerous.
3 Most joyriders die in accidents.
4 Young people learn joyriding at *Wheels*.

5 At *Wheels* members drive on roads.
6 *Wheels* is only for joyriders.
7 *Wheels* doesn't need any money.
8 Supporters should give equipment to *Wheels*.

LISTENING 🎧 *Wheels*

Martin is new at *Wheels*. Jason and Linda are telling him about the project. Listen.

EXERCISE 11 ■ Which poster is right?

A **WHEELS**
... is for everybody, from 9 – 99
... meets every day, Mon – Fri
... costs nothing

B **WHEELS**
... is for people over 18
... meets every month
... costs £15 per session

C **WHEELS**
... is for young people under 23
... meets two days a week
... costs £1 per session

EXERCISE 12 ■ Listen again. What's right?

1 *50/15/5* members are usually at *Wheels*.
2 The youngest member is *12/30/13*.
3 The oldest member is *14/24/21*.
4 Members pay *10p/£10/£1* per session.

5 Jason goes there *on Mondays / two evenings a week / on Sundays*.
6 The Rover is *Linda's/Jason's/Martin's* favourite car.

Tip: Listen to the cassette/CD again and check your answers.

96

F ## LETTERS ABOUT *WHEELS*

People have different opinions about the *Wheels* project.
Here are some letters from the local newspaper.

Why should we support people who steal cars? I want car thieves to go to prison. Or they should pay a fine.
I give donations to young people who work hard. For example, some teenagers want to go to college but they don't have enough money. They need our support. *Wheels* is a silly idea!

Clare Palmer

Wheels gives teenagers an alternative. The young people who go to *Wheels* learn about cars. Perhaps some of them will get jobs as drivers or mechanics. That's good for them.
I want them to have a chance. And they'll all become better drivers. That's good for everybody. I've already given my donation. I want *Wheels* to support young people.

Stephen Hardy

In my part of the town young people have nothing to do. Many don't have a job. Many are bored. Going to the cinema is too expensive. That's why they take cars.
Of course joyriding isn't OK. But complaining doesn't help. I want everybody to help young car thieves. That's why I think *Wheels* is a great idea. I want all young people to know about the project.

Jody Canfield

What do the young people learn at *Wheels*? I'm sure they learn about breaking into cars. And then they learn to drive fast – so that the police can't stop them. No, I'm not going to give a donation. I want *Wheels* to stop its work.

Rod Longhurst

EXERCISE 13 ■ Who supports *Wheels?* Who doesn't support it?
1 Clare Palmer …   2 Stephen Hardy …   3 Jody Canfield …   4 Rod Longhurst …

EXERCISE 14 ■ What do the readers want? Make sentences with *want to*.
1 Stephen thinks people should give car thieves a chance.
   Stephen wants people to give car thieves a chance.
2 He thinks *Wheels* should help young people. – He wants *Wheels* to …
3 Clare thinks car thieves should pay for their crimes. – Clare wants car thieves to …
4 Jody thinks everybody should help young people with problems. – Jody wants everybody …
5 She thinks all young people should find out about the project. – She wants all young people …
6 Rod thinks people shouldn't give *Wheels* money. – Rod doesn't want people …

EXERCISE 15 ■ What do you know about *Wheels*?
Who goes to *Wheels?* What do the members do there? What does *Wheels* need? Why is *Wheels* a good idea?

Tip: Look at the information on page 96.

EXERCISE 16 ■ What's your opinion?
Write a letter to the newspaper.
What's your opinion of *Wheels?*
Is it a good project?
Say why / why not.

Tip: Look at the letters on this page.

W 60, 7-9

A | A NEW START

It isn't easy to leave everything behind and start a new life in a new place. It's tough to say goodbye to friends and relatives. It's sometimes difficult to settle in a new country, where people speak another language and have another culture – where people are just different. Jutta Lang from Germany knows all this. Her home is in England now.

After Jutta's father, an engineer, had lost his job in a factory, he tried to get other work. But he was unsuccessful. He was depressed about this. Jutta's mother was a chemist in another factory, but she didn't like her job very much. So one day Mrs Lang had an idea – they should start looking for jobs outside Germany. "Jobs in foreign countries are often in the German newspapers," she said to her husband. "Today more people move to other countries to work and live. It could be a new start for us, too."

5

10

It didn't take long to find something. After they had both found jobs at a chemical factory near Bristol, they decided that the whole family should move to England. Jutta (16) and her two younger brothers Sven (10) and Paul (8) were very excited about moving.

In the first weeks in England the Langs were very busy. They found a nice house with a large garden. They were very happy in their new home.

15

20

But not everything was easy for the Langs. They had to get used to a new school, lessons in English, school lunches, different food and new neighbours. And they missed a lot of things from home: the visits to their relatives, seeing their friends, German food – especially the bread!
"Will we ever really settle here?" Jutta asked herself.

25

EXERCISE 1 ■ Find the words in the text for:
1 difficult – tough
2 people in your family – ...
3 get used to a new place
4 somebody who plans, makes or repairs things
5 very unhappy
6 other countries
7 go to live in a new place
8 feel sad about something that isn't there

EXERCISE 2 ■ A *Bristol News* interview
A reporter from the *Bristol News* spoke to Jutta Lang. Here are Jutta's answers. What were the questions?
1 Germany.
2 Last year.
3 My parents wanted new jobs – a new start.
4 Sven is 10 and Paul is 8.
5 School, lessons in English, ...
6 Oh, lots of things – like German food, ...

EXERCISE 3 ■ A *Bristol News* report   Tip: Exercise 2 can help you.
Write a report (60 words). Describe Jutta and her family.

W 61, 1

EXERCISE 4 ■ **Finish the sentences. Use the past perfect form.**

1 After Mr Lang … his job, he tried to get other work.
  After Mr Lang *had lost* his job, he tried to get other work.
2 After the Langs … an advert in a German newspaper, they applied for jobs in Bristol.
3 After they … jobs in a chemical factory, they decided to move to Bristol.
4 After they … goodbye to friends and relatives, the Langs left Germany.
5 After they … in England for a few weeks, they found a nice house.
6 After they … to their new house, they tried to get used to life in England.

 **CHECKPOINT**

> **Mit der *past perfect*-Form (Vorvergangenheit) drückst du aus, welches von zwei Ereignissen in der Vergangenheit weiter zurückliegt.**
> He saw the advert. Then he applied for the job.
> ➔ After he had seen the advert, he applied for the job.
> **Das *past perfect* bildest du mit *had* und dem Partizip Perfekt des Verbs.**

W 61, 2

 ## A YEAR LATER

How do the Langs feel about their new home after a year?

MRS LANG
People are nice. They speak very politely in shops and they queue at bus-stops. But on the roads it's sometimes different. People don't always drive very carefully. And you can't drive very fast – not like in Germany.

JUTTA
School is difficult. My teacher in Germany always spoke slowly. Here people speak quickly and I sometimes can't understand them. Some people in school think my accent is funny and they laugh about it. And sometimes I miss my old friends in Germany.

MR LANG
I like it here. In Germany we lived in a small flat. Here we live in a house – and the rent isn't too high. We live well here.

SVEN
The food is very different here, but you get used to it. People eat a lot of white bread. You can eat cheaply in fish and chip shops. The cakes aren't very good. But the different puddings are delicious!

PAUL
Sport is fun here. I've started playing rugby. I can't play very well – yet.

EXERCISE 5 ■ **What the Langs like and don't like in England. Finish the sentences.**

1 The Langs live … in their new house.
2 People speak … in shops.
3 You can eat … in fish and chip shops.

4 People don't always drive …
5 You can't drive … on English roads.
6 People don't speak … They speak …

EXERCISE 6 ■ **And you?**

What can people from other countries say about Germany?

People are …   People eat …
People live …   People drive …
People speak …   The cakes are …

People don't queue.

W 61, 3

99

TIMES HAVE CHANGED ... AND JOBS TOO!

Find the right words for photos A-D.

growing and selling food ▪ spraying cars ▪ working hours ▪ selling food

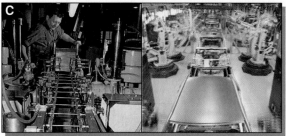

1 I'm a farmer and my father was a farmer, too. He used lots of chemicals and grew bigger vegetables. Today I don't use any chemicals. I grow organic vegetables. It's more work so I have to sell them for more money.

2 I started work when I was 16. I worked in a baker's shop in the town centre. Today most small baker's shops have closed. People buy their bread in a supermarket. I still sell bread and cakes – in a supermarket.

3 My uncle started work in the car industry in 1960. In those days spraying parts of cars was dangerous. Today lots of the dangerous jobs are done by robots.

4 When I started work here, we closed at 5.30 every evening. And we weren't open on Sundays. But now the chemist's is open every Sunday from 11.00 till 4.00 and on three evenings a week till 8.00.

EXERCISE 7 ■ Find the photos.

Text 1: Photos …

Text 2: Photos …

EXERCISE 8 ■ Who are they?

shop assistant ▪ farmer
factory worker ▪ chemist

1 His shop is open 7 days a week.
2 She grows vegetables without chemicals.
3 He doesn't spray cars today.
4 Today she has the same job in a different shop.

EXERCISE 9 ■ Write what these people said about their jobs.

Tip: The texts (1–4) will help you.

1 I – bus driver – my mother – bus driver, too – she just drove bus – today – I – drive bus – and sell tickets – more work

2 started – 14 – toy shop – town centre – today – closed – shopping centre – still sell

3 aunt – travel agency – 1975 – booking tickets – not so fast – today – is done – computer

4 started work here – 5.30 – every evening – not Sundays – now supermarket – open – Sundays – every evening – 10 pm

W 62, 4a

D OLD JOBS, NEW JOBS

Bill Rogers was a butcher for almost 50 years. He usually enjoyed the
job, but when the new supermarket opened, he decided to retire.

His daughter Kate wanted to take over his job, but Bill pointed out that
running a small butcher's shop had become very difficult. He told her
5 that he had lost a lot of customers because they could buy cheaper meat
at the supermarket. So Kate closed the butcher's shop and opened a
sandwich bar in its place. Kate's customers are office workers who don't have a long
lunch break. She sells sandwiches, crisps, chocolate and cans of lemonade and cola. She earns
more money than a butcher, but she doesn't have to work so hard.

When Ben Toft left school five years ago, he didn't know what he 10
wanted to do. His parents and grandparents worked in the steel industry.
They said that they had had a good life there, so Ben got a job in the
steel industry, too. But last year the factory needed fewer workers
because more and more jobs were done by robots. It was a sad day
when Ben's boss had to tell him – and a lot of other workers – that 15
they had lost their jobs. Ben tried for two months to find work. Then
one day he came home and said he had found a new job. He was going
to train to be a lorry driver. Now Ben earns more money than before. He often has to be away
from home. But he's happy and pleased to have a job.

EXERCISE 10 ■ All about Bill and Kate: Put the sentences in the right order.

> Kate took over Bill's shop. ▪ Office workers came to Kate's sandwich bar.
> Bill retired. ▪ Kate earns more money than a butcher. ▪ Kate opened a sandwich bar.
> A new supermarket opened. ▪ Bill Rogers was a butcher.

EXERCISE 11 ■ All about Ben

Write ten sentences about Ben. Five should be right, five wrong. Give the sentences to a partner.
Can he/she tell you which sentences are right and which ones are wrong?

EXERCISE 12 ■ What did they say?

1 Bill Rogers said	that Ben had lost his job.
2 Kate Rogers said	that he had lost a lot of customers.
3 Bill's customers told him	that he had found a new job.
4 Ben Toft's grandparents said	that they had found cheaper meat at the supermarket.
5 Ben's boss told him	that they had had a good life in the steel industry.
6 Ben said	that she had opened a sandwich bar.

---

* Die Vorvergangenheit in der indirekten Rede

Direkte Rede – *present perfect*	**Indirekte Rede – *past perfect***
"Running a small shop has become very difficult."	Bill said that running a small shop had become very difficult.

---

* Siehe auch *Option 9*, S.114

W 62, 4b

E MOBILE PHONES

When mobile phones were introduced, they were used by people in mobile jobs, for example, TV engineers, plumbers and travelling salespeople.

But today talking to family and friends, when you like and where you like, has become part of life for lots of people – not just people in mobile jobs.

And more and more young people are seen with mobiles – in shops, at school, everywhere. Teenagers are often

15 given mobiles by their parents. They can then phone them if they miss the last bus home, for example. And mum and dad can always find out where their children are.

But there are problems, too. Teachers aren't
20 happy when mobiles are used in lessons, especially when students phone friends to get the answers to the test they're doing! So why don't schools ban mobiles? – Because parents think their children are safer on the way to
25 and from school if they can get help quickly. In many schools the rule is: You can bring a mobile to school, but you mustn't use it there. But how many students follow this rule …?

Mobiles help to make life easier for people with disabilities and old people when they're 30 outside the home. They don't have to walk a long way to a public phone. And the numbers they often need – relatives, doctors, friends – can be programmed on their mobiles. So they don't have to remember 35 and enter long numbers. And they can always phone for help if they need it.

But mobile phones aren't popular everywhere. In cinemas and restaurants, trains and buses, there are more and more complaints about 40 people with mobiles. And in some places, petrol stations and planes, for example, mobiles can be very dangerous. That oh-so-important call might be the last call you ever make … 45

"I've told you before: Don't phone me at work."

EXERCISE 13 ■ Talking about mobile phones

INTERVIEWER You're a plumber. What do you think about mobile phones?

PLUMBER They're very useful. My firm can phone me while I'm travelling from job to job.

Make more dialogues. Ask these people:
teenager – parent – teacher – old person – person on a train/plane

> **THAT ISN'T ENGLISH!**
> 'Handy' is only used in German for 'mobile phone' or 'mobile'.

EXERCISE 14 ■ Put in the verbs in the passive form.

1 Today mobile phones (use) by lots of people. – Today mobile phones *are used* by lots of people.

2 Business people bought the first mobile phones. Today they (buy) by everybody.

3 Many young people (give) mobile phones by their parents.

4 Life (make) easier for old people by mobiles.

5 People get angry when mobiles (use) in cinemas or restaurants.

Phoning and driving

Last Tuesday Sam Gordon, a travelling salesman for a toy company, was on the road from Oxford to Stratford. A friend phoned him on his mobile phone. Sam was very interested in what his friend was saying. He didn't notice that a bus in front of him had stopped at the traffic lights in Woodstock. He crashed into the bus. His legs were hurt and he couldn't get out of the car. He used his mobile to phone the emergency services. They arrived and took Sam to hospital. He's getting better now, but he's still in hospital – with his mobile, of course.

EXERCISE 15 ■ Sam's phone call to the emergency services: Write the dialogue.

EXERCISE 16 ■ Tell the story. Use the right form of the verbs.

1 last Saturday / Sally and John / go / important football match
2 be / long queue / outside / stadium
3 suddenly / John / remember / the tickets
4 they / be / other jeans / at home
5 John / phone / father / tickets

6 his father / bring / tickets / stadium
7 Sally and John / be / happy
8 they / not lose / place / long queue

1 Last Saturday Sally and John went to an important football match.
2 There was a long queue …
3 …

W 63, 6-7

LISTENING  Mobile phone users

You're going to hear five people. They're speaking on their mobiles. Listen.

EXERCISE 17 ■ Which photo (A-E) goes with which person?

1st person: …   3rd person: …   5th person: …
2nd person: …   4th person: …

EXERCISE 18 ■ Listen again. Who are they (1st person–5th person) phoning?

a mother ▪ a friend ▪ a shop manager ▪ somebody from the same company ▪ a girlfriend

Tip: Listen to the cassette/CD again and check your answers.

*OPTION 1

AN AMERICAN MAGAZINE

Seventeen is one of the most popular magazines in the USA.

It comes out every month and costs $3.50.
There are usually 250 pages, many with adverts!
Look at these pages from the magazine.

A

B

C

D

E

F

G

H

EXERCISE ■ **Which page (A–H) is it? This page …**

1 … is about problems with other people. – G.
2 … has readers' letters to the magazine.
3 … is about holidays.
4 … is about boyfriends.

5 … has tips for teenagers with cars.
6 … tells you about your future (your stars).
7 … tells you what's in the magazine.
8 … has an article about problems at a dance.

W 64, 1-3

*OPTION 2

MUSIC – MADE IN THE USA

Think of a hit from the last few years and there's a very good chance that the music came from the USA. Maybe the singer or group isn't American. They could be British, German or Swedish. But it's still OK to say that their music came from the other side of the Atlantic.

■ **Why? Think of an answer.**

Pop, rock, blues, country, rap, hip hop, heavy metal, punk, reggae. All these kinds of music have rhythm. To be popular, music has to have rhythm. American music has always had rhythm, especially from the Fifties, when rock 'n' roll started.

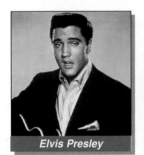

1998 Spice Girls: Goodbye

■ **What are these American hits from the Fifties to the Eighties?**

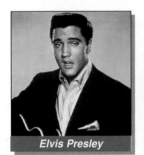

Elvis Presley

The Beach Boys

Joni Mitchell

Madonna

1956
SHOESSUEDEBLUE

1964
AROUNDIGET

1970
YELLOWBIGTAXI

1987
THATWHO'SGIRL?

■ **Who are the two African-American stars in the photos on the right?**

Tip: These photos were taken when they were much younger.

There have been very many famous black musicians from the USA. Their ancestors contributed not only to black American music, but to white American music, too.

■ **How? Think of an answer.**

Blacks were once slaves on the farms of the south. They sang songs about their hard lives. When they became free, they moved to other parts of the USA and took their music with them. This music became rhythm and blues, then rock 'n' roll, then pop, rock, heavy metal and most kinds of popular music.
That's why all pop stars should really say thank you to people like the man in this picture.

W 65, 1-3

*OPTION 3

"ONE NATION UNDER GOD"

Every morning in American schools
students stand, look at the American flag
in their classroom, put their right hands on
their hearts and say they'll be loyal to the
5 USA, "one nation under God".

"In God we trust" – that's the motto of the
United States. You can find it on American
money, for example. Over 90% of Americans
say they believe in God. And for many this
10 means they believe in America, too. For them
the USA is "God's own country".

"I pledge allegiance to the Flag of the
United States of America and to the Republic
for which it stands, one Nation under God,
indivisible, with liberty and justice for all."

**Religion has been important in America from
the start.** One of the early groups of settlers
were Puritans, very strict Protestants. They left
England because their religion wasn't allowed
there. Today, about 400 years later, 61% of 15
Americans are active members of one of the
hundreds of different religious groups. It's easy
to find one where you can meet people like
yourself. It's almost like belonging to a club. 20

**Going to church in the USA can be very
different.** Churches that black people go to,
for example, are often full. And the happy
atmosphere there isn't what you usually
25 find in a church.

■ What's wrong? Say what's right.

1 In American schools students have to say they'll be loyal to their school.
2 You can find the motto of the United States on the American flag.
3 For many Americans the USA is "Our own country".
4 The Puritans were one of the last groups of settlers in the USA.
5 The Puritans came from France.
6 There aren't many different religious groups in the USA.
7 The atmosphere in churches that black people go to is usually sad.

W 66, 1-4

*OPTION 4

THE AMISH – MORE THAN A TOURIST ATTRACTION

TRAVEL AGENT You must go to Lancaster County when you're in Pennsylvania. There are lots of Amish people there. And don't forget your camera. It's like an outdoor museum.

CUSTOMER Amish people?

5 **TRAVEL AGENT** Yes, you know, that religious group with the funny clothes that doesn't have cars or electricity. They still live in the 17th century.

CUSTOMER Is that really true?

– Well, most of it is true. The Amish came from Europe
10 almost 300 years ago. They have names like *Stolzfuss* and *Oberholtzer* and some still speak a little German. They're farmers who believe in hard work. They wear traditional clothes and still use horse-drawn buggies. How have the Amish kept the modern world out of their lives?

They have little to do with the world around them. Children only go to the local school –
15 and not for long! Farmers don't move far from home. They never want help from *Draussigers*, but they always help each other. They aren't interested in politics and they hate fighting.

The family is very important.
There are usually about seven children. Their parents almost
20 always stay together all their lives.
Their life is very simple and traditional. Modern things aren't allowed. But some Amish people have been very good at finding
25 compromises.
Here are some examples:

AMISH COMPROMISES

Not allowed:	But it's allowed if ...
a car	somebody who isn't Amish drives, or you live a long way from your family.
electricity	it comes from a generator.
an electric tool	you use it outside the house.
a tractor	it doesn't have tyres.
a phone	it's a public phone.

Not everything is perfect. Some Amish teenagers take drugs, for example.
The Amish say there must be *Ordnung*.
But they also say that teenagers (boys
30 only!) should be free to decide if they want to stay Amish or not. And 80% stay Amish.

And then? They marry early and parents often move into
35 the *Grossdaadi Haus* next door.
And the tourists? They come to Lancaster County and take their photos – even when there are signs like this one …

■ Tasks

1 Describe how you live. (Lines 14–25 will help you.)
2 What isn't allowed in your home (or a friend's home)? Find compromises.

W 67, 1-3

*OPTION 5

THE COMMONWEALTH

Canada, Australia, India and many countries in Africa once belonged to Britain. When they became independent, most of these countries became members of an English-speaking "club", the Commonwealth. The Queen is called the "Head of the Commonwealth", but Britain isn't the most important member. Every country, large or small, has the same rights. A quarter of the world's population lives in the Commonwealth countries. Here's one of them:

- **New Zealand** is 1,600 km east of Australia. It has two big islands, North Island and South Island.
- New Zealand is about as big as Britain, but only about 3 million people live there.
- It's mild in New Zealand. January is the warmest month and July is the coldest, because it's winter then.
- The first people were the Maoris (9% of the population today). They belong to the poorer parts of society.

QUIZ ■ New Zealand

1 86% of the people came from Europe. From which country did most of them come?
a) Ireland; b) Holland; c) Britain.

2 Auckland is the biggest city, but it isn't the capital. What *is* the capital?
a) Wellington; b) Nelson; c) Hamilton.
Tip: Look at the map above.

3 This is New Zealand's famous bird. What is it?
a) An emu; b) a kiwi; c) an Aussie.
Tip: The name sounds like a fruit.

4 Rugby is the most popular sport in New Zealand. What's the country's team called?
a) The Maoris; b) the Zealis;
c) the All Blacks.   Tip: Look at the photo.

EXERCISE ■ How long have they been in the Commonwealth?

1 New Zealand (1931): New Zealand has been in the Commonwealth for … years.
2 Jamaica (1962): Jamaica …
3 Canada (1931)   4 India (1947)   5 Kenya (1963)   6 Malta (1964)

W 68, 1

CLASS PROJECT Fast facts cards

Make a card with photos and information about your country or a country you know. *Example:*

JAMAICA

IMPORTANT FACTS
Independent Commonwealth country
Population: 2,600,000
Capital: Kingston
Holiday place: Montego Bay
Languages: English, Creole

CULTURAL FACTS
Famous singer: Bob Marley
National sport: Cricket
Big events: Reggae Sunsplash Festival; Carnival

FOOD FACTS
Breakfast: Ackee and saltfish
Snack: Jerk
Drink: Ting

Bob Marley

Phrases (English–Creole)
Hallo – *Everyt'ing cool, mon?*
Thanks – *T'anks*
No problem – *Cool runnings*
Goodbye – *One love.*

Tips for tourists
Relax.
Ask before taking photos.
Don't call Jamaicans "natives".
Don't be unfriendly and loud.

Ting

Ackee and saltfish

Jerk

W 68, 2

QUIZ Trivial Pursuit

"Trivial Pursuit" comes from Canada, but most people think the game is American. You have to answer questions about lots of different things. Do you know the answers to these questions?

■ **Who are the famous people in these photos?**
What country do they all come from? Answers: page 137.

ONE LAST THING

Some people say there are Americans who don't know much about Canada. But they probably know more than this man knew ...

Al Capone was a gangster in Chicago in the 1920s.

*OPTION 6

NUMBER ONE LANGUAGE

English is a world language. It's the language of business, computers, science, pop music, sport and advertising. People use words like *yes, goodbye, weekend, girl* and *welcome* all
5 over the world. About a quarter of the world's people speak English today. Most of them have learned it as a foreign language. About 75% of the world's letters and e-mails are in English.

So how did this happen? 400 years ago English was spoken only in Britain. But then 10 the people from these islands started to travel all over the world. They became the rulers in many places – India, large parts of Africa and North America, for example. And the language of the British rulers became the 15 language of their colonies. One of these colonies left the British Empire over two hundred years ago and became independent as "The United States of America". Today the USA is the most influential country in the 20 world. And that's why English is the number one language for international communication.

> **Where do people speak English?**
> **How many countries do you know?**
> **How many can you find out?**

■ **Who uses English?**

English is the language of …? Find the right word for each picture.   Tip: Look at lines 1–3.

Taiwan Film Festival 1999

W 69, 1-3

*OPTION 7

ENGLISH AND …

In some English-speaking countries English isn't the only language. For example:

USA: English and Spanish

English is the official language of the USA – right or wrong? Well, there's no rule that says this, but the USA *is* an English-speaking country! Many people think Spanish (and English, of course) should be an official language. 11 million people in the USA speak Spanish at home. Other people are against the idea. They say that English should be the only official language because it makes people American.

South Africa: English and Afrikaans

Only 14% of people in South Africa are white, but for many years they had all the power in the country. This was because of apartheid, the system that discriminated against black people. "Apartheid" is an Afrikaans word. Afrikaans is the language of 60%, English the language of 34% of the white people. The black people have their own languages, but many of them speak English or Afrikaans, too.

Ireland: English and Irish

When the English came to Ireland, they brought their language with them and "pushed out" the Irish language. Now only 1–2% of people in Ireland use Irish every day. And nobody today speaks only Irish. But Irish is one of the two official languages of the Republic of Ireland. Signs are often in English and Irish, places often have two different names – and everybody has to learn Irish at school.

■ **Where do they come from?**

Everybody here speaks English, and we all have to learn our other official language at school.

English isn't our official language but most people here speak it.

There are many different languages in my country. My people speak their own language. I speak English, too.

W 70, 1-3

*OPTION 8

WORKING AND LIVING IN A FOREIGN COUNTRY

A lot of Germans find jobs in other countries. What's it like to live away from your family and home? What's it like to speak a foreign language every day? Is it easy to make friends? Do people miss their old friends and neighbours? Here are some young people who are talking about their lives in other countries.

SABINE

My family lives near Winterberg. When I left school I became a skiing instructor.

My aunt lives in Canada. With her help I found a job here. I teach skiing in Canada now. Skiing in Germany is great, but the mountains in Canada are the best! I teach swimming in the summer.

Canadians are very friendly – they always talk to strangers. I feel at home here, but I miss my old friends and my family. I have my own life here. I have a Canadian boyfriend and I want to stay in Canada.

■ **Why does Sabine want to stay in Canada?**

JÜRGEN

I live in Jamaica. When I was nine, my father started a new job with an American fruit company in Jamaica. The weather is great and I can swim in the sea every day. I like the food, too.

Some people are very poor here and there's a lot of crime. It can sometimes be dangerous on the streets at night. But most people here are friendly. I've made a lot of friends at school and I speak English well now. I play in the school cricket team.

I don't want to go back to Germany.

■ **What does Jürgen like in Jamaica? What doesn't he like there?**

FRANZISKA

I was born in Germany and I started school in Münster. When I was 13, my mother married my stepfather. He's Indian, so we moved to India and my mother became a teacher at a German language school in Chennai (Madras). I spoke German with my mother and English at school. My Indian friends taught me a lot of Tamil words. But we usually spoke English. I'm 28 now and I'm an engineer. I went to college in Germany. After college I came back to India because I found a job with a German company that has big projects in India. I enjoy living in India.

■ **What languages did Franziska speak when she was a teenager in India? When did she speak them?**

ANDREAS

When I was a teenager in Trier, I often worked in the vineyards. I left school two years ago and I work in a vineyard in Australia now. I can work here for a year.
In the first few weeks here I didn't understand the Australian accent. Now I understand everybody but I can't speak English with an Australian accent yet!
The people are very friendly. Australia is very beautiful, but I often miss Germany. Australia is so big and Germany is so far away. I'm looking forward to going back to Germany next year.

■ **What problem did Andreas have when he arrived in Australia?**

■ **Who's speaking?**
1 "I like living in a beautiful country with friendly people."
2 "I went to college in Germany."
3 "I teach skiing on the best mountains in the world!"
4 "When I was 13 we moved to the country where my stepfather was born."
5 "Sun and sea! It's great. I can go swimming every day."
6 "I like it here, but I want to go back to Germany next year."
7 "You have to be careful. It isn't always safe on the streets at night."
8 "I miss my friends and family, but I like it here. I don't want to go back to Germany."

W 71, 1-3

*OPTION 9 – SUMMARY 1

Direkte und indirekte Rede

Sowohl mit der direkten als auch mit der indirekten Rede kann man wiedergeben, was jemand gesagt hat.

Hi, everybody!
Jay Bird is my favourite star.
He's a great singer.
I often listen to his music.
I can't stop listening to his new CD.
His new single will be a big hit.
* His last single was a big hit, too.
* I've just seen his new video on TV.

Direkte Rede

- *Hier stehen die tatsächlich gesprochenen Wörter zwischen Anführungsstrichen.*
  "Hi, everybody!" said Tracy.

- *Die Pronomen bleiben unverändert.*
  "Jay Bird is **my** favourite star," said Tracy.

- *Auch die Verbformen bleiben hier unverändert.*
  "He**'s** a great singer," she told us.
  "I often **listen** to his music."
  "I **can't** stop listening to his new CD."
  "His new single **will** be a big hit."
  * "His last single **was** a big hit, too."
  * "**I've** just **seen** his new video on TV."

Indirekte Rede

- *Hier handelt es sich um einen Bericht, bei dem manchmal andere Wörter benutzt werden.*
  → Tracy said hallo to everybody.

- *Die Pronomen werden oft verändert.*
  → She said Jay Bird was **her** favourite star.

- *Die Verbformen werden oft verändert, wenn das einleitende Verb (z.B.* say, tell) *im* simple past *steht.*
  → She told us he **was** a great singer.
  → She mentioned that she often **listened** to his music.
  → She said she **couldn't** stop listening to his new CD.
  → She said that his new single **would** be a big hit.
  → She said that his last single **had been** a big hit, too.
  → She said that she **had** just **seen** his new video on TV.

- *Verschiedene Verben können die indirekte Rede einleiten, zum Beispiel:*

say	mention	add
tell	point out	remark

- *Das Wort* that *kann weggelassen werden*:
  She said (that) it was very late.
  He told us (that) the firm made cameras.

He said there was something really interesting in this street.

Yes.
He said we would be very surprised.

Present progressive – Simple present

Die beiden Zeitformen werden unterschiedlich verwendet.

Present progressive form

- Was gerade geschieht

What are you doing at the moment?
– I'm watching TV.
  Was machst du gerade? – Ich sehe fern.
I'm not watching TV. I'm still doing my homework.
  Ich sehe nicht fern. Ich mache noch meine
  Hausaufgaben.

> **Zeitangaben, die oft vorkommen:**
> at the moment ▪ now ▪ still ▪ today

- Was man plant oder vorhat

What are you doing this afternoon?
– I'm not leaving the camp-site. I'm tired.
  Was machst du heute Nachmittag? – Ich verlasse
  den Campingplatz nicht. Ich bin müde.
I'm meeting Don at the Rio Grande at 4 pm.
  Ich treffe Don um 16 Uhr am Rio Grande.

> **Zeitangaben, die oft vorkommen:**
> tomorrow ▪ next week/month/year ▪ after school
> at 4 pm / ... ▪ this morning/afternoon/evening

Simple present form

- Gewohnheiten, Zustände, Vorlieben und Abneigungen, Berufe und Hobbys

Jennifer works at a gas station at the weekend.
  Jennifer arbeitet am Wochenende an einer
  Tankstelle.
She often buys CDs with the money she gets.
  Sie kauft oft CDs von dem Geld, das sie bekommt.
She lives in Arizona but she doesn't like the "Canyon
Rockers".
  Sie wohnt in Arizona, aber sie mag die „Canyon
  Rockers" nicht.

> **Zeitangaben, die oft vorkommen:**
> every day/week/month/year ▪ on Tuesdays
> at the weekend ▪ in the mornings
> always ▪ often ▪ sometimes ▪ never ▪ usually

*OPTION 11 – SUMMARY 3

Modale Hilfsverben

Modale Hilfsverben *(modal verbs)* drücken aus, dass jemand etwas tun kann, darf, muss usw. Sie werden in Verbindung mit der Grundform eines anderen Verbs gebraucht.

- Was jemand tun kann

Fans can see Robbie tomorrow.

can
I can play tennis.
 Ich kann Tennis spielen.
Dave can't find his money.
 Dave kann sein Geld nicht finden.
Can you come to town with me?
 Kannst du mit mir in die Stadt kommen?

- Was jemand tun darf

Can I see your tickets, please?

can
I can stay up late today.
 Ich darf heute lange aufbleiben.
Sue can't come home alone.
 Sue darf nicht allein nach Hause kommen.
Can I use your phone, please?
 Darf ich bitte Ihr Telefon benutzen?

- Was jemand tun muss

You must leave your camera here.

must
I really must help my parents this evening.
 Heute abend muss ich wirklich meinen Eltern helfen.

⚠ *must* wird häufig durch *have to* ersetzt.
I have to meet Jill and Kate in town.
 Ich muss Jill und Kate in der Stadt treffen.

⚠ Bei der Verneinung gibt es zwei Möglichkeiten:
mustn't = nicht dürfen:
We mustn't be noisy. Wir dürfen nicht laut sein.
doesn't/don't have to = nicht brauchen:
You don't have to wait. Du brauchst nicht zu warten.

- Was jemand vielleicht tut

might
Paul might visit his uncle in the USA.
 Paul besucht vielleicht seinen Onkel in den USA.

- Was jemand tun sollte

should
You should go out. You shouldn't watch TV.
 Du solltest ausgehen. Du solltest nicht fernsehen.

Bedingungssätze

Bedingungssätze drücken aus, was unter bestimmten Bedingungen geschehen wird oder würde. Ein Bedingungssatz besteht aus zwei Teilen: einem Nebensatz mit *if* (*if*-Satz) und einem Hauptsatz. Es geht in den Sätzen um verschiedene Arten von Ereignissen, zum Beispiel:

Ereignisse, die möglich sind:

If you buy one box of *Wheatos*, we'll give you another box free.

If you clean your bike in the kitchen, dad will be very angry.

If mum and dad are too busy this evening, my brother will cook the evening meal.
  Wenn Mutti und Vati heute Abend zu beschäftigt sind, wird mein Bruder das Abendessen kochen.
If Tom helps Jane with her homework, she'll give him a dollar.
  Wenn Tom Jane bei den Hausaufgaben hilft, wird sie ihm einen Dollar geben.
If you have a computer, you can buy lots of different games for it.
  Wenn du einen Computer hast, kannst du viele verschiedene Spiele dafür kaufen.
If you go to a birthday party, you should take a present.
  Wenn du zu einer Geburtstagsfeier gehst, solltest du ein Geschenk mitnehmen.

> Der *if*-Satz steht in der *simple present*-Form. Im Hauptsatz steht *will*.
> Auch *can, must* oder *should* können im Hauptsatz stehen.

Ereignisse, die unwahrscheinlich oder unmöglich sind:

If I won the money, I'd (= I would) travel.

If I lived in the USA, I'd speak a lot of English.
  Wenn ich in den USA lebte / leben würde, würde ich viel Englisch sprechen.
If the tickets were cheaper, Jill would go to the concert.
  Wenn die Karten billiger wären, würde Jill in das Konzert gehen.
If Bob was rich, he'd buy a big house.
  Wenn Bob reich wäre, würde er sich ein grosses Haus kaufen.

> Der *if*-Satz steht in der *simple past*-Form. Im Hauptsatz steht *would*.

The English alphabet

a	[eɪ]	j	[dʒeɪ]	s	[es]
b	[biː]	k	[keɪ]	t	[tiː]
c	[siː]	l	[el]	u	[juː]
d	[diː]	m	[em]	v	[viː]
e	[iː]	n	[en]	w	['dʌbljuː]
f	[ef]	o	[əʊ]	x	[eks]
g	[dʒiː]	p	[piː]	y	[waɪ]
h	[eɪtʃ]	q	[kjuː]	z	[zed]
i	[aɪ]	r	[ɑː]		

English sounds

[iː]	team, see, he	[eɪ]	eight, name, play, great	[b]	bike,hobby, table, job
[ɑː]	ask, class, start	[aɪ]	I, time, right, my	[p]	pen, pupil, shop
[ɔː]	or, ball, four, door	[ɔɪ]	boy, toilet	[d]	day, window, good
[uː]	ruler, blue, too, two, you	[əʊ]	old, no, road, yellow	[t]	ten, matter, at
[ɜː]	girl, her, early, work	[aʊ]	house, now	[k]	car, lucky, book
[ɪ]	in, big, enough	[ɪə]	near, here, we're	[g]	go, again, bag
[e]	yes, bed	[eə]	there, repair	[ŋ]	wrong, morning
[æ]	cat, black	[ʊə]	you're, plural	[l]	like, old, small
[ʌ]	bus, colour			[r]	ruler, friend, biro
[ɒ]	on, dog, what			[v]	very, seven, have
[ʊ]	put, good, woman			[w]	we, where, quarter
[ə]	again, sister, today			[s]	six, poster, yes
[i]	radio, video, coffee, happy			[z]	zoo, present, his
[u]	July, usually			[ʃ]	she, station, English
				[tʃ]	child, teacher, match
				[dʒ]	jeans, German, badge
				[ʒ]	garage, usually
				[j]	yes, you, young
				[θ]	thing, maths, tooth
				[ð]	the, father, with

Vocabulary

Dieses Wörterverzeichnis enthält alle neuen Wörter des Buches in der Reihenfolge,
in der sie im Buch zum ersten Mal vorkommen.

In der eckigen Klammer
steht, wie die Wörter
ausgesprochen werden.

Der Pfeil bedeutet:
Schau in die rechte
Spalte.

Dieses Zeichen
bedeutet
„Aufgepasst!".

Diese Zahl gibt die
Seite an, auf der die
Wörter zum ersten
Mal vorkommen.

Die ganz schwarz
gedruckten Wörter
sind besonders wichtig.

Hier sind Wörter in
Gruppen zusammen-
gefasst. Das macht
das Lernen leichter.

Normal gedruckte
Wörter sind wichtig
für das Kapitel, in
dem sie vorkommen.

Schräg gestellte
Wörter kommen
z. B. in Liedern
und Projekten vor.

Ein Sternchen
heißt: Die drei
Formen dieses
unregelmäßigen
Verbs findest du
in dem grauen
Kasten auf der
rechten Seite.

(AE) bedeutet
American English.

In diesem Ab-
schnitt kannst
du selbst über-
prüfen, ob du
Wörter richtig
verstanden
hast.

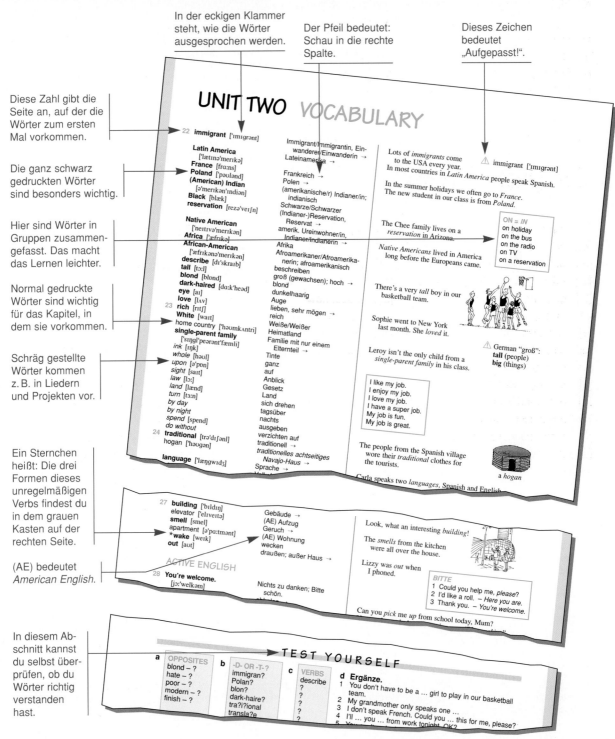

UNIT TWO   VOCABULARY

22 **immigrant** ['ɪmɪgrənt]

Latin America
['lætɪnə'merɪkə]
France [frɑːns]
Poland ['pəʊlənd]
(American) Indian
[ə'merɪkən'ɪndiən]
Black [blæk]
reservation [rezə'veɪʃn]

Native American
['neɪtɪvə'merɪkən]
Africa ['æfrɪkə]
African-American
['æfrɪkənə'merɪkən]
describe [dɪ'skraɪb]
tall [tɔːl]
blond [blɒnd]
dark-haired [dɑːk'heəd]
eye [aɪ]
love [lʌv]
23 **rich** [rɪtʃ]
White [waɪt]
home country ['həʊmkʌntri]
single-parent family
['sɪŋgl'peərənt'fæmli]
ink [ɪŋk]
whole [həʊl]
upon [ə'pɒn]
sight [saɪt]
law [lɔː]
land [lænd]
turn [tɜːn]
by day
by night
spend [spend]
do without
24 **traditional** [trə'dɪʃənl]
hogan ['həʊgən]

language ['læŋgwɪdʒ]

Immigrant/Immigrantin, Ein-
wanderer/Einwanderin →
Lateinamerika →

Frankreich →
Polen →
(amerikanische/r) Indianer/in;
indianisch
Schwarze/Schwarzer
(Indianer-)Reservation,
Reservat →
amerik. Ureinwohner/in,
Indianer/Indianerin →
Afrika
Afroamerikaner/Afroamerika-
nerin; afroamerikanisch
beschreiben
groß (gewachsen); hoch →
blond
dunkelhaarig
Auge
lieben, sehr mögen →
reich
Weiße/Weißer
Heimatland
Familie mit nur einem
Elternteil →
Tinte
ganz
auf
Anblick
Gesetz
Land
sich drehen
tagsüber
nachts
ausgeben
verzichten auf
traditionell →
traditionelles achtseitiges
Navajo-Haus →
Sprache

Lots of *immigrants* come
to the USA every year.
In most countries in *Latin America* people speak Spanish.

In the summer holidays we often go to *France*.
The new student in our class is from *Poland*.

The Chee family lives on a
reservation in Arizona.

Native Americans lived in America
long before the Europeans came.

There's a very *tall* boy in our
basketball team.

Sophie went to New York
last month. She *loved* it.

Leroy isn't the only child from a
single-parent family in his class.

I like my job.
I enjoy my job.
I love my job.
I have a super job.
My job is fun.
My job is great.

The people from the Spanish village
wore their *traditional* clothes for
the tourists.

Carla speaks two *languages*, Spanish and English.

⚠ immigrant ['ɪmɪgrənt]

ON = IN
on holiday
on the bus
on the radio
on TV
on a reservation

⚠ German "groß":
tall (people)
big (things)

a hogan

27 **building** ['bɪldɪŋ]
elevator ['elɪveɪtə]
smell [smel]
apartment [ə'pɑːtmənt]
*wake [weɪk]
out [aʊt]

ACTIVE ENGLISH

28 **You're welcome.**
[jɔː'welkəm]

Gebäude →
(AE) Aufzug
Geruch →
(AE) Wohnung
wecken
draußen; außer Haus →

Nichts zu danken; Bitte
schön.

Look, what an interesting *building*!

The *smells* from the kitchen
were all over the house.

Lizzy was *out* when
I phoned.

Can you *pick* me *up* from school today, Mum?

BITTE
1 Could you help me, *please*?
2 I'd like a roll. — Here you are.
3 Thank you. – You're welcome.

TEST YOURSELF

a | OPPOSITES
blond – ?
hate – ?
poor – ?
modern – ?
finish – ?

b | -D- OR -T-?
immigran?
Polan?
blon?
dark-haire?
tra?i?ional
transla?e

c | VERBS
describe
?
?
?
?
?

d Ergänze.
1 You don't have to be a ... girl to play in our basketball
team.
2 My grandmother only speaks one ...
3 I don't speak French. Could you ... this for me, please?
4 I'll ... you ... from work tonight, OK?

119

UNIT ONE VOCABULARY

6	**media** ['miːdiə]	Medien →
	web site ['websaɪt]	Website *(Gesamtangebot eines Anbieters im Internet bzw. im World Wide Web)*
	viewer ['vjuːə]	Fernsehzuschauer/Fernsehzuschauerin
7	**less** [les]	weniger →
	advert ['ædvɜːt]	Anzeige; Werbespot; Reklame
	local ['ləʊkl]	örtlich; Lokal-; Regional- →
	TV/radio station	Fernseh-/Radiosender
	teenage ['tiːneɪdʒ]	Jugend-, Teenager-
	power ['paʊə]	Macht
	you've yet to have your finest hour ['faɪnɪst]	deine beste Stunde steht dir noch bevor
	someone ['sʌmwʌn]	jemand
	love [lʌv]	lieben, sehr mögen
	"standard" ['stændəd]	Klassiker, Oldie
	the top five [tɒp]	die Top fünf, die wichtigsten fünf *(einer Bestenliste)*
	chose: I chose [tʃəʊz]	ich suchte aus / ich habe ausgesucht
	aerobics [eəˈrəʊbɪks]	Aerobic
	beat [biːt]	Rhythmus, Beat
	message ['mesɪdʒ]	Botschaft, Aussage
	words (of a song)	Text *(eines Liedes)*
8	**business** ['bɪznəs]	Geschäft; Betrieb
	guitarist [gɪˈtɑːrɪst]	Gitarrist/Gitarristin
	talent ['tælənt]	Talent
	energy ['enədʒi]	Energie, Kraft →
	luck [lʌk]	Glück
	career [kəˈrɪə]	Karriere, berufliche Laufbahn →
	mention ['menʃn]	erwähnen →
	in the right place at the right time	zur richtigen Zeit am richtigen Ort
	add [æd]	hinzufügen →
	hall [hɔːl]	Halle, Saal
	musician [mjuːˈzɪʃn]	Musiker/Musikerin
	the only way of learning	die einzige Art zu lernen →
	agent ['eɪdʒənt]	Agent/Agentin
	point out [pɔɪntˈaʊt]	hinweisen auf; betonen →
	hang up [hæŋˈʌp]	aufhängen
	decide [dɪˈsaɪd]	beschließen, (sich) entscheiden →
	remark [rɪˈmɑːk]	bemerken, anmerken
	Good luck!	Viel Glück!
	adjective ['ædʒɪktɪv]	Adjektiv, Eigenschaftswort
	adverb ['ædvɜːb]	Adverb, Umstandswort
9	**publicity** [pʌbˈlɪsəti]	Werbung; Publicity
	TV and radio would … [wʊd]	Fernsehen und Radio würden … →
	recording contract [rɪˈkɔːdɪŋkɒntrækt]	Plattenvertrag
	little ['lɪtl]	wenig →
	member ['membə]	Mitglied

STORY

10	**as** [əz]	als →
	screen [skriːn]	Leinwand; Bildschirm →
	decision [dɪˈsɪʒn]	Entscheidung

All the *media* are talking about her – she's a star!

I think "CompuNews" is *less* interesting than "Online". – Yes, but it costs *less* money.

We're new in this town. – Just read the *local* newspaper to find out what's happening.

VERB + -ER	
listen	– listener
play	– player
read	– reader
sing	– singer
work	– worker
dance	– dancer
drive	– driver
run	– runner

STATION
▪ *Bahnhof:*
bus station
railway station
underground station
▪ *Sender:*
radio station
TV station
▪ *Tankstelle:*
gas station (AE)
▪ *Wache:*
police station

I should really tidy my room now, but I just don't have the *energy*.

I'd like a *career* in the film industry.

Did Anne *mention* me in her letter? – No, she only talked about Paul.

"Be careful," her father said. "And don't be late," her mother *added*.

The best *way of learning* English is to spend some time in Britain or the USA.
Mr Fox *pointed out* the mistakes in my test.

So which T-shirt would you like? – I don't know. I can't *decide*.

⚠ guitarist [gɪˈtɑːrɪst]
talent ['tælənt]
energy ['enədʒi]

⚠ ich hatte Glück
= I was lucky

⚠ hang
I hung
I've hung

add
explain
mention
point out
remark
say
tell

She said my parents *would* win lots of money soon!

A big man sat in front of me, so I saw very *little*.

Phil has a new job. He works *as* a guitarist for "Crash".
Is the "Mega" a big cinema? – Yes, it has ten *screens*.

least [liːst]	wenigste/wenigster/wenigstes; am wenigsten →	Every year "Tim's Teashop" sells the *least* tea. It's the *least* popular tea shop in town.
quick [kwɪk]	schnell	⚠ little – less – least
stupid ['stjuːpɪd]	dumm, blöd	
worse – worst [wɜːs, wɜːst]	schlechter, schlimmer – schlechteste/r/s, schlimmste/r/s; am schlechtesten →	The weather in May was *worse* than in April. But June was the *worst* month of all!
latest ['leɪtɪst]	neueste/neuester/neuestes →	⚠ bad – worse – worst
snack bar ['snækbaː]	Imbissstube, Imbissstand	Have you heard the *latest* news? Tina is going out with Rick!
farther – farthest ['faːðə, 'faːðɪst]	weiter – am weitesten →	I can run *farther* than you, but Jane can run *farthest*.
11 stay out of [steɪ'autəv]	sich heraushalten aus	
whisper ['wɪspə]	flüstern	

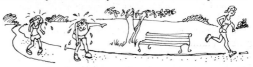

ACTIVE ENGLISH

⚠ far – farther – farthest

12 **When's the programme on?**	Wann läuft die Sendung?	Emma asked *if* you'd like to come to her party next week.
programme ['prəʊɡræm]	programmieren	
if [ɪf]	ob	
violence ['vaɪələns]	Gewalttätigkeit, Gewalt	
attractive [ə'træktɪv]	attraktiv, ansprechend	
parental guidance [pə'rentl'ɡaɪdns]	Begleitung durch die Eltern	
suggested [sə'dʒestɪd]	empfohlen	
inappropriate [ɪnə'prəʊprɪət]	nicht geeignet	
13 **cinema-goer** ['sɪnəməɡəʊə]	Kinobesucher/Kinobesucherin	Let's go dancing tonight.
brilliant ['brɪlɪənt]	toll, glänzend, großartig →	– That's a *brilliant* idea!

TV AND RADIO
watch TV
listen to the radio
on TV / on the radio
video-recorder
cassette-recorder
The programme is on at …
I'll programme the recorder.
(TV/radio) station
(TV/radio) programme
(TV/radio) news
TV screen

PRACTICE PAGES

15 **preposition** [prepə'zɪʃn]	Präposition, Verhältniswort

TEST YOURSELF

a PEOPLE
viewer
?
?
?
?
?

b [ɜː] AND [iː]
m?dia
adv??t
adv??b
scr??n
l??st
w??se
w??st

c Ergänze.
1 Kyte's new CD isn't very good. It's … interesting than her old one.
2 You get all the news about our town on KLIC, our … radio station.
3 I couldn't … which T-shirt I wanted, so I didn't buy one.
4 My teacher said that everybody … have computers soon.
5 little – … – …; bad – … – …; far – … – …
6 I don't know … I can come to the party. I'm very busy at the moment.

TIPS

Auf S. 120 lernst du die englischen Ausdrücke für das Verb „(sich) entscheiden" und das dazugehörige Nomen „Entscheidung". Die beiden Wörter sind sich auch im Englischen ähnlich: *decide* und *decision*. (Achte aber auf die unterschiedliche Aussprache: [dɪ'saɪd] und [dɪ'sɪʒn].)

Wenn du das Gefühl hast, dass zwei Wörter ähnlich sind oder irgendwie zusammengehören, schreibe sie auch zusammen auf. Dann behältst du sie besser.

An welche bekannten Wörter erinnern dich die neuen Wörter rechts?

guitarist luck

musician

UNIT TWO VOCABULARY

22 immigrant ['ɪmɪgrənt]
Immigrant/Immigrantin, Einwanderer/Einwanderin →
Lots of *immigrants* come to the USA every year.
⚠ immigrant ['ɪmɪgrənt]

Latin America ['lætɪnə'merɪkə]
Lateinamerika →
In most countries in *Latin America* people speak Spanish.

France [frɑːns]
Frankreich →

Poland ['pəʊlənd]
Polen →
In the summer holidays we often go to *France*.
The new student in our class is from *Poland*.

(American) Indian [ə'merɪkən'ɪndiən]
(amerikanische/r) Indianer/in; indianisch

Black [blæk]
Schwarze/Schwarzer

reservation [rezə'veɪʃn]
(Indianer-)Reservation, Reservat →
The Chee family lives on a *reservation* in Arizona.

ON = IN
on holiday
on the bus
on the radio
on TV
on a reservation

Native American ['neɪtɪvə'merɪkən]
amerik. Ureinwohner/in, Indianer/Indianerin →
Native Americans lived in America long before the Europeans came.

Africa ['æfrɪkə]
Afrika

African-American ['æfrɪkənə'merɪkən]
Afroamerikaner/Afroamerikanerin; afroamerikanisch

describe [dɪ'skraɪb]
beschreiben

tall [tɔːl]
groß (gewachsen); hoch →
There's a very *tall* boy in our basketball team.

blond [blɒnd]
blond

dark-haired [dɑːk'heəd]
dunkelhaarig

eye [aɪ]
Auge

love [lʌv]
lieben, sehr mögen →
Sophie went to New York last month. She *loved* it.

⚠ German "groß":
tall (people)
big (things)

23 rich [rɪtʃ]
reich

White [waɪt]
Weiße/Weißer

home country ['həʊmkʌntri]
Heimatland

single-parent family ['sɪŋgl'peərənt'fæmli]
Familie mit nur einem Elternteil →
Leroy isn't the only child from a *single-parent family* in his class.

ink [ɪŋk]
Tinte

whole [həʊl]
ganz

upon [ə'pɒn]
auf

I like my job.
I enjoy my job.
I love my job.
I have a super job.
My job is fun.
My job is great.

sight [saɪt]
Anblick

law [lɔː]
Gesetz

land [lænd]
Land

turn [tɜːn]
sich drehen

by day
tagsüber

by night
nachts

spend [spend]
ausgeben

do without
verzichten auf

24 traditional [trə'dɪʃənl]
traditionell →
The people from the Spanish village wore their *traditional* clothes for the tourists.

a *hogan*

hogan ['həʊgən]
traditionelles achtseitiges Navajo-Haus →

language ['læŋgwɪdʒ]
Sprache →
Carla speaks two *languages*, Spanish and English.

fair [feə]
Volksfest, Kirmes

tip [tɪp]
Trinkgeld →
In the USA you always give the waiter or waitress a *tip*.

attraction [ə'trækʃn]
Attraktion →
The biggest *attraction* in our town is the old castle.

horse [hɔːs]
Pferd

25 translate [træns'leɪt]
übersetzen →
My father doesn't speak English, so I have to *translate* when tourists come.

Cuba ['kjuːbə]
Kuba

minority group [maɪ'nɒrətigruːp]
Minderheit →
Joe belongs to a *minority group* in England. He's a Catholic.

LANGUAGE
read
speak
translate
understand
write

STORY

26 reason ['riːzn]
Grund

*begin: I began [bɪ'gɪn, bɪ'gæn]
beginnen, anfangen: ich begann, fing an / ich habe begonnen, angefangen →
The story *begins* in a small village in the mountains of Mexico.

each other [iːtʃ'ʌðə]
einander, sich →

Christmas ['krɪsməs]
Weihnachten
You're good at French and I'm good at maths – let's help *each other* with our homework.

in a car park
auf einem Parkplatz

IN = AUF
in English
in my photo
in the country
in the world
in a car park

27	**building** [ˈbɪldɪŋ]	Gebäude →
	elevator [ˈelɪveɪtə]	(AE) Aufzug
	smell [smel]	Geruch →
	apartment [əˈpɑːtmənt]	(AE) Wohnung
	★wake [weɪk]	wecken
	out [aʊt]	draußen; außer Haus →

ACTIVE ENGLISH

28	**You're welcome.**	Nichts zu danken; Bitte
	[jɔːˈwelkəm]	schön.
	pick up [pɪkˈʌp]	abholen →
	smoke [sməʊk]	rauchen →
	teen curfew [tiːnˈkɜːfjuː]	Ausgangssperre für Teenager
	trouble [ˈtrʌbl]	Schwierigkeiten, Ärger
	jail [dʒeɪl]	Gefängnis
29	**earring** [ˈɪərɪŋ]	Ohrring →

PRACTICE PAGES

33	**Dear Sir or Madam, ...**	Sehr geehrte Damen und
	[dɪəˈsɜːrɔːˈmædəm]	Herren, ...
	Yours faithfully, ...	Mit freundlichen Grüßen ...
	[jɔːzˈfeɪθfəli]	

Look, what an interesting *building*!

The *smells* from the kitchen were all over the house.

Lizzy was *out* when I phoned.

> **BITTE**
> 1 Could you help me, *please*?
> 2 I'd like a roll. – *Here you are.*
> 3 Thank you. – *You're welcome.*

Can you *pick* me *up* from school today, Mum?
You can't *smoke* here. The sign says "No *smoking*".

I can't wear these big *earrings*. My ears are too small.

eye
ear
arm
hand
finger
back
leg
knee
foot

★ IRREGULAR VERBS

INFINITIVE FORM	SIMPLE PAST FORM	PRESENT PERFECT FORM
begin [bɪˈgɪn]	I began [bɪˈgæn]	I've begun [bɪˈgʌn]
wake [weɪk]	I woke [wəʊk]	I've woken [ˈwəʊkən]

AMERICAN ENGLISH VOCABULARY

AE (AMERICAN ENGLISH)	BE (BRITISH ENGLISH)	
apartment [əˈpɑːtmənt]	flat	Wohnung
elevator [ˈelɪveɪtə]	lift	Aufzug

TEST YOURSELF

a OPPOSITES
blond – ?
hate – ?
poor – ?
modern – ?
finish – ?

b -D- OR -T-?
immigran?
Polan?
blon?
dark-haire?
tra?i?ional
transla?e
minori?y group

c VERBS
describe
?
?
?
?
?
?

d Ergänze.
1 You don't have to be a ... girl to play in our basketball team.
2 My grandmother only speaks one ...
3 I don't speak French. Could you ... this for me, please?
4 I'll ... you ... from work tonight. OK?
5 You can't ... in this restaurant. Look at the sign.
6 I usually wear these modern ... . I think they look great.

38	**Canadian** [kə'neɪdiən]	kanadisch; Kanadier/Kana- → dierin	The *Canadian* winter is very long.
	few [fjuː]	wenige →	There were *fewer* people at the party than last time.
	border ['bɔːdə]	Grenze →	A lot of people cross the *border* from Mexico to the USA every day.
	gun [gʌn]	Schußwaffe; Gewehr	
	allowed [ə'laud]	erlaubt →	Eating isn't *allowed* in the library.
39	**war** [wɔː]	Krieg	
	the British	die Briten und Britinnen →	*The British* drink more tea than the Germans or the French.
	queen [kwiːn]	Königin	
	province ['prɒvɪns]	Provinz	
	Chinese [tʃaɪ'niːz]	chinesisch; Chinesisch; Chinese/Chinesin →	My *Chinese* friend thinks that German is a very difficult language.
	Italian [ɪ'tæliən]	italienisch; Italienisch; Italiener/Italienerin →	Enrico is *Italian*, but he speaks a little Spanish, too.

⚠ a few *(ein paar)*
few *(wenige)*
little *(wenig)*

	smile [smaɪl]	Lächeln
	Hold me captive ... [həʊld, 'kæptɪv]	Halte mich gefangen ...
	just a while [waɪl]	nur eine Weile lang
	cloud [klaʊd]	Wolke
	qualm [kwɑːm]	ungutes Gefühl, Bedenken
	burst into sunshine [bɜːst, 'sʌnʃaɪn]	in Sonnenschein aufgehen
	animal rights [raɪts]	Tierrechte, Tierschutz
	charity ['tʃærəti]	Wohltätigkeitsverein
	typical ['tɪpɪkl]	typisch
	moose [muːs]	amerikanischer Elch, amerikanische Elche
	shy [ʃaɪ]	scheu

America	– American
Britain	– British
Canada	– Canadian
China	– Chinese
France	– French
Germany	– German
Ireland	– Irish
Italy	– Italian
Japan	– Japanese

⚠ take – I took – I've taken

The wedding *took place* in January.

My favourite winter sport is *ice-skating*.

40	**Jamaica** [dʒə'meɪkə]	Jamaika
	take place [teɪk'pleɪs]	stattfinden →
	downtown Toronto [daʊntaʊntə'rɒntəʊ]	(AE) die Stadtmitte von Toronto
	mall [mɔːl]	Einkaufszentrum
	ice-skating ['aɪsskeɪtɪŋ]	Schlittschuhlaufen →
	city hall ['sɪti'hɔːl]	(AE) Rathaus
	flavour ['fleɪvə]	Geschmack
	cover ['kʌvə]	verhüllen; bedecken →
	I could [kʊd]	ich konnte →
	Caribbean [kærə'biːən]	1. Karibik; 2. karibisch

Let's *cover* the food to protect it.
Paula *couldn't* speak English when she was younger.

WINTER SPORTS
ice hockey
ice-skating
skiing

STORY

42	**noisy** ['nɔɪzi]	laut, lärmend →
	boastful ['bəʊstfl]	angeberisch, prahlerisch
	relative ['relətɪv]	Verwandte/Verwandter
	I'd rather ... ['rɑːðə]	ich würde lieber ... →
	maple syrup ['meɪpl'sɪrəp]	Ahornsirup
	sound [saʊnd]	klingen, sich anhören →
	guy [gaɪ]	Typ, Kerl
	tough [tʌf]	hart
	lie [laɪ]	Lüge
43	**while** [waɪl]	während →
	after that [ɑːftə'ðæt]	danach
	agree on many things [ə'griː]	sich in vielen Dingen einig sein

The new neighbours have very *noisy* children.

⚠ noisy ['nɔɪzi]

I'd rather watch TV than go out tonight.

Mick *sounded* unhappy when I talked to him on the phone yesterday.

I always listen to music *while* I'm in the bathroom.

ACTIVE ENGLISH

44	**..., aren't you?**	..., nicht wahr? →
	Pleased to meet you.	Freut mich, dich/Sie kennen zu lernen.

You like dogs, *don't you?*
– Yes, I do.

..., NICHT WAHR?
..., aren't you?
..., isn't he/she/it?
..., don't you?
..., doesn't he/she/it?

Would you like anything else? [els]	Möchtest du / Möchten Sie sonst noch etwas?
direct [də'rekt]	direkt
queue [kju:]	Schlange stehen, sich anstellen →
45 helpful ['helpfl]	hilfsbereit; hilfreich
favour ['feɪvə]	Gefallen →
ask for	bitten um →

In Britain and America it's very important to *queue*.

Can you do me a *favour*?
I'm going to *ask* my boss *for* more money tomorrow.

AMERICAN ENGLISH VOCABULARY

AE (AMERICAN ENGLISH)	BE (BRITISH ENGLISH)	
city hall ['sɪti'hɔ:l]	town hall	Rathaus
downtown [daʊn'taʊn]	town centre	Stadtmitte

TEST YOURSELF

a PEOPLE
Canadian
?
?
?
?
?

b [i:] AND [ɔ:]
b??der
w??
qu??n
Chin?se
m?ll
Caribb?an
agr??

c [ə] AM ENDE
bord??
Jamaic?
flav???
cov??
rath??
fav???

d Ergänze.
1 You can't ride your bike here. It isn't …
2 Last year the fair … … in April.
3 I … write a postcard because I didn't have a pen.
4 … … go by bus than walk.
5 People in Germany don't usually … at bus-stops.
6 I had to … other people … help in New York.

TIPS

Ist dir dies auch schon einmal passiert: du liest einen englischen Text und stolperst über ein Wort, das du eigentlich kennst, das aber plötzlich nicht so richtig passt? Dann handelt es sich vielleicht um ein Wort, das als Verb und als Nomen gleich ist. Zum Beispiel „antworten" und „Antwort" – beides heißt *answer*. Schreibe dir solche Wörter zusammen auf und lerne sie gut.

Einige solcher Wörter kennst du auch schon. Schreibe auf, wie
1 das Verb und
2 das Nomen
zu den Wörtern rechts auf Deutsch heißt.

Nun schaue dir alle Wörter in den Listen dieser beiden Seiten gut an. Darin sind zwei Verben, zu denen es Nomen gibt, die genauso lauten (die Nomen stehen aber nicht in der Liste!). Auf Deutsch heißen die Nomen:
1 Klang
2 (Warte-)Schlange
Wie lauten die englischen Wörter?

54	**difference** ['dɪfrəns]	Unterschied
	cricket ['krɪkɪt]	Kricket →
	fashion ['fæ ʃn]	Mode
	improve [ɪm'pru:v]	verbessern →
	demonstration [demən'streɪʃn]	Demonstration
	charity ['tʃærəti]	Wohlfahrt; wohltätige Zwecke
55	**right** [raɪt]	Recht →
	★ride a moped ['məʊped]	Moped fahren
	cigarette [sɪgə'ret]	Zigarette
	lottery ticket ['lɒtərɪtɪkɪt]	Los
	get married ['mærid]	heiraten →
	★ride a motor bike ['məʊtəbaɪk]	Motorrad fahren
	credit card ['kredɪtkɑ:d]	Kreditkarte
	vote [vəʊt]	wählen →
	age [eɪdʒ]	Alter →
	I'm bored [bɔːd]	ich langweile mich
	I don't want to be nobody's fool [fu:l]	ich will mir nichts vormachen lassen
	sweet [swi:t]	süß; lieb
	neat [ni:t]	ordentlich
	I don't want someone living my life for me ['sʌmwʌn]	ich will nicht, dass jemand anders mein Leben für mich lebt
	turn [tɜ:n]	(um)drehen, (um)krempeln
	inside out ['ɪnsaɪd'aʊt]	auf links
	suburbia [sʌ'bɜ:bɪə]	Vorstadt
	turn upside down ['ʌpsaɪd'daʊn]	auf den Kopf stellen
	walk the streets	durch die Straßen laufen
	scream [skri:m]	schreien
	crawl [krɔ:l]	kriechen
	alley-way ['æliweɪ]	Gasse
	survey ['sɜ:veɪ]	Umfrage
	millionaire [mɪljə'neə]	Millionär/Millionärin
56	**whatever** [wɒt'evə]	was auch immer, egal was
	nose [nəʊz]	Nase
	everywhere ['evriweə]	überall →
	sponsor ['spɒnsə]	1. sponsern; 2. Sponsor/in, Geldgeber/in →
	walk [wɔ:k]	Spaziergang, Wanderung
	crazy ['kreɪzi]	verrückt →
	notice-board ['nəʊtɪsbɔ:d]	Anschlagbrett, schwarzes Brett
	for nothing	umsonst
57	**take part (in)** [teɪk'pɑ:t]	teilnehmen (an), mitmachen (bei) →
	protest ['prəʊtest]	Protest
	destroy [dɪ'strɔɪ]	zerstören
	protest [prə'test]	protestieren
	underground ['ʌndəgraʊnd]	unterirdisch, unter der Erde
	successful [sək'sesfl]	erfolgreich
	it's worth it [wɜ:θ]	es lohnt sich →
	serious ['sɪəriəs]	seriös; ernst, ernsthaft
	popular newspapers	Massenblätter
	international [ɪntə'næʃnəl]	international

Cricket is a very popular sport in England.

I'm going to France for a year to *improve* my French.

In my country people have the *right* to say what they think.

So when are you two *getting married*?

Sheila can't *vote* yet. She's only 15.
Do you know the *age* of that building?
It's beautiful!

⚠ get
I got
I've got

baseball
basketball
cricket
football
hockey
rugby
soccer
tennis
table-tennis
volleyball

drive a car
go by car
go by bus/train
go by plane – fly
ride a bike – cycle
ride a moped
ride a motor bike

⚠ nose [nəʊz]

I've looked *everywhere* for my pen, but I can't find it.

every *(jede/r/s)*
everybody *(alle, jeder)*
everything *(alles)*
everywhere *(überall)*

A local company *is sponsoring* our sports club.
But we need more *sponsors*.
I paid £50 for this T-shirt. – You must be *crazy*!

⚠ take – I took – I've taken

Last year I *took part in* a sponsored walk.
It was lots of fun.

⚠ protest: 1 ['prəʊtest] *(Protest)*
2 [prə'test] *(protestieren)*

-FUL
beautiful
boastful
careful
helpful
successful
useful

I won't wash my car again.
It isn't worth it.

4

STORY

58	**he changed his mind** [maɪnd]	er änderte seine Meinung →	Where's Maggie?

58 **he changed his mind** [maɪnd] — er änderte seine Meinung →
a waste of time [weɪst] — Zeitverschwendung
megaphone ['megəfəʊn] — Megaphon
crowd [kraʊd] — (Menschen-)Menge
59 **typical** ['tɪpɪkl] — typisch →

Where's Maggie?
– She *changed her mind*. She isn't coming.

We couldn't go to the concert because Melanie left the tickets at home. – Oh no! That's so *typical*!

⚠ typical ['tɪ̱pɪkl]

ACTIVE ENGLISH

60 **he cheers her up** — er muntert sie auf →
down [daʊn] — „down", bedrückt
I'm fed up with going to the cinema. — Ich habe es satt, ins Kino zu gehen. →
61 **grumpy** ['grʌmpi] — schlecht gelaunt, mürrisch
That's what friends are for. — Dazu sind Freunde/Freundinnen da.
order ['ɔːdə] — Reihenfolge

I've tried to *cheer him up* but he's still very sad.

I'm *fed up with surfing* the Internet – I never find what I'm looking for.

angry
down
fed up
frightened
grumpy
sad
unhappy
worried

PRACTICE PAGES

64 What do you **like about** …? — Was gefällt dir an …? →

There's one thing I *like about* Ricky: He's always helpful.

★ IRREGULAR VERBS

INFINITIVE FORM	SIMPLE PAST FORM	PRESENT PERFECT FORM
ride [raɪd]	I rode [rəʊd]	I've ridden ['rɪdn]

TEST YOURSELF

a -V- OR -W-?
impro?e
?ote
e?ery?here
?alk
it's ?orth it
a ?aste of time

b [d] AND [t]
righ?
cigare???
get marrie?
vo??
notice-boar?
crow?

c [s] AND [z]
differen??
no??
spon?or
cra?y
succe??ful
seriou?

d Ergänze.
1 Aida wants to … her English, so she's going to Canada for six months.
2 That's a beautiful old tree. Do you know its …?
3 I couldn't … … … the demonstration. I was ill.
4 Tim was late, so we missed the bus. – That's so …!
5 Simon is so unhappy. Nobody can … … …

TIPS

Manchmal siehst oder hörst du ein neues englisches Wort, das dich an ein bekanntes Wort erinnert. Dann versuche zuerst einmal zu erraten, was das Wort bedeuten könnte. Das kannst du üben.

Du kennst z. B. bereits das Wortpaar *help* (= Hilfe) und *helpful* (= hilfsbereit; hilfreich). Auf S. 126 lernst du das Wort *successful* (= erfolgreich). Kannst du jetzt erraten, was das englische Wort *success* [sək'ses] auf Deutsch heißt?

UNIT FIVE VOCABULARY

70 **work experience**
['wɜːkɪk'spɪəriəns'] — Berufspraktikum →

earn [ɜːn] — verdienen →

courier ['kʊriə] — Kurier/Kurierin, Bote/Botin →

garage ['gærɑːʒ] — (Reparatur-)Werkstatt

an apprentice bricklayer [ə'prentɪs] — ein Maurerlehrling →

mechanic [mə'kænɪk] — Mechaniker/Mechanikerin

college ['kɒlɪdʒ] — Berufsschule, Fach(hoch)- schule

cashier [kæ'ʃɪə] — Kassierer/Kassiererin

(working) hours — Arbeitszeit →

71 **diary** ['daɪəri] — Tagebuch

manic ['mænɪk] — manisch; verrückt

middle ['mɪdl] — Mitte

dream [driːm] — Traum

crystal blue ['krɪstl'bluː] — kristallblau

stream [striːm] — Bach

I guess ... [ges] — Ich nehme an, ...

wish [wɪʃ] — wünschen

I wish it was ... — Ich wünschte, es wäre ...

dirty ['dɜːti] — schmutzig

guess [ges] — erraten

72 **answer the phone** — ans Telefon gehen →

heavy ['hevi] — schwer →

envelope ['envələʊp] — Briefumschlag

day centre ['deɪsentə] — Altentagesstätte, Seniorentreff

nervous ['nɜːvəs] — nervös, ängstlich

serve [sɜːv] — 1. servieren; 2. bedienen →

chat [tʃæt] — sich unterhalten, plaudern →

bookshelf, bookshelves ['bʊkʃelf, 'bʊkʃelvz] — Bücherregal, Bücherregale

73 **careers teacher** [kə'rɪəztiːtʃə] — Lehrer/Lehrerin für die Berufs- beratung

cook [kʊk] — Koch/Köchin

prepare [prɪ'peə] — vorbereiten →

vegetable ['vedʒtəbl] — Gemüse

fill in [fɪl'ɪn] — ausfüllen →

application form [æplɪ'keɪʃnfɔːm] — Bewerbungsformular →

practise ['præktɪs] — üben, trainieren →

(job) interview ['ɪntəvjuː] — Vorstellungsgespräch

I'm training to be a ... — ich mache eine Ausbildung zum/zur ... →

pass the exam [pɑːs, ɪg'zæm] — die Prüfung bestehen

job centre ['dʒɒbsentə] — Arbeitsamt

apply (to/for) [ə'plaɪ] — sich bewerben (bei/um) →

government training scheme ['gʌvənmənt'treɪnɪŋskiːm] — staatliches Ausbildungs- programm

plumber ['plʌmə] — Installateur/Installateurin, Klempner/Klempnerin

STORY

74 **coffee pot** ['kɒfipɒt] — Kaffeekanne →

in the end [ɪnðɪ'end] — schließlich →

waitress ['weɪtrəs] — Kellnerin →

it's called [kɔːld] — es (er/sie) heißt →

★bet [bet] — wetten

You learn a lot about a job in *work experience*.
Peter didn't *earn* much money in his old job.
Peggy loves cycling. She's a bike *courier*.

Rita is *an apprentice* TV engineer. She's learning to repair TVs.

The *working hours* in an office are usually from 9 to 5.

JOBS		
bank clerk	musician	shop assistant
bricklayer	nurse	teacher
bus/... driver	police officer	TV engineer
chemist	postman	waiter
farmer	reporter	warden

Mike, can you *answer the phone*, please? I'm busy.
I can't carry your bag. It's too *heavy*.

address
envelope
letter
postcard
postman
post office
stamp

A waiter has to *serve* meals.
   A shop assistant has to *serve* customers.
I love *chatting* with my old friends.

⚠ nervous ['nɜːvəs]

⚠ one shel**f** – two shel**ves**

Can you *prepare* the salad while I'm setting the table?

For a successful application you have to *fill in* the *application form* carefully.

You have to *practise* a lot to be a good guitarist.

⚠ vegetable ['vedʒtəbl]

Robby *is training to be a* bike mechanic.

Last week Anita *applied to* "The Car Company".
Today she*'s applying for* a job at "Tesco's".

⚠ plumber ['plʌmə]

a *coffee pot*

First they hated each other. *In the end* they became friends.
The new restaurant is looking for waiters and *waitresses*.
My dog is my best friend. *He's called* Jet.

| **I can't stand it** | ich kann es nicht aus-stehen → | I *can't stand* big crowds. They make me nervous. |
| 75 **advertise** ['ædvətaɪz] | Reklame machen (für), werben (für) → | They *advertised* their new game in computer magazines. |

ACTIVE ENGLISH

| 76 **fill** [fɪl] | (auf)füllen, voll machen → | Could you *fill* this glass for me, please? |

*IRREGULAR VERBS

INFINITIVE FORM	SIMPLE PAST FORM	PRESENT PERFECT FORM
bet [bet]	I bet [bet]	I've bet [bet]

TEST YOURSELF

a MORE JOBS
courier
?
?
?
?
?

b FIND THE VERBS
? money – earn money
? the phone
? lunch (or customers)
? vegetables
? ? an application form
? a job interview
? the exam
? for a job

c Ergänze.
1 It's a nice job, but you don't … enough money.
2 We're moving soon. We need people who can carry … things.
3 Could you help me to … the food for the party tonight?
4 If you want to be a good singer, you have to … every day.
5 Have you seen the new fashion magazine? … … "Flash".
6 You like "Fan's World"? … … … that magazine! It's terrible.
7 The company … their new car in many international newpapers.

TIPS

Wenn dich neue Wörter an bereits bekannte Wörter erinnern, aber du nicht sicher bist, ob sie wirklich zusammengehören, schau im *Dictionary* nach. Meistens sind einige Anfangsbuchstaben gleich.
Damit du ein wenig Übung bekommst, kannst du die folgende Aufgabe lösen.

Du kennst die folgenden Verben und Adjektive. Nun suche die dazugehörigen Nomen im *Dictionary* (ab S. 138). Manche kennst du auch schon. Schreibe die Paare auf.

build   cloudy   different   attractive   decide   interested

feel   lucky   independent   invite   empty

traditional

86	**face** [feɪs]	Gesicht
	ask for	bitten um →
	rain [reɪn]	Regen
	on the corner [ˈkɔːnə]	an der Ecke
	real [ˈriːəl]	echt, richtig →
	Walk of Fame [ˈwɔːkəvˈfeɪm]	Weg des Ruhms
	sound [saʊnd]	klingen, sich anhören →
	pavement [ˈpeɪvmənt]	Bürgersteig
	star [stɑː]	Stern →
	handprint [ˈhændprɪnt]	Handabdruck
	cement [sɪˈment]	Zement
	Lots of love from, …	Viele liebe Grüße …
	security guard [sɪˈkjʊərətigɑːd]	Wachperson, Angestellte/r beim Sicherheitsdienst
	climb the hills [klaɪm]	auf die Hügel klettern →
	impossible [ɪmˈpɒsəbl]	unmöglich →
87	**shabby** [ˈʃæbi]	schäbig
88	**rest** [rest]	Rest
	act [ækt]	spielen (in einem Film/Theaterstück) →
	play [pleɪ]	Theaterstück →
	actor [ˈæktə]	Schauspieler/Schauspielerin
	accident [ˈæksɪdənt]	Unfall
	amputate [ˈæmpjuteɪt]	amputieren
	★**wake: I woke** [weɪk, wəʊk]	aufwachen: ich wachte auf / ich bin aufgewacht →
	politics [ˈpɒlətɪks]	Politik
	governor [ˈgʌvənə]	Gouverneur/Gouverneurin
	what sort of governor [sɔːt]	was für ein Gouverneur →
	free enterprise [ˈentəpraɪz]	freies Unternehmertum
	government [ˈgʌvənmənt]	Regierung →
	strong [strɒŋ]	stark →
	military [ˈmɪlətri]	Militär
	minority group [maɪˈnɒrətigruːp]	Minderheit
	★**begin: I began** [bɪˈgɪn, bɪˈgæn]	beginnen, anfangen: ich begann, fing an / ich habe begonnen, angefangen →
	disease [dɪˈziːz]	Krankheit
	★**lead** [liːd]	führen →
	sunset [ˈsʌnset]	Sonnenuntergang
90	**mobile** [ˈməʊbaɪl]	mobil, beweglich
	the old favourites [ˈfeɪvrətsl]	die alten Lieblingshits/Lieblings…
	live on little money	von wenig Geld leben
	answer to	antworten auf
	answering machine [ˈɑːnsərɪŋməʃiːn]	(AE) Anrufbeantworter
	first-aid kit [fɜːstˈeɪdkɪt]	Verbandskasten →
	sewing kit [ˈsəʊɪŋkɪt]	Nähzeug →
	hairspray [ˈheəspreɪ]	Haarspray
	hair gel [ˈheədʒel]	Haargel
	van [væn]	Lieferwagen
	insect spray [ˈɪnsektspreɪ]	Insektenspray
	go wrong	schief gehen →
91	**romantic** [rəʊˈmæntɪk]	romantisch
	refugee [refjuˈdʒiː]	Flüchtling →
	sort [sɔːt]	Art, Sorte
	beat [biːt]	Rhythmus, Beat
	beetle [ˈbiːtl]	Käfer

I *asked* Frank *for* help, but he said he didn't have time.

real
really
reality

"Sunny" isn't her *real* name. It's Sandra.

Mick *sounded* nervous when I talked to him on the phone.

a *star*

⚠ climb [kla<u>ɪ</u>m]

Our cat *climbs* every tree in the garden.
You can't eat ten large cakes – it's *impossible*!

I'd love to *act* in the next school *play*.

act
actor
film
film star
play
western

Mandy usually *wakes* early on Sundays.

What sort of music do you like?
– I like rap.

He's so *strong* that he can carry a dishwasher!

⚠ politi**c**s (Politik)

⚠ military [ˈmɪlə<u>tri</u>]

We *began* writing to each other in 1996.

The dog *is leading* the police officer to a bag full of drugs.

a *first-aid kit*

a *sewing kit*

⚠ sewing kit [ˈs<u>əʊ</u>ɪŋkɪt]

How was your holiday? – Not so good.
So many things *went wrong*.

⚠ go
I went
I've gone

Some *refugees* came to the USA because of a war in their own country.

EXTRA 1

*IRREGULAR VERBS

INFINITIVE FORM	SIMPLE PAST FORM	PRESENT PERFECT FORM
begin [bɪˈgɪn]	I began [bɪˈgæn]	I've begun [bɪˈgʌn]
lead [liːd]	I led [led]	I've led [led]
wake [weɪk]	I woke [wəʊk]	I've woken [ˈwəʊkən]

AMERICAN ENGLISH VOCABULARY

AE (AMERICAN ENGLISH)	BE (BRITISH ENGLISH)	
answering machine [ˈɑːnsərɪŋməʃiːn]	answerphone	Anrufbeantworter

TEST YOURSELF

a ADJECTIVES
real
?
?
?
?

b -EA- OR -EE-?
r??l
dis??se
l??d
refug??
b??t
b??tle

c Ergänze.
1 This isn't a … cat, of course. It's only a toy.
2 Sheila phoned. She … really happy.
3 I can't do this difficult exercise – it's …!
4 Tom wants to be an actor. He loves to … in our school plays.
5 I love bananas. … … … fruit do you like?
6 The woman is … the old man across the street.

EXTRA WORDS

COMPUTERS

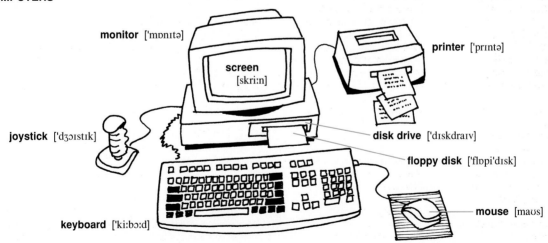

monitor [ˈmɒnɪtə]

screen [skriːn]

printer [ˈprɪntə]

joystick [ˈdʒɔɪstɪk]

disk drive [ˈdɪskdraɪv]

floppy disk [ˈflɒpiˈdɪsk]

mouse [maʊs]

keyboard [ˈkiːbɔːd]

92	**make friends**	Freundschaft(en) schließen →
	annual ['ænjʊəl]	jährlich →
	membership ['membəʃɪp]	Mitgliedschaft
	fee [fiː]	Gebühr
	non-members [nɒn'membəz]	Nicht-Mitglieder
	per [pɜː]	pro
	session ['seʃn]	Treffen; Sitzung
	swimming club	Schwimmverein
	['swɪmɪŋklʌb]	
	fill in [fɪl'ɪn]	ausfüllen
	form [fɔːm]	Formular
	aerobics [eə'rəʊbɪks]	Aerobic
93	**short** [ʃɔːt]	kurz; klein →
	outdoor centre ['aʊtdɔːsentə]	Ferienlager
	postcode ['pəʊstkəʊd]	Postleitzahl
	formal ['fɔːməl]	offiziell; formell →
	like this [laɪk'ðɪs]	so, auf diese Weise
	at the end of October [end]	Ende Oktober →
	go potholing ['pɒthəʊlɪŋ]	Höhlen erkunden gehen
94	**alternative** [ɔːl'tɜːnətɪv]	1. alternativ; 2. Alternative →
	lifestyle ['laɪfstaɪl]	Lebensstil
	prize [praɪz]	Preis, Gewinn
	put on	aufführen (Theaterstück, Show)
	puppet show ['pʌpɪtʃəʊ]	Puppentheater →
	college ['kɒlɪdʒ]	Berufsschule, Fach(hoch)-schule
	nine-to-five job	Bürojob (mit fester Arbeitszeit)
	uncomfortable [ʌn'kʌmftəbl]	unbequem; ungemütlich →
	luxury ['lʌkʃəri]	Luxus
	earn [ɜːn]	verdienen
95	**in the last few** years	in den letzten paar Jahren
	increase [ɪn'kriːs]	ansteigen, zunehmen →
	doorway ['dɔːweɪ]	Eingang
	argue ['ɑːgjuː]	(sich) streiten →
	he was drunk [drʌŋk]	er war betrunken
	one day	eines Tages
	★**hit: I hit** [hɪt]	schlagen: ich schlug / ich habe geschlagen →
	★**sleep rough** [rʌf]	im Freien übernachten
	hostel ['hɒstl]	Wohnheim; Obdachlosenheim
	frightening ['fraɪtnɪŋ]	beängstigend →
	lonely ['ləʊnli]	einsam
96	**joyriding** ['dʒɔɪraɪdɪŋ]	Fahren eines gestohlenen Autos (zum Vergnügen) →
	joyrider ['dʒɔɪraɪdə]	Fahrer/in eines für eine (Vergnügungs-)Fahrt gestohlenen Autos
	illegal [ɪ'liːgl]	ungesetzlich, illegal →
	garage ['gærɑːʒ]	(Reparatur-)Werkstatt
	track [træk]	Rennstrecke
	legal ['liːgl]	gesetzlich, legal
	support [sə'pɔːt]	unterstützen, fördern →
	donation [dəʊ'neɪʃn]	Spende →
	supporter [sə'pɔːtə]	Förderer/Förderin
	correct [kə'rekt]	korrigieren, berichtigen →
97	**opinion** [ə'pɪnjən]	Meinung
	I want them to …	Ich will, dass sie … →
	thief, thieves [θiːf, θiːvz]	Dieb/Diebin, Diebe/Diebinnen →
	fine [faɪn]	Geldstrafe →
	mechanic [mə'kænɪk]	Mechaniker/Mechanikerin

I*'ve made* a lot of *friends* in my new job.
The *annual* dog show always takes place in May.

⚠ make
I made
I've made

> meet
> like each other
> make friends
> go out together
> get married

Lisa has *short* hair, but Jenny has long hair.

E-mail letters are often less *formal* than letters you send by post.
I'm going to the Caribbean *at the end of* the year.
We've heard John's idea, and Kate's *alternative* suggestion. Are there other *alternatives*?

⚠ go
I went
I've gone

⚠ price (Preis, Kaufpreis)
prize (Preis, Gewinn)

For a good *puppet show* you need an attractive puppet.

This couch is a little *uncomfortable.* – Yes, but the comfortable ones are more expensive.

The number of people without a job *has increased* again.

⚠ put
I put
I've put

It's terrible! The children *are arguing* again.

What happened?
– We argued. Then he *hit* me.

I watched a *frightening* film last night. After that I couldn't sleep.

Joyriding is a serious crime.

In Britain it's *illegal* to buy cigarettes if you're under 16.

> crime
> drugs
> legal
> illegal
> jail
> joyriding
> police
> prison
> steal

My boss *supports* lots of local charity groups.
We need *donations* for the refugees. Food and clothes are the most important things.
When my teacher *corrected* my homework, he found five mistakes.
I *want my children to* have a better life.

She didn't have to go to prison, but she had to pay a high *fine.*

⚠ one thie**f**
two thie**ves**

chance [tʃɑːns]	Chance, Gelegenheit	Mum, I'm so *bored*. What can I do?
they're bored [bɔːd]	sie langweilen sich →	The neighbours *complained* about our dog.
complain [kəm'pleɪn]	sich beschweren →	Somebody *broke into* our flat while we were on holiday.
*break into [breɪk'ɪntu]	aufbrechen, einbrechen (in) →	

*IRREGULAR VERBS

INFINITIVE FORM	SIMPLE PAST FORM	PRESENT PERFECT FORM
break [breɪk]	I broke [brəʊk]	I've broken ['brəʊkən]
hit [hɪt]	I hit [hɪt]	I've hit [hɪt]
sleep [sliːp]	I slept [slept]	I've slept [slept]

TEST YOURSELF

a

OPPOSITES
member – ?
long – ?
comfortable – ?
legal – ?

b

[ɜː] AND [iː]
f??
p??
???n
incr??se
ill?gal
th??f

c Ergänze.
1. This chair looks nice, but it's very …
2. Mark had a … dream last night, so he couldn't sleep.
3. The number of people who don't smoke has … in the last years.
4. You can't drive a car before you're 17 in Britain. It's …
5. We've organised an animal rights group and we're looking for people who want to … us.

EXTRA WORDS

THE HEAD [hed]

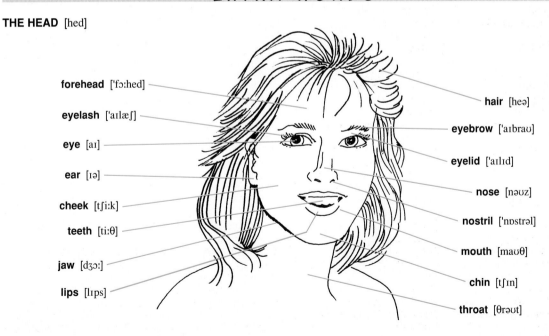

forehead ['fɔːhed]

eyelash ['aɪlæʃ]

eye [aɪ]

ear [ɪə]

cheek [tʃiːk]

teeth [tiːθ]

jaw [dʒɔː]

lips [lɪps]

hair [heə]

eyebrow ['aɪbraʊ]

eyelid ['aɪlɪd]

nose [nəʊz]

nostril ['nɒstrəl]

mouth [maʊθ]

chin [tʃɪn]

throat [θrəʊt]

98	**leave behind**	zurücklassen, hinter sich lassen →
	settle ['setl]	sich niederlassen; sich einleben
	culture ['kʌltʃə]	Kultur
	After **he had lost** his job, …	Nachdem er seine Arbeits-stelle verloren hatte, … →
	depressed [dɪ'prest]	deprimiert, niedergeschlagen
	chemist ['kemɪst]	Chemiker/Chemikerin
	like **very much**	sehr mögen
	foreign countries ['fɒrən'kʌntriz]	fremde Länder, Ausland
	husband ['hʌzbənd]	Ehemann
	both [bəʊθ]	beide →
	chemical factory ['kemɪkl'fæktri]	Chemiefabrik
	whole [həʊl]	ganz →
	excited [ɪk'saɪtɪd]	aufgeregt
	get used to [ju:st]	sich gewöhnen an →
99	**How do they feel about …?**	Was halten sie von …?
	rent [rent]	Miete
	pudding ['pʊdɪŋ]	Nachtisch
	delicious [dɪ'lɪʃəs]	köstlich, lecker
100	**grow** [grəʊ]	anbauen; heranziehen →
	spray [spreɪ]	(be)sprühen, sprayen
	chemical ['kemɪkl]	Chemikalie
	organic [ɔ:'gænɪk]	biodynamisch, Bio- *(natürlich behandelt)* →
	baker's shop ['beɪkəzʃɒp]	Bäckerladen →
	robot ['rəʊbɒt]	Roboter
101	**butcher** ['bʊtʃə]	Fleischer/Fleischerin
	retire [rɪ'taɪə]	sich zur Ruhe setzen, in Rente gehen
	take over [teɪk'əʊvə]	übernehmen →
	★run a shop	ein Geschäft führen
	butcher's shop ['bʊtʃəzʃɒp]	Fleischerei
	meat [mi:t]	Fleisch
	sandwich bar ['sænwɪtʃbɑ:]	„Sandwichladen", Stehcafé
	office worker ['ɒfɪsw3:kə]	Büroangestellte/r
	steel [sti:l]	Stahl →
102	**mobile phone** ['məʊbaɪl'fəʊn]	Mobiltelefon, Handy
	introduce [ɪntrə'dju:s]	einführen →
	mobile job ['məʊbaɪl'dʒɒb]	*Arbeit, bei der man viel unter-wegs ist*
	travelling salespeople ['seɪlzpi:pl]	Handelsreisende, Vertreter/Vertreterinnen →
	ban [bæn]	verbieten →
	disability [dɪsə'bɪləti]	Behinderung
	public ['pʌblɪk]	öffentlich
	doctor ['dɒktə]	Arzt/Ärztin, Doktor
	enter ['entə]	eingeben →
	complaint [kəm'pleɪnt]	Beschwerde
	petrol station ['petrəlsteɪʃn]	Tankstelle →
	(phone) call [kɔ:l]	Anruf
	person ['p3:sn]	Person, Mensch →
	passive ['pæsɪv]	Passiv
103	**notice** ['nəʊtɪs]	bemerken
	crash into a bus [kræʃ'ɪntu]	auf einen Bus auffahren →
	emergency services [ɪ'm3:dʒənsi's3:vɪsɪz]	Notdienst
	he's getting better	es geht ihm schon besser

When their holiday was over, they had to *leave* their new friends *behind*.

⚠ leave – I left – I've left

After they *had moved* to England, they felt lonely.

Luke doesn't like tennis *very much*.

MAN	– WOMAN
husband	– wife
father	– mother
son	– daughter
brother	– sister
uncle	– aunt
cousin	– cousin

There are shops on *both* sides of the street.

I was so thirsty, I drank a *whole* bottle of water.

The food wasn't very good, but I soon *got used to* it.

HE'S/SHE'S/IT'S …ED	
bored	frightened
closed	interested
depressed	surprised
excited	worried

⚠ get – I got – I've got

I *grew* these tomatoes myself.

⚠ grow – I grew – I've grown

You can't buy *organic* vegetables in every supermarket.
This *baker's shop* is always full.
– Well, Alice is a very good baker.

⚠ robot ['rəʊbɒt]   ⚠ butcher ['bʊtʃə]

Mrs Brown was ill, so Mr Carr *took over* her class.

⚠ take – I took – I've taken

cereals
fruit
vegetables
fish
meat

Knives are made of *steel*.

The company *is introducing* a new car this year.

MADE OF …
glass
metal
plastic
steel
wood

Mrs Harris is a *travelling saleswoman*. She sells books all over the country.
The government *has banned* smoking in schools.

Could you *enter* this text into the computer, please?

Today most *petrol stations* don't only sell petrol.

One *person* at the party talked so much that all the other people were quiet.
I was talking to my mum. Then I *crashed into* a tree.

★IRREGULAR VERBS

INFINITIVE FORM	SIMPLE PAST FORM	PRESENT PERFECT FORM
run [rʌn]	I ran [ræn]	I've run [rʌn]

TEST YOURSELF

a 2 WORDS
? countries
? factory
? phone
travelling ?
? station
? services

b 2 OR 3 WORDS
? behind
? ? to
take ?
? ? shop
? into

c [ʃ] AND [ʃə]
cult???
deli????s
but????
petrol sta???n
cra??

d Ergänze.
1 I was so hungry, I ate a … cake.
2 The music wasn't very good, but she … … … it.
3 You can't break these. They're made of …
4 We're … a fantastic new hair gel next week.
5 The police have … demonstrations here.
6 At this … … you can buy everything, even food.

EXTRA WORDS

THE BODY ['bɒdi]

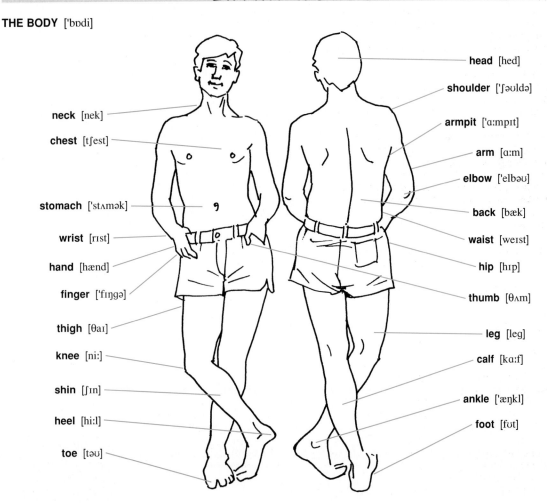

neck [nek]
chest [tʃest]
stomach ['stʌmək]
wrist [rɪst]
hand [hænd]
finger ['fɪŋgə]
thigh [θaɪ]
knee [ni:]
shin [ʃɪn]
heel [hi:l]
toe [təʊ]

head [hed]
shoulder ['ʃəʊldə]
armpit ['ɑːmpɪt]
arm [ɑːm]
elbow ['elbəʊ]
back [bæk]
waist [weɪst]
hip [hɪp]
thumb [θʌm]
leg [leg]
calf [kɑːf]
ankle ['æŋkl]
foot [fʊt]

OPTIONS VOCABULARY

OPTION 1

104 *star* [stɑː]   Stern

OPTION 2

105 *the last few years*   die letzten Jahre
there's a good chance   die Wahrscheinlichkeit ist
  [tʃɑːns]   groß
Swedish ['swiːdɪʃ]   schwedisch; Schwede/
     Schwedin
still [stɪl]   trotzdem
Atlantic [ət'læntɪk]   Atlantik
think of an answer   sich eine Antwort ausden-
     ken
kind [kaɪnd]   Art
rhythm ['rɪðəm]   Rhythmus
the Fifties ['fɪftiz]   die fünfziger Jahre
African-American   Afroamerikaner/in;
  ['æfrɪkənə'merɪkən]   afroamerikanisch
ancestor ['ænsestə]   Vorfahr/Vorfahrin
contribute [kən'trɪbjuːt]   beitragen
Black [blæk]   Schwarze/Schwarzer
once [wʌns]   einmal, einst
slave [sleɪv]   Sklave/Sklavin

OPTION 3

106 *nation* ['neɪʃn]   Nation
God [gɒd]   Gott
flag [flæg]   Fahne, Flagge
heart [hɑːt]   Herz
loyal ['lɔɪəl]   treu
In God we trust. [trʌst]   Wir vertrauen auf Gott.
motto ['mɒtəʊ]   Motto, Wahlspruch
believe in   glauben an
religion [rɪ'lɪdʒən]   Religion
settler ['setlə]   Siedler/Siedlerin
Puritan ['pjʊərɪtən]   Puritaner/Puritanerin
strict [strɪkt]   streng
allowed [ə'laʊd]   erlaubt
active ['æktɪv]   aktiv
religious [rɪ'lɪdʒəs]   religiös
atmosphere ['ætməsfɪə]   Stimmung, Atmosphäre

OPTION 4

107 *the Amish* ['ɑːmɪʃ]   die „Amischen" (Amish-
     Mennoniten)
travel agent ['trævleɪdʒənt]   Reisebüroangestellte/r
outdoor museum   Freilichtmuseum
  ['aʊtdɔːmjuːˈziːəm]
religious [rɪ'lɪdʒəs]   religiös
electricity [ɪlek'trɪsəti]   Elektrizität, Strom
century ['sentʃəri]   Jahrhundert
believe in   glauben an
horse-drawn ['hɔːsdrɔːn]   von Pferden gezogen
buggy ['bʌgi]   leichter Wagen
politics ['pɒlətɪks]   Politik
simple ['sɪmpl]   einfach
allowed [ə'laʊd]   erlaubt
compromise ['kɒmprəmaɪz]   Kompromiss
generator ['dʒenəreɪtə]   Generator, Stromerzeuger
electric [ɪ'lektrɪk]   elektrisch
tractor ['træktə]   Traktor
tyre ['taɪə]   Reifen
public ['pʌblɪk]   öffentlich
also ['ɔːlsəʊ]   auch
marry ['mæri]   heiraten

OPTION 5

108	*Australia* [ɒ'streɪlɪə]	Australien
	India ['ɪndɪə]	Indien
	once [wʌns]	einmal, einst
	head [hed]	Oberhaupt
	right [raɪt]	Recht
	population [pɒpju'leɪʃn]	Bevölkerung
	New Zealand [nju:'zi:lənd]	Neuseeland
	island ['aɪlənd]	Insel
	mild [maɪld]	mild
	Kenya ['kenjə]	Kenia
109	*fact* [fækt]	Tatsache
	Creole ['kri:əʊl]	kreolisch
	cultural ['kʌltʃərəl]	kulturell
	cricket ['krɪkɪt]	Kricket
	event [ɪ'vent]	Veranstaltung; Ereignis
	festival ['festɪvl]	Festival; Fest
	ackee ['æki]	Baumfrucht
	saltfish ['sɔ:ltfɪʃ]	eingelegter Fisch
	jerk [dʒɜːk]	mariniertes, gegrilltes Fleisch
	relax [rɪ'læks]	(sich) entspannen
	Jamaican [dʒə'meɪkən]	jamaikanisch; Jamaikaner/Jamaikanerin
	"native" ['neɪtɪv]	„Eingeborene/Eingeborener"
	1920s [naɪnti:n'twentiz]	zwanziger Jahre

OPTION 6

110	*business* ['bɪznəs]	Wirtschafts- und Geschäftswelt
	advertising ['ædvətaɪzɪŋ]	Werbung
	foreign language ['fɒrən'læŋgwɪdʒ]	Fremdsprache
	island ['aɪlənd]	Insel
	ruler ['ru:lə]	Herrscher/Herrscherin
	India ['ɪndɪə]	Indien
	colony ['kɒləni]	Kolonie
	the British Empire ['empaɪə]	das britische Kolonialreich
	influential [ɪnflu'enʃl]	einflussreich
	communication [kəmju:nɪ'keɪʃn]	Kommunikation

OPTION 7

111	*official language* [ə'fɪʃl'læŋgwɪdʒ]	Amtssprache
	power ['paʊə]	Macht
	system ['sɪstəm]	System
	discriminate against [dɪ'skrɪmɪneɪt]	diskriminieren, benachteiligen
	push out [pʊʃ'aʊt]	hinausdrängen

OPTION 8

112	*foreign language* ['fɒrən'læŋgwɪdʒ]	Fremdsprache
	make friends	Freundschaft(en) schließen
	skiing instructor ['ski:ɪŋɪnstrʌktə]	Skilehrer/Skilehrerin
	teach [ti:tʃ]	beibringen, unterrichten
	stranger ['streɪndʒə]	Fremde/Fremder
	sea [si:]	Meer
113	*marry* ['mæri]	heiraten
	Indian ['ɪndɪən]	Inder/Inderin; indisch
	India ['ɪndɪə]	Indien
	Tamil ['tæmɪl]	tamilisch
	vineyard ['vɪnjəd]	Weinberg
	Australia [ɒ'streɪlɪə]	Australien
	Australian [ɒ'streɪlɪən]	australisch

Answers to the quiz on page 109:
1 William Shatner; 2 Alanis Morissette; 3 Bryan Adams; 4 Celine Dion;
5 Michael J. Fox; 6 Pamela Anderson. They all come from Canada.

Answer to the question on page 91: The Fugees.

Dictionary

Alphabetische Liste der Wörter aus den Bänden 1– 5

(AE): Angegeben sind grundsätzlich Schreibweise und Aussprache des britischen Englisch; Wörter, die vorwiegend im amerikanischen Englisch benutzt werden, sind mit (AE) gekennzeichnet.

A

a [ə] ein/eine; **£2 a week** 2 Pfund pro Woche

about [ə'baʊt] **1.** über, von; **2.** wegen; **3.** ungefähr; **crazy about** verrückt nach; **The programme is about …** Die Sendung handelt von …; **What about …?** Wie wäre es mit …? Was ist mit …? **What do you like about …?** Was gefällt dir an …?

above [ə'bʌv] über

accent ['æksənt] Akzent

accident ['æksɪdənt] Unfall

accommodation [əkɒmə'deɪʃn] Unterkunft

ackee ['æki] *Baumfrucht*

across [ə'krɒs] (quer) durch, über

act [ækt] **1.** sich benehmen, sich verhalten; **2.** spielen *(in einem Film/Theaterstück)*

action ['ækʃn] Handlung, Tätigkeit

active ['æktɪv] aktiv

activity [æk'tɪvəti] Tätigkeit, Aktivität; Unternehmung

actor ['æktə] Schauspieler/in

add [æd] hinzufügen

address [ə'dres] Adresse

adjective ['ædʒɪktɪv] Adjektiv, Eigenschaftswort

adult ['ædʌlt] Erwachsene/Erwachsener

adverb ['ædvɜːb] Adverb, Umstandswort

advert ['ædvɜːt] Anzeige; Werbespot; Reklame

advertise ['ædvətaɪz] Reklame machen (für), werben (für)

advertising ['ædvətaɪzɪŋ] Werbung

aerobics [eə'rəʊbɪks] Aerobic

Africa ['æfrɪkə] Afrika

African-American ['æfrɪkənə'merɪkən] Afroamerikaner/in; afroamerikanisch

after ['ɑːftə] **1.** nach; **2.** nachdem; **after school** nach der Schule; **after that** danach

afternoon ['ɑːftə'nuːn] Nachmittag; **Good afternoon.** Guten Tag. *(nachmittags)*; **in the afternoon(s)** nachmittags; am Nachmittag; **this afternoon** heute Nachmittag

again [ə'gen] (schon) wieder; noch einmal

against [ə'genst] gegen

age [eɪdʒ] Alter; **of the right age** im richtigen Alter

agency ['eɪdʒənsi]: **travel agency** Reisebüro

agent ['eɪdʒənt] Agent/Agentin; **travel agent** Reisebüroangestellte/r

ago [ə'gəʊ]: **400 years ago** vor 400 Jahren

agree [ə'griː]: **agree on many things** sich in vielen Dingen einig sein

ahead [ə'hed]: **straight ahead** geradeaus

airport ['eəpɔːt] Flughafen

Albania [æl'beɪniə] Albanien

alcohol ['ælkəhɒl] Alkohol

all [ɔːl] alle; alles; **all Canada** ganz Kanada; **all day/month/…** den ganzen Tag/Monat/… (lang); **all over** überall (in/auf); **all the time** die ganze Zeit

alley-way ['æliweɪ] Gasse

allowed [ə'laʊd] erlaubt

almost ['ɔːlməʊst] fast, beinahe

alone [ə'ləʊn] allein

along [ə'lɒŋ] entlang

already [ɔːl'redi] schon

also ['ɔːlsəʊ] auch

alternative [ɔːl'tɜːnətɪv] **1.** alternativ; **2.** Alternative

always ['ɔːlweɪz] immer

a m ['eɪ'em] morgens, vormittags

am [æm]: **I am** ich bin

America [ə'merɪkə] Amerika

American [ə'merɪkən] amerikanisch; Amerikaner/in; **American Indian** (amerik.) Indianer/in; indianisch

Amish ['ɑːmɪʃ]: **the Amish** die „Amischen" *(Amish-Mennoniten)*

amputate ['æmpjuteɪt] amputieren

an [ən] ein/eine

ancestor ['ænsestə] Vorfahr/Vorfahrin

and [ænd, ənd] und

angry ['æŋgri] böse, wütend

animal ['ænɪməl] Tier; **animal home** Tierheim

annual ['ænjuəl] jährlich

another [ə'nʌðə] ein anderer / eine andere / ein anderes; noch ein/eine/eins

answer ['ɑːnsə] **1.** antworten, beantworten; **answer to** antworten auf; **answer the phone** ans Telefon gehen, einen Anruf entgegennehmen; **2.** Antwort; Lösung

answering machine ['ɑːnsərɪŋməʃiːn] (AE) Anrufbeantworter

answerphone ['ɑːnsəfəʊn] Anrufbeantworter

any ['eni]: **not … any** kein/keine; keine/keiner/keines; **not any more** nicht mehr

anybody ['enibɒdi]: **not … anybody** niemand

anything ['eniθɪŋ]: **not … anything** nichts; **Would you like anything else?** Möchtest du / Möchten Sie sonst noch etwas?

apart [ə'pɑːt]: **miles apart** meilenweit voneinander entfernt

apartheid [ə'pɑːthaɪt] Apartheid

apartment [ə'pɑːtmənt] (AE) Wohnung

apple ['æpl] Apfel

application [æplɪ'keɪʃn] Bewerbung; **application form** Bewerbungsformular

apply (for/to) [ə'plaɪ] sich bewerben (um/bei)

apprentice [ə'prentɪs]: **an apprentice bricklayer** ein Maurerlehrling

April ['eɪprəl] April

are [ɑː]: **you are** du bist; ihr seid; Sie sind; **we/they are** wir/sie sind

argue ['ɑːgjuː] (sich) streiten

arm [ɑːm] Arm

army ['ɑːmi] Armee, Heer

around [ə'raʊnd]: **around Manhattan** um Manhattan herum; **turn around** sich umdrehen

arrive [ə'raɪv] ankommen

art [ɑːt] Kunst

article ['ɑːtɪkl] Artikel

as [æz, əz] **1.** als; **2.** wie; **3.** während; **as near as** so nah wie

Asian ['eɪʃn] asiatisch; Asiat/Asiatin

ask [ɑːsk] fragen; bitten; **ask about** fragen nach; **ask for** bitten um; **ask a question** eine Frage stellen

asleep [ə'sliːp]: **I was asleep** ich schlief / ich habe geschlafen

assistant [ə'sɪstənt]: **shop assistant** Verkäufer/Verkäuferin

at [æt, ət] bei; an; in; **at 6 o'clock** um 6 Uhr / 18 Uhr; **at 16** mit 16 (Jahren); **at Dave's house / Asif's flat** bei Dave/Asif zu Hause; **at home** zu Hause, daheim; **at least** zumindest; mindestens; **at night** nachts, in der Nacht; **at school** in der Schule; **at that time** damals; **at the moment** zurzeit, im Augenblick; **at the top** auf der Spitze; **at the weekend** am Wochenende; **at work** bei der Arbeit

ate [et]: **I ate** ich aß / ich habe gegessen

Atlantic [ət'læntɪk] Atlantik

atmosphere ['ætməsfɪə] Stimmung, Atmosphäre

attack [ə'tæk] angreifen

attraction [ə'trækʃn] Attraktion

attractive [ə'træktɪv] attraktiv, ansprechend

auction ['ɔːkʃn] Versteigerung

audience ['ɔːdɪəns] Publikum

August ['ɔːgəst] August

aunt [ɑːnt] Tante

Australia [ɒ'streɪlɪə] Australien

Australian [ɒ'streɪlɪən] australisch

autumn ['ɔːtəm] Herbst

avenue ['ævənjuː] Straße *(in einer Stadt)*

awake [ə'weɪk]: **I'm awake** ich bin wach

away [ə'weɪ] weg, entfernt; fort

B

baby ['beɪbi] Baby

back [bæk] **1.** zurück; **2.** Rücken

backpack ['bækpæk] Rucksack

backwards ['bækwədz] rückwärts; nach hinten

bacon ['beɪkən] Speck

bad [bæd] schlecht, schlimm; **too bad** schade

badge [bædʒ] Abzeichen; Anstecker, Button

bag [bæg] (Schul-)Tasche, Tüte

baker ['beɪkə] Bäcker/Bäckerin; **baker's shop** Bäckerladen

ball [bɔːl] Ball

ban [bæn] verbieten

banana [bə'nɑːnə] Banane

band [bænd] Band, (Musik-)Gruppe

bank [bæŋk] Bank, Sparkasse; **bank clerk** Bankangestellte/r

bar [bɑː] Bar, Kneipe; **sandwich bar** „Sandwichladen", Stehcafé

barbecue ['bɑːbɪkjuː] Grill; Grillfest

bark [bɑːk] bellen

baseball ['beɪsbɔːl] Baseball

basket ['bɑːskɪt] Korb

basketball ['bɑːskɪtbɔːl] Basketball

bathroom ['bɑːθruːm] Bad, Badezimmer

battery ['bætəri] Batterie

be [biː] sein

beach [biːtʃ] Strand

beads [biːdz] Perlenkette, -ketten

bean [biːn] Bohne

bear [beə] Bär; **black bear** ['blækbeə] Schwarzbär; **grizzly bear** ['grɪzlibeə] Grislibär

beat [biːt] **1.** schlagen; **I beat** ich schlug / ich habe geschlagen; **2.** Rhythmus, Beat

beaten ['biːtn]: **I've beaten** ich habe geschlagen

beautiful ['bjuːtɪfl] schön, wunderschön

beaver ['biːvə] Biber

became [bɪ'keɪm]: **I became** ich wurde / ich bin geworden

because [bɪ'kɒz] weil; **because of** wegen

become [bɪ'kʌm] werden; **I've become** ich bin geworden

bed [bed] Bett; **go to bed** ins Bett gehen; **in bed** im Bett; **bed and breakfast** [bedən'brekfəst] Zimmer mit Frühstück *(in kleiner Frühstückspension)*

bedroom ['bedruːm] Schlafzimmer

been [biːn, bɪn]: **I've been** ich bin gewesen

beetle ['biːtl] Käfer

before [bɪ'fɔː] **1.** vor; **2.** bevor; **3.** vorher, schon einmal

began [bɪ'gæn]: **I began** ich begann, fing an / ich habe begonnen, angefangen

begin [bɪ'gɪn] beginnen, anfangen

beginning [bɪ'gɪnɪŋ] Anfang

begun [bɪ'gʌn]: **I've begun** ich habe begonnen, angefangen

behind [bɪ'haɪnd] hinter

believe (in) [bɪ'liːv] glauben (an)

belong to [bɪ'lɒŋtu, bɪ'lɒŋtə] gehören (zu)

bench [bentʃ] (Garten-, Park-)Bank

best [best] beste/bester/bestes; der/die/das Beste

bet [bet] wetten; **I bet** ich wettete / ich habe gewettet; **I've bet** ich habe gewettet

better ['betə] besser

between [bɪ'twiːn] zwischen

big [bɪg] groß

bike [baɪk] Fahrrad; **ride a bike** Rad fahren; **bike path** Fahrradweg

bingo ['bɪŋgəʊ] Bingo(spiel)

biology [baɪ'ɒlədʒi] Biologie

bird [bɜːd] Vogel

biro ['baɪrəʊ] Kugelschreiber

birth [bɜːθ]: **place of birth** Geburtsort

birthday ['bɜːθdeɪ] Geburtstag; **Happy birthday (to you)!** Herzlichen Glückwunsch zum Geburtstag!

bit [bɪt]: **a bit** ein bisschen, ein wenig

black [blæk] schwarz; **black bear** ['blækbeə] Schwarzbär

Black [blæk] Schwarze/Schwarzer

block [blɒk] Häuserblock

blond [blɒnd] blond

blue [bluː] blau

blues [bluːz] Blues(musik)

board [bɔːd] Tafel

boastful ['bəʊstfl] angeberisch, prahlerisch

boat [bəʊt] Schiff, Boot

bomb [bɒm] Bombe

book [bʊk] **1.** Buch; Heft; **2.** buchen, reservieren (lassen), vorbestellen

bookshelf, bookshelves ['bʊkʃelf, 'bʊkʃelvz] Bücherregal, Bücherregale

border ['bɔːdə] Grenze

bored [bɔːd] gelangweilt; **I'm bored** ich langweile mich

boring ['bɔːrɪŋ] langweilig

born [bɔːn]: **I was born ...** ich wurde ... geboren

borrow ['bɒrəʊ] (sich) borgen, (sich) ausleihen

Bosnia ['bɒzniə] Bosnien

boss [bɒs] Boss

both [bəʊθ] beide

bottle ['bɒtl] Flasche

bought [bɔːt]: **I bought** ich kaufte / ich habe gekauft; **I've bought** ich habe gekauft

box [bɒks] Kiste, Karton, Schachtel, Dose

boy [bɔɪ] Junge

boycott ['bɔɪkɒt] Boykott

boyfriend ['bɔɪfrend] (fester) Freund

brain [breɪn] Gehirn

bread [bred] Brot

break [breɪk] **1.** brechen, zerbrechen, kaputtmachen; **break into** aufbrechen, einbrechen (in); **break up** sich (von jemandem) trennen; **2.** Pause; **have a break** (eine) Pause machen; **lunch break** Mittagspause

breakfast ['brekfəst] Frühstück; **for breakfast** zum Frühstück; **have breakfast** frühstücken

bricklayer ['brɪkleɪə] Maurer/in

bridge [brɪdʒ] Brücke

brilliant ['brɪliənt] toll, glänzend, großartig

bring [brɪŋ] bringen, mitbringen

Britain ['brɪtn] Großbritannien

British ['brɪtɪʃ] britisch; Brite/Britin; **the British** die Briten und Britinnen

brochure ['brəʊʃə] Broschüre

broke [brəʊk]: **I broke** ich zerbrach / ich habe zerbrochen (usw.)

broken ['brəʊkən] gebrochen, zerbrochen, kaputt; **I've broken** ich habe zerbrochen (usw.)

brother ['brʌðə] Bruder

brought [brɔːt]: **I brought** ich brachte (mit) / ich habe (mit)gebracht; **I've brought** ich habe (mit)gebracht

brown [braʊn] braun

budgie ['bʌdʒi] Wellensittich

buffalo, buffaloes ['bʌfələʊ, 'bʌfələʊz] Büffel

buffet ['bʊfeɪ] Büffet

buggy ['bʌgi] leichter Wagen

build [bɪld] bauen

building ['bɪldɪŋ] Gebäude

built [bɪlt]: **I built** ich baute / ich habe gebaut; **I've built** ich habe gebaut

burst [bɜːst]: **burst into sunshine** in Sonnenschein aufgehen

bus [bʌs] Bus; **bus station** Bushof, Busbahnhof

bus-stop ['bʌstɒp] Bushaltestelle

business ['bɪznəs] 1. Geschäft; Betrieb; 2. Wirtschafts- und Geschäftswelt

busy ['bɪzi] beschäftigt; hektisch, belebt

but [bʌt] aber

butcher ['bʊtʃə] Fleischer/Fleischerin; **butcher's shop** Fleischerei

buy [baɪ] kaufen; **I'll buy you a meal.** Ich spendiere dir ein Essen.

by [baɪ] von, durch; **by bike/bus/ car/...** mit dem Rad/Bus/Auto/...; **by day** tagsüber; **by night** nachts

Bye. / Bye-bye. [baɪ, baɪ'baɪ] Tschüs. Wiedersehen.

C

café ['kæfeɪ] Café

cafeteria [kæfə'tɪəriə] Selbstbedienungsrestaurant, Cafeteria

cake [keɪk] (kleiner) Kuchen

calculator ['kælkjuleɪtə] Taschenrechner

California [kælɪ'fɔːniə] Kalifornien

call [kɔːl] 1. nennen; **it's called** es (er/sie) heißt; **a man called ...** ein Mann, der ... heißt/hieß; 2. rufen, herbeirufen; 3. **(phone) call** Anruf

came [keɪm]: **I came** ich kam / ich bin gekommen

camel ['kæml] Kamel

camera ['kæmrə] Fotoapparat, Kamera

camp [kæmp] zelten; **go camping** zelten gehen

camp-site ['kæmpsaɪt] Campingplatz; Zeltplatz

can[1] [kæn, kən] können, dürfen; **can't** [kɑːnt] (= **cannot** ['kænɒt]) nicht können, nicht dürfen

can[2] [kæn] Dose, Büchse

Canada ['kænədə] Kanada

Canadian [kə'neɪdiən] kanadisch; Kanadier/Kanadierin

canoe [kə'nuː] 1. Kanu; 2. Kanu fahren

capital ['kæpɪtl] Hauptstadt

captive ['kæptɪv]: **Hold me captive ...** Halte mich gefangen ...

car [kɑː] Auto; **car park** (großer) Parkplatz, Parkhaus; **in a car park** auf einem Parkplatz

caravan ['kærəvæn] Wohnwagen

card [kɑːd] (Spiel-, Post-)Karte; **youth hostel card** Jugendherbergsausweis

career [kə'rɪə] Karriere, berufliche Laufbahn; **careers teacher** Lehrer/in für die Berufsausbildung

careful ['keəfl] vorsichtig; sorgfältig

Caribbean [kærə'biːən] 1. Karibik; 2. karibisch

caribou ['kærɪbuː] Karibu

carry ['kæri] tragen; befördern

cashier [kæ'ʃɪə] Kassierer/in

casino [kə'siːnəʊ] (Spiel-)Kasino

cassette [kə'set] Cassette

castle ['kɑːsl] Burg; Schloss

cat [kæt] Katze

Catholic ['kæθlɪk] Katholik/Katholikin

cattle ['kætl] Vieh, Rinder

cave [keɪv] Höhle

CD [siː'diː] CD

CD-ROM [siːdiː'rɒm] CD-ROM

celebrate ['selɪbreɪt] feiern

cement [sɪ'ment] Zement

cent **(¢)** [sent] Cent (nordamerikanisches Geld)

centimetre ['sentɪmiːtə] Zentimeter

central heating [sentrəl'hiːtɪŋ] Zentralheizung

centre ['sentə] Zentrum, Mitte; Center; **day centre** Altentagesstätte, Seniorentreff; **job centre** Arbeitsamt; **outdoor centre** Ferienlager

century ['sentʃəri] Jahrhundert

cereal ['sɪəriəl] Getreide-, Frühstücksflocken

certainly ['sɜːtnli] sicherlich, bestimmt

chair [tʃeə] Stuhl

chance [tʃɑːns] Chance, Gelegenheit; **there's a good chance** die Wahrscheinlichkeit ist groß

change [tʃeɪndʒ] (sich) ändern, verändern; **I've changed my mind** ich habe meine Meinung geändert; **change (trains/...)** umsteigen; (den Zug/...) wechseln

charity ['tʃærəti] 1. Wohlfahrt; wohltätige Zwecke; 2. Wohltätigkeitsverein

chat [tʃæt] sich unterhalten, plaudern

cheap [tʃiːp] billig, preiswert

check [tʃek] (über)prüfen, kontrollieren

cheer [tʃɪə]: **he cheers her up** er muntert sie auf; **Cheer up!** Kopf hoch!

cheerleader ['tʃɪəliːdə] *Person, die das Publikum bei einem Wettkampf zum Beifall anfeuert*

cheese [tʃiːz] Käse

cheeseburger ['tʃiːzbɜːgə] Cheeseburger

chemical ['kemɪkl] Chemikalie; **chemical factory** Chemiefabrik

chemist ['kemɪst] 1. Apotheker/in, Drogist/in; 2. Chemiker/in; **at the chemist's** in der Apotheke/Drogerie

chewing gum ['tʃuːɪŋgʌm] Kaugummi

chicken ['tʃɪkɪn] Huhn; (Brat-)Hähnchen

chief [tʃiːf] Häuptling

child, children [tʃaɪld, 'tʃɪldrən] Kind, Kinder

Chinese [tʃaɪ'niːz] chinesisch; Chinesisch; Chinese/Chinesin

chip shop ['tʃɪpʃɒp] Pommes-frites-Bude

chips [tʃɪps] Pommes frites

chocolate ['tʃɒklət] Trinkschokolade; Schokolade

chose [tʃəʊz]: **I chose** ich suchte aus / ich habe ausgesucht

Christmas ['krɪsməs] Weihnachten

church [tʃɜːtʃ] Kirche, Kirchen-

cigarette [sɪgə'ret] Zigarette
cinema ['sɪnəmə] Kino
cinema-goer ['sɪnəməgəʊə] Kinobesucher/Kinobesucherin
city ['sɪti] Stadt, Großstadt; **city hall** (AE) Rathaus
Civil Rights movement [sɪvl'raɪtsmuːvmənt] Bürgerrechtsbewegung
class [klɑːs] Klasse
classroom ['klɑːsruːm] Klassenzimmer
clean [kliːn] 1. sauber machen, putzen; **I clean my teeth.** Ich putze mir die Zähne. 2. sauber
clear ['klɪə]: **clear the table** den Tisch abräumen
clerk [klɑːk]: **bank clerk** Bankangestellte/Bankangestellter
clever ['klevə] schlau, klug
climb [klaɪm]: **climb the hills** auf die Hügel klettern
clock [klɒk] Uhr
close [kləʊz] zumachen, schließen
closed [kləʊzd] geschlossen, zu
clothes [kləʊðz] Kleidung, Kleider
clothing ['kləʊðɪŋ] Kleidung
cloud [klaʊd] Wolke
cloudy ['klaʊdi] bewölkt
club [klʌb] Club, Verein
coach [kəʊtʃ] Trainer/Trainerin
coal [kəʊl] Kohle
coffee ['kɒfi] Kaffee; **coffee pot** ['kɒfipɒt] Kaffeekanne
coke [kəʊk] Cola
cola ['kəʊlə] Cola
cold [kəʊld] 1. kalt; **I'm cold** ich friere; 2. Erkältung
collect [kə'lekt] (ein)sammeln
college ['kɒlɪdʒ] 1. Berufsschule, Fach(hoch)schule; 2. Hochschule (in Nordamerika)
colony ['kɒləni] Kolonie
"Colored" ['kʌləd] „Farbige/Farbiger" (BE: "Coloured")
colour ['kʌlə] Farbe; **What colour is ...?** Welche Farbe hat ...?
come [kʌm] kommen; **I've come** ich bin gekommen; **Come on!** Komm/Kommt schon! Los!
come true wahr werden; **they come in boxes** sie sind in Schachteln erhältlich
comfortable ['kʌmftəbl] bequem; gemütlich
comic ['kɒmɪk] Comic(heft)
communication [kəmjuːnɪ'keɪʃn] Kommunikation
company ['kʌmpəni] Gesellschaft, Firma

complain [kəm'pleɪn] sich beschweren
complaint [kəm'pleɪnt] Beschwerde
compromise ['kɒmprəmaɪz] Kompromiss
computer [kəm'pjuːtə] Computer, Rechner
concert ['kɒnsət] Konzert
continued [kən'tɪnjuːd]: **To be continued.** Fortsetzung folgt.
contract ['kɒntrækt]: **recording contract** Plattenvertrag
contribute [kən'trɪbjuːt] beitragen
cook [kʊk] 1. kochen; 2. Koch/Köchin
cool [kuːl] kühl; ruhig, überlegen
corner ['kɔːnə] Ecke
cornflakes ['kɔːnfleɪks] Cornflakes
correct [kə'rekt] korrigieren, berichtigen
cost [kɒst] (Geld) kosten
costume ['kɒstjuːm] Kostüm
couch [kaʊtʃ] Couch, Sofa
cough [kɒf] Husten
could [kʊd]: **I could** 1. ich könnte; 2. ich konnte
count [kaʊnt] zählen
country ['kʌntri] 1. Land; **in the country** auf dem Land; 2. Country(musik)
couple ['kʌpl] Paar
courier ['kʊriə] Kurier/in, Bote/Botin
course [kɔːs] Kurs, Lehrgang; **of course** natürlich, selbstverständlich
cousin ['kʌzn] Cousin/Cousine, Vetter
cover ['kʌvə] verhüllen; bedecken
cow [kaʊ] Kuh
cowboy ['kaʊbɔɪ] Cowboy
crash [kræʃ]: **crash into a bus** auf einen Bus auffahren
crawl [krɔːl] kriechen
crazy (about) ['kreɪzi] verrückt (nach)
credit card ['kredɪtkɑːd] Kreditkarte
Creole ['kriːəʊl] kreolisch
cricket ['krɪkɪt] Kricket
crime [kraɪm] Verbrechen
crisps [krɪsps] Kartoffelchips
Croatia [krəʊ'eɪʃə] Kroatien
cross [krɒs] überqueren
crowd [kraʊd] (Menschen-)Menge
cry [kraɪ] weinen
crystal ['krɪstl]: **crystal blue** kristallblau
Cuba ['kjuːbə] Kuba
cultural ['kʌltʃərəl] kulturell
culture ['kʌltʃə] Kultur
cup [kʌp] Tasse
cupboard ['kʌbəd] Schrank

curfew ['kɜːfjuː]: **teen curfew** Ausgangssperre für Teenager
customer ['kʌstəmə] Kunde/Kundin
cv [siː'viː] (= **curriculum vitae** [kə'rɪkjələm'viːtaɪ]) Lebenslauf
cycle ['saɪkl] Rad fahren
cycling ['saɪklɪŋ] Radfahren
Czech Republic [tʃekrɪ'pʌblɪk] Tschechische Republik

D

dad [dæd] Papa, Vati
dance [dɑːns] 1. tanzen; 2. Tanz; Tanzveranstaltung, Ball
dancer ['dɑːnsə] Tänzer/Tänzerin
dangerous ['deɪndʒərəs] gefährlich
dark [dɑːk] dunkel
dark-haired [dɑːk'heəd] dunkelhaarig
date [deɪt] Datum
daughter ['dɔːtə] Tochter
day [deɪ] Tag; **day centre** Altentagesstätte, Seniorentreff; **day return** Tagesrückfahrkarte; **open day** Tag der offenen Tür
dead [ded] tot
Dear ... [dɪə] Liebe/Lieber ...; **Dear Sir or Madam, ...** Sehr geehrte Damen und Herren, ...
December [dɪ'sembə] Dezember
decide [dɪ'saɪd] beschließen, (sich) entscheiden
decision [dɪ'sɪʒn] Entscheidung
decoration [dekə'reɪʃn] Dekoration, Verzierung
degree [dɪ'griː] Grad
delicious [dɪ'lɪʃəs] köstlich, lecker
deliver [dɪ'lɪvə] austragen, zustellen; liefern
demonstration [demən'streɪʃn] Demonstration
dentist ['dentɪst] Zahnarzt/Zahnärztin; **at the dentist's** beim Zahnarzt / bei der Zahnärztin
department store [dɪ'pɑːtməntstɔː] Kaufhaus
depressed [dɪ'prest] deprimiert, niedergeschlagen
describe [dɪ'skraɪb] beschreiben
desert ['dezət] Wüste
design [dɪ'zaɪn]: **design and technology** künstlerisches Gestalten und Werken
dessert [dɪ'zɜːt] Nachtisch, Nachspeise
destroy [dɪ'strɔɪ] zerstören
detention [dɪ'tenʃn] Nachsitzen
dialogue ['daɪəlɒg] Dialog, Gespräch
diary ['daɪəri] Tagebuch

did [dɪd]: **I did** ich tat / ich habe
getan
die [daɪ] sterben
difference ['dɪfrəns] Unterschied
different ['dɪfrənt] andere/anderer/
anderes; verschieden, anders;
different from anders als; sich
unterscheiden von
difficult ['dɪfɪkəlt] schwierig, schwer
dinner ['dɪnə] Festessen
direct [də'rekt] direkt
dirty ['dɜːti] schmutzig
disability [dɪsə'bɪləti] Behinderung
disaster [dɪ'zɑːstə] Katastrophe
disc jockey (DJ) ['dɪskdʒɒki, 'diː'dʒeɪ]
Diskjockey
disco ['dɪskəʊ] Disko(thek)
discriminate [dɪ'skrɪmɪneɪt]:
discriminate against diskrimi-
nieren, benachteiligen
discrimination [dɪskrɪmɪ'neɪʃn]
Diskriminierung, Benachteiligung
disease [dɪ'ziːz] Krankheit
disguise [dɪs'gaɪz] verkleiden
dishes ['dɪʃɪz]: **wash dishes**
Geschirr spülen
dishwasher ['dɪʃwɒʃə] Geschirrspül-
maschine
divide [dɪ'vaɪd] teilen
dizzy ['dɪzi] schwindlig
do [duː] tun, machen; schaffen;
do sports Sport treiben;
do without verzichten auf
doctor ['dɒktə] Arzt/Ärztin, Doktor
dog [dɒg] Hund
dollar ($) ['dɒlə] Dollar
donation [dəʊ'neɪʃn] Spende
done [dʌn]: **I've done** ich habe
getan
door [dɔː] Tür
doorway ['dɔːweɪ] Eingang
doughnut ['dəʊnʌt] Doughnut *(eine
Art Krapfen oder Berliner)*
down [daʊn] 1. hinunter/herunter,
hinab/herab; 2. „down", bedrückt
downhill [daʊn'hɪl] bergab
downtown [daʊn'taʊn] (AE) Stadtmitte; **downtown Toronto** (AE)
die Stadtmitte von Toronto
drank [dræŋk]: **I drank** ich trank /
ich habe getrunken
draw [drɔː] zeichnen
drawn [drɔːn]: **I've drawn** ich habe
gezeichnet
dream [driːm] Traum
dress [dres] Kleid
drew [druː]: **I drew** ich zeichnete /
ich habe gezeichnet
drink [drɪŋk] 1. trinken; 2. Getränk
drive [draɪv] fahren

driven ['drɪvn]: **I've driven** ich bin
gefahren
driver ['draɪvə] Fahrer/Fahrerin
driving test ['draɪvɪŋtest] Führerscheinprüfung; **take a driving test**
die Führerscheinprüfung machen
drop [drɒp] fallen lassen
drove [drəʊv]: **I drove** ich fuhr / ich
bin gefahren
drown [draʊn] ertränken
drug [drʌg] 1. Droge, Rauschgift;
2. Medikament
drunk [drʌŋk]: **I've drunk** ich habe
getrunken; **he was drunk** er war
betrunken
dry [draɪ] trocknen, abtrocknen
dump [dʌmp] Müllkippe
during ['djʊərɪŋ] während
duty ['djuːti]: **on duty** im Dienst

E

e-mail ['iːmeɪl] (= **electronic mail**
[ɪlek'trɒnɪk'meɪl]) E-Mail (= elek-
tronische Post)
each [iːtʃ] jede/jeder/jedes; je;
each other einander, sich
ear [ɪə] Ohr
early ['ɜːli] früh; vorzeitig, zu früh
earn [ɜːn] verdienen
earring ['ɪərɪŋ] Ohrring
east [iːst] Ost-; (nach) Osten; östlich
easy ['iːzi] einfach, leicht
eat [iːt] essen
eaten ['iːtn]: **I've eaten** ich habe
gegessen
edge [edʒ] Rand, Kante
egg [eg] Ei
Eiffel Tower ['aɪfəl'taʊə] Eiffelturm
electric [ɪ'lektrɪk] elektrisch
electricity [ɪlek'trɪsəti] Elektrizität,
Strom
elevator ['elɪveɪtə] (AE) Aufzug
else [els]: **Would you like anything
else?** Möchtest du / Möchten Sie
sonst noch etwas?
emergency [ɪ'mɜːdʒənsi]:
emergency repair Notreparatur;
emergency services Notdienst
empire ['empaɪə]: **the British
Empire** das britische Kolonialreich
emptiness ['emptɪnəs] Leere
empty ['empti] 1. leer; 2. leeren,
ausräumen
emu ['iːmjuː] Emu
end [end] 1. enden; 2. Ende;
at the end of October Ende
Oktober; **in the end** schließlich
energy ['enədʒi] Energie, Kraft

engineer [endʒɪ'nɪə] Techniker/Tech-
nikerin; Ingenieur/Ingenieurin
England ['ɪŋglənd] England
English ['ɪŋglɪʃ] englisch; Englisch;
Engländer/in
enjoy [ɪn'dʒɔɪ] genießen, Spaß
haben an, gern haben/tun; **I'm
enjoying myself** ich amüsiere
mich, ich habe viel Spaß; **Enjoy
your meal.** Guten Appetit.
enormous [ɪ'nɔːməs] riesig
enough [ɪ'nʌf] genug
enter ['entə] eingeben
enterprise ['entəpraɪz]: **free enterprise** freies Unternehmertum
entrance ['entrəns] Eingang
envelope ['envələʊp] Briefumschlag
environment [ɪn'vaɪrənmənt] Umge-
bung; Umwelt
equipment [ɪ'kwɪpmənt] Ausrüstung
especially [ɪ'speʃəli] besonders
Europe ['jʊərəp] Europa
European [jʊərə'piːən] europäisch;
Europäer/Europäerin
even ['iːvn] sogar; **not even** nicht
einmal
evening ['iːvnɪŋ] Abend; **Good
evening.** Guten Abend. **in the
evening(s)** abends; am Abend;
this evening heute Abend
event [ɪ'vent] Veranstaltung;
Ereignis
ever ['evə] schon einmal, jemals
every ['evri] jede/jeder/jedes
everybody ['evrɪbɒdi] jeder, alle
everything ['evriθɪŋ] alles
everywhere ['evriweə] überall
exam [ɪg'zæm] Prüfung
example [ɪg'zɑːmpl] Beispiel;
for example zum Beispiel
except [ɪk'sept] außer
excited [ɪk'saɪtɪd] aufgeregt
exciting [ɪk'saɪtɪŋ] aufregend,
spannend
excuse [ɪk'skjuːz]: **Excuse me, ...**
Entschuldigen Sie, ...
exercise ['eksəsaɪz] Übung
exhibition ['eksɪ'bɪʃn] Ausstellung
expensive [ɪk'spensɪv] teuer
experience [ɪk'spɪərɪəns]: **work
experience** Berufspraktikum
explain [ɪk'spleɪn] erklären
extra ['ekstrə] extra, zusätzlich
eye [aɪ] Auge

F

face [feɪs] Gesicht
fact [fækt] Tatsache

factory ['fæktrɪ] Fabrik

fair[1] [feə] fair, gerecht

fair[2] [feə] Volksfest, Kirmes

faithfully ['feɪθfəlɪ]: **Yours faithfully, …** Mit freundlichen Grüßen …

fall [fɔːl] fallen; umstürzen; **fall off** hinunter-/herunterfallen; **fall over** umfallen, hinfallen; **fall in love** sich verlieben

fallen ['fɔːlən]: **I've fallen** ich bin gefallen

fame [feɪm]: **Walk of Fame** Weg des Ruhms

family ['fæmlɪ] Familie; **family name** Familienname

famous ['feɪməs] berühmt

fan [fæn] Fan, Anhänger/Anhängerin

fantastic [fæn'tæstɪk] fantastisch

far [fɑː] weit; **so far** bisher

farm [fɑːm] Bauernhof, Farm

farmer ['fɑːmə] Landwirt/Landwirtin

farther ['fɑːðə] weiter

farthest ['fɑːðɪst] am weitesten

fashion ['fæʃn] Mode

fast [fɑːst] schnell; **fast food** [fɑːst'fuːd] Fastfood *(schnell verzehrbare kleinere Gerichte)*

fasten ['fɑːsn]: **Fasten your seatbelts.** Schnallen Sie sich an.

father ['fɑːðə] Vater

fault [fɔːlt] Schuld

favour ['feɪvə] Gefallen; **she owes me a favour** sie schuldet mir einen Gefallen

favourite ['feɪvrət] Lieblings-; **the old favourites** die alten Lieblingshits/Lieblings…

fax [fæks] Fax; **fax machine** [fæksmə'ʃiːn] Faxgerät

February ['februərɪ] Februar

fed up [fed'ʌp]: **I'm fed up** ich habe die Nase voll; **I'm fed up with going to the cinema.** Ich habe es satt, ins Kino zu gehen.

fee [fiː] Gebühr

feed [fiːd] füttern, zu essen geben

feel [fiːl] (sich) fühlen; **How do you feel about …?** Was hältst du von …?

feeling ['fiːlɪŋ] Gefühl

fell [fel]: **I fell** ich fiel / ich bin gefallen

felt [felt]: **I felt** ich fühlte (mich) / ich habe (mich) gefühlt

felt-tip ['felttɪp] Filzstift

festival ['festɪvl] Festival; Fest

few [fjuː] wenige; **a few** ein paar, einige; **the last few years** die letzten (paar) Jahre

field [fiːld] Feld, Wiese

fifties ['fɪftɪz]: **the Fifties** die fünfziger Jahre

fight [faɪt] 1. bekämpfen; 2. Kampf; Schlägerei

fighting ['faɪtɪŋ] Kämpfe

fill [fɪl] (auf)füllen, voll machen; **fill in** [fɪl'ɪn] ausfüllen

film [fɪlm] Film; **film-maker** Filmemacher/Filmemacherin

find [faɪnd] finden; **find out (about)** herausfinden, sich erkundigen (nach)

fine [faɪn] Geldstrafe

finest ['faɪnɪst]: **your finest hour** deine beste Stunde

finger ['fɪŋgə] Finger; **fish finger** Fischstäbchen

finish ['fɪnɪʃ] aufhören (mit); beenden

fire ['faɪə] Feuer

fireworks ['faɪəwɜːks] Feuerwerk

firm [fɜːm] Firma

first [fɜːst] 1. erste/erster/erstes; 2. zuerst; zum ersten Mal

first-aid kit [fɜːst'eɪdkɪt] Verbandskasten

fish [fɪʃ] 1. fischen, angeln; 2. Fisch, Fische; **fish and chips** Fisch und Pommes frites; **fish finger** Fischstäbchen

fit [fɪt] fit

fitness ['fɪtnəs]: **fitness centre** Fitnesscenter; **fitness training** ['fɪtnəstreɪnɪŋ] Fitnesstraining

flag [flæg] Fahne, Flagge

flat [flæt] Wohnung

Flatiron Building ['flætaɪənbɪldɪŋ] „Bügeleisengebäude"

flavour ['fleɪvə] Geschmack

flew [fluː]: **I flew** ich flog / ich bin geflogen

flight [flaɪt] Flug

floor [flɔː] Stock(werk); **on the first floor** im ersten Stock(werk)

flower ['flaʊə] Blume

flower-bed ['flaʊəbed] Blumenbeet

flown [fləʊn]: **I've flown** ich bin geflogen

flu [fluː] Grippe

fly [flaɪ] fliegen

follow ['fɒləʊ] (ver)folgen; befolgen

food [fuːd] Essen; Lebensmittel; Futter

fool [fuːl]: **I don't want to be nobody's fool.** Ich will mir nichts vormachen lassen.

foot, feet [fʊt, fiːt] Fuß, Füße; **on foot** zu Fuß

football ['fʊtbɔːl] Fußball

for [fɔː, fə] für; zu; **for 15 years** 15 Jahre lang; seit 15 Jahren; **for a long time** lange; **for breakfast / for lunch** zum Frühstück / zum Mittagessen; **for example** zum Beispiel; **for meeting friends** um Freunde zu treffen; **for nothing** umsonst; **for the first time** zum ersten Mal; **I'm late / in time for school.** Ich komme zu spät / rechtzeitig zur Schule. **look for** suchen

forecast ['fɔːkɑːst]: **weather forecast** Wettervorhersage

foreign ['fɒrən]: **foreign countries** fremde Länder, Ausland; **foreign language** Fremdsprache; **foreign travel** Auslandsreisen

forever [fər'evə] für immer

forget [fə'get] vergessen

forgiven [fə'gɪvn]: **I've forgiven** ich habe vergeben

forgot [fə'gɒt]: **I forgot** ich vergaß / ich habe vergessen

forgotten [fə'gɒtn]: **I've forgotten** ich habe vergessen

fork [fɔːk] Gabel

form [fɔːm] 1. Form; 2. Formular

formal ['fɔːməl] offiziell; formell

forward ['fɔːwəd]: **look forward to** sich freuen auf; **I'm looking forward to meeting you.** Ich freue mich darauf, Sie kennen zu lernen.

fought [fɔːt]: **I fought** ich bekämpfte / ich habe bekämpft; **I've fought** ich habe bekämpft

found [faʊnd]: **I found** ich fand / ich habe gefunden; **I've found** ich habe gefunden

France [frɑːns] Frankreich

free [friː] frei; kostenlos, umsonst; **free time** Freizeit

French [frentʃ] französisch; Französisch; Franzose/Französin; **French fries** [frentʃ'fraɪz] Pommes frites

Friday ['fraɪdeɪ, 'fraɪdɪ] Freitag

friend [frend] Freund/Freundin; **make friends** Freundschaft(en) schließen; **That's what friends are for.** Dazu sind Freunde/Freundinnen da.

friendly ['frendlɪ] freundlich

fries [fraɪz]: **French fries** [frentʃ'fraɪz] Pommes frites

frighten ['fraɪtn] erschrecken

frightened ['fraɪtnd]: **I'm frightened** ich erschrecke, ich habe Angst

frightening ['fraɪtnɪŋ] beängstigend

from [frɒm, frəm] von; aus; **from 8 till 10** von 8 (Uhr) bis 10 (Uhr); **from July 13th** ab dem 13. Juli, vom 13. Juli an

front [frʌnt]: **front of the train** Zugspitze; **in front of** vor

frozen ['frəʊzn] gefroren, zugefroren

fruit [fru:t] Obst, Früchte

full [fʊl] voll; vollständig

fun [fʌn] Spaß; **... is/are fun.** ... macht/machen Spaß. **She's great fun.** Es macht großen Spaß, mit ihr zusammen zu sein. **fun park** Vergnügungspark, Freizeitpark

funny ['fʌni] lustig, komisch

fur [fɜ:] Fell, Pelz

future ['fju:tʃə] Zukunft

G

game [geɪm] Spiel

gangster ['gæŋstə] Gangster

garage ['gæra:ʒ] 1. Garage; 2. (Reparatur-)Werkstatt

garbage ['ga:bɪdʒ] (AE) Abfall, Müll

garden ['ga:dn] Garten

gardening ['ga:dnɪŋ] Gartenarbeit

gas [gæs] 1. Gas; 2. (AE) Benzin; **gas station** (AE) Tankstelle

gate [geɪt] Tor; Sperre, Schranke

gave [geɪv]: **I gave** ich gab / ich habe gegeben (usw.)

gel [dʒel]: **hair gel** Haargel

generator ['dʒenəreɪtə] Generator, Stromerzeuger

gentlemen ['dʒentlmən]: **Ladies and gentlemen!** Meine Damen und Herren!

geography [dʒi'ɒgrəfi] Erdkunde, Geographie

German ['dʒɜ:mən] deutsch; Deutsch; Deutsche/Deutscher

Germany ['dʒɜ:məni] Deutschland

get [get] 1. bekommen; 2. besorgen, holen; 3. werden; 4. kommen, gelangen; **he's getting better** es geht ihm schon besser; **get married** heiraten; **get off the train/bus/...** aus dem Zug/Bus/... aussteigen; **get on** aufsteigen, einsteigen; **get out of the car/taxi** aus dem Auto/Taxi aussteigen; **get to know** kennen lernen; **get up** aufstehen; sich erheben; **get used to** sich gewöhnen an

ghost [gəʊst] Gespenst, Geist

girl [gɜ:l] Mädchen

girlfriend ['gɜ:lfrend] (feste) Freundin

give [gɪv] geben; schenken; spenden

given ['gɪvn]: **I've given** ich habe gegeben (usw.)

glamour ['glæmə] Glanz

glass [gla:s] Glas, Trinkglas

go [gəʊ] gehen, fahren; führen; **go for a walk** spazieren gehen; **go home** nach Hause gehen; **go off** ausgehen, erlöschen; **go on** fortfahren, weiterreden; **go out** ausgehen, weggehen; **go out (together)** miteinander gehen; **go to bed** ins Bett gehen; **go to Dave's house** zu Dave (nach Hause) gehen; **go to school** zur Schule gehen; **go to the shops / go shopping** einkaufen gehen; **go to town** in die Stadt gehen; **go to work** arbeiten gehen; **go window-shopping** einen Schaufensterbummel machen; **go wrong** schief gehen

God [gɒd] Gott

going to ['gəʊɪŋtu, 'gəʊɪŋtə]: **I'm going to win** ich werde gewinnen / ich gewinne

gold [gəʊld] Gold

gone [gɒn]: **I've gone** ich bin gegangen, gefahren

good [gʊd] gut; **good at** gut in, geschickt in; **Good afternoon.** Guten Tag. *(nachmittags)*; **Good morning/evening/night.** Gute/n Morgen/Abend/Nacht. **Good luck!** Viel Glück!

good-looking [gʊd'lʊkɪŋ] gut aussehend

Goodbye. [gʊd'baɪ] Auf Wiedersehen.

gossip ['gɒsɪp] Klatsch, Tratsch

got [gɒt]: **I got** ich bekam / ich habe bekommen (usw.); **I've got** ich habe bekommen (usw.)

government ['gʌvənmənt] Regierung **government training scheme** ['gʌvənmənt'treɪnɪŋski:m] staatliches Ausbildungsprogramm

governor ['gʌvənə] Gouverneur/in

gram [græm] Gramm

grandfather ['grænfa:ðə] Großvater

grandma ['grænma:] Oma, Großmutter

grandmother ['grænmʌðə] Großmutter

grandparents ['grænpeərənts] Großeltern

grass [gra:s] Gras; Rasen

great [greɪt] toll, großartig

great [greɪt]: **great-great grandparents** Ururgroßeltern

Greece [gri:s] Griechenland

green [gri:n] grün

greetings ['gri:tɪŋz] Grüße

grew [gru:]: **I grew** ich wuchs / ich bin gewachsen (usw.)

grizzly bear ['grɪzlibeə] Grislibär

ground [graʊnd] (Erd-)Boden

group [gru:p] Gruppe

grow [grəʊ] 1. wachsen; 2. anbauen; heranziehen

grown [grəʊn]: **I've grown** ich bin gewachsen (usw.)

grumpy ['grʌmpi] schlecht gelaunt, mürrisch

guess [ges] erraten; **I guess ...** Ich nehme an, ...

guest [gest] Gast

guest-house ['gesthaʊs] Pension

guidance ['gaɪdns]: **parental guidance** Begleitung durch die Eltern

guide [gaɪd] (Fremden-)Führer/Führerin

guitar [gɪ'ta:] Gitarre; **play the guitar** Gitarre spielen

guitarist [gɪ'ta:rɪst] Gitarrist/in

gun [gʌn] Schußwaffe; Gewehr

gunfight ['gʌnfaɪt] Schießerei

guy [gaɪ] Typ, Mann

H

had [hæd]: **I had** ich hatte / ich habe gehabt; **I've had** ich habe gehabt; **I had gone** ich war gegangen

hair [heə] Haar, Haare; **hair gel** ['heədʒel] Haargel

hair-drier ['heədraɪə] Föhn

hairspray ['heəspreɪ] Haarspray

half [ha:f]: **half an hour** eine halbe Stunde; **half of the job** die Hälfte des Jobs; **half past two** halb drei

halfway [ha:f'weɪ] auf halbem Wege

hall [hɔ:l] Halle, Saal; **city hall** (AE) Rathaus; **town hall** Rathaus

Hallo. [hə'ləʊ] Hallo. Guten Tag.

ham [hæm] Schinken

hamburger ['hæmbɜ:gə] Hamburger

hamster ['hæmstə] Hamster

hand [hænd] Hand

handball ['hændbɔ:l] Handball

handbook ['hændbʊk] Handbuch

handprint ['hændprɪnt] Handabdruck

hang (from) [hæŋ] aufhängen (an), hängen (an); **hang up** [hæŋ'ʌp] aufhängen

happen ['hæpən] passieren, geschehen; **happen to the environment** mit der Umwelt geschehen

happy ['hæpi] glücklich, froh; **Happy birthday (to you)!** Herzlichen Glückwunsch zum Geburtstag!

hard [hɑːd] hart; schwer

hate [heɪt] hassen; **hate to wait** sehr ungern warten

have [hæv] haben; **have a break** Pause machen; **have a shower** duschen; **have a wash** sich waschen; **have breakfast** frühstücken; **have lunch** zu Mittag essen; **have sandwiches / a cola** Sandwiches essen / eine Cola trinken

have to ['hævtu, 'hævtə] müssen

he [hiː] er

head [hed] Oberhaupt

headache ['hedeɪk] Kopfschmerzen

hear [hɪə] hören

heard [hɜːd]: **I heard** ich hörte / ich habe gehört; **I've heard** ich habe gehört

heart [hɑːt] Herz

heating ['hiːtɪŋ]: **central heating** Zentralheizung

heavy ['hevi] schwer; **heavy metal** Heavy Metal

helmet ['helmɪt] Helm

help [help] 1. helfen; **help out** helfen, aushelfen; **Help yourselves (to coffee)!** Bedient euch! Nehmt euch selbst Kaffee! 2. Hilfe

helper ['helpə] Helfer/Helferin

helpful ['helpfl] hilfsbereit; hilfreich

her [hɜː] 1. ihr/ihre; 2. ihr/sie

here [hɪə] hier; hierhin/hierher; **Here you are.** Hier, bitte.

hers [hɜːz] ihre/ihrer/ihres

herself [hɜːˈself] sich (selbst); selbst

Hi. [haɪ] Hallo.

high [haɪ] hoch; **high school** Oberschule *(in Nordamerika)*

highlight ['haɪlaɪt] Höhepunkt

hike [haɪk] wandern

hiker ['haɪkə] Wanderer/Wanderin

hill [hɪl] Hügel, *(kleiner)* Berg

him [hɪm] ihm/ihn

himself [hɪmˈself] sich (selbst); selbst

hind leg [haɪnd'leg] Hinterbein

hip hop ['hɪphɒp] Hip-Hop

hire ['haɪə] 1. mieten; 2. vermieten

his [hɪz] 1. sein/seine; 2. seine/seiner/seines

Hispanic [hɪˈspænɪk] Hispano-Amerikaner/in; hispanisch; spanischsprachig

history ['hɪstri] Geschichte

hit [hɪt] 1. schlagen; **I hit** ich schlug / ich habe geschlagen; **I've hit** ich habe geschlagen; 2. Hit

hobby ['hɒbi] Hobby

hockey ['hɒki] Hockey

hogan ['həʊgən] *traditionelles achtseitiges Navajo-Haus*

hold [həʊld]: **Hold me captive …** Halte mich gefangen …

holiday ['hɒlədeɪ] Feiertag; Ferien, Urlaub; **on holiday** in/im Urlaub; **public holiday** gesetzlicher Feiertag

home [həʊm] 1. Heim, Zuhause; Haushalt; 2. nach Hause, heim; 3. Heimat-; **at home** zu Hause, daheim

homeless ['həʊmləs] heimatlos; obdachlos

homepage ['həʊmpeɪdʒ] Eingangsseite *(einer Website im Internet)*

homework ['həʊmwɜːk] Hausaufgaben, Schularbeiten

hope [həʊp] hoffen

horror ['hɒrə] Horror

horse [hɔːs] Pferd

horse-drawn ['hɔːsdrɔːn] von Pferden gezogen

hospital ['hɒspɪtl] Krankenhaus

hostel ['hɒstl] Wohnheim; Obdachlosenheim; **youth hostel** Jugendherberge

hot [hɒt] heiß; **hot dog** ['hɒt'dɒg] Hot Dog *(heißes Würstchen mit Ketchup im Brötchen)*

hotel [həʊˈtel] Hotel

hour ['aʊə] Stunde; **(working) hours** Arbeitszeit

house [haʊs] Haus; **Come to my house.** Komm zu mir (nach Hause).

how [haʊ] wie; **How did you know …?** Woher wusstest du …? **How do you feel about …?** Was hältst du von …? **How long?** Wie lange? Wie lang? **How many?** Wie viele? **How much?** Wie viel? **How much is/are …?** Was kostet/kosten …? **How old are you?** Wie alt bist du? / Wie alt sind Sie?

humour ['hjuːmə]: **a sense of humour** (Sinn für) Humor

hump [hʌmp] Höcker, Buckel

hung [hʌŋ]: **I hung** ich hängte (auf) / ich habe (auf)gehängt; **I've hung** ich habe (auf)gehängt

hungry ['hʌŋgri] hungrig; **I'm hungry.** Ich habe Hunger.

hunt [hʌnt] jagen

hurry ['hʌri] sich beeilen; **in a hurry** in (großer) Eile

hurt [hɜːt] verletzen; wehtun; **I hurt** ich verletzte / ich habe verletzt (usw.); **I've hurt** ich habe verletzt (usw.)

husband ['hʌzbənd] Ehemann

I

I [aɪ] ich; **I'd** [aɪd] (= **I would**): **I'd like …** Ich möchte / hätte gern …; **I'd like to go.** Ich möchte gehen.

ice [aɪs] Eis *(gefrorenes Wasser)*; **ice hockey** ['aɪshɒki] Eishockey

ice-cream [aɪs'kriːm] (Speise-)Eis

ice-rink ['aɪsrɪŋk] Eisbahn, Schlittschuhbahn

ice-skating ['aɪsskeɪtɪŋ] Schlittschuhlaufen

idea [aɪˈdɪə] Idee, Einfall; Meinung; Vorstellung

if [ɪf] 1. wenn, falls; 2. ob

igloo ['ɪgluː] Iglu

ill [ɪl] krank

illegal [ɪˈliːgl] ungesetzlich, illegal

imagine [ɪˈmædʒɪn] sich vorstellen

immigrant ['ɪmɪgrənt] Immigrant/in, Einwanderer/Einwanderin

important [ɪmˈpɔːtnt] wichtig

impossible [ɪmˈpɒsəbl] unmöglich

improve [ɪmˈpruːv] verbessern

in [ɪn] 1. in; 2. hinein/herein; **in 1850** (im Jahre) 1850; **in a car park** auf einem Parkplatz; **in English** auf Englisch; **in front of** vor; **in love (with)** verliebt (in); **in my photo** auf meinem Foto; **in October** im Oktober; **in the country** auf dem Land; **in the morning(s)/afternoon(s)/evening(s)** morgens/nachmittags/abends; am Morgen/Nachmittag/Abend; **in the right place at the right time** zur richtigen Zeit am richtigen Ort; **in the world** auf der (ganzen) Welt; **in time** rechtzeitig; **in town** in der (Innen-)Stadt

inappropriate [ɪnəˈprəʊpriət] nicht geeignet

increase [ɪnˈkriːs] ansteigen, zunehmen

independence [ɪndɪˈpendəns] Unabhängigkeit, Unabhängigkeits-

independent [ɪndɪˈpendənt] unabhängig

India ['ɪndiə] Indien

Indian ['ɪndiən] 1. Inder/in; indisch; 2. Indianer/in; indianisch

indoors [ɪnˈdɔːz] in der Halle, drinnen

industry ['ɪndəstri] Industrie

influential [ɪnflu'enʃl] einflussreich

information [ɪnfə'meɪʃn] Informationen, Auskunft

ink [ɪŋk] Tinte

inline-skates ['ɪnlaɪnskeɪts] Inline Skates

inline-skating ['ɪnlaɪn'skeɪtɪŋ] Inline-Skating

inner city ['ɪnə'sɪti] Innenstadt

insect spray ['ɪnsektspreɪ] Insektenspray

inside out ['ɪnsaɪd'aʊt] auf links

instructor [ɪn'strʌktə]: **skiing instructor** Skilehrer/Skilehrerin

interest ['ɪntrəst] Interesse

interested (in) ['ɪntrəstɪd] interessiert (an)

interesting ['ɪntrəstɪŋ] interessant

international [ɪntə'næʃnəl] international

interstate ['ɪntəsteɪt] Autobahn *(durch mehrere US-Bundesstaaten)*

interview ['ɪntəvjuː] Interview; **(job) interview** Vorstellungsgespräch

interviewer ['ɪntəvjuːə] Interviewer/in

into ['ɪntu, 'ɪntə] in (… hinein/herein)

introduce [ɪntrə'djuːs] einführen

invention [ɪn'venʃn] Erfindung

invitation [ɪnvɪ'teɪʃn] Einladung

invite [ɪn'vaɪt] *(Gäste)* einladen

Ireland ['aɪələnd] Irland

Irish ['aɪrɪʃ] irisch; Irisch; Ire/Irin

is [ɪz]: **he/she/it is** er/sie/es ist

island ['aɪlənd] Insel

it [ɪt] es (er/sie; *nicht bei Personen*)

Italian [ɪ'tæliən] italienisch; Italienisch; Italiener/Italienerin

Italy ['ɪtəli] Italien

its [ɪts] sein/seine; ihr/ihre

J

jail [dʒeɪl] Gefängnis

Jamaica [dʒə'meɪkə] Jamaika

Jamaican [dʒə'meɪkən] jamaikanisch; Jamaikaner/Jamaikanerin

January ['dʒænjuəri] Januar

Japanese [dʒæpə'niːz] japanisch; Japanisch; Japaner/Japanerin

jazz [dʒæz] Jazz(musik)

jeans [dʒiːnz] Jeans

jeep [dʒiːp] Jeep

jerk [dʒɜːk] *mariniertes, gegrilltes Fleisch*

Jewish ['dʒuːɪʃ] jüdisch

job [dʒɒb] Arbeit, Beruf; Arbeitsstelle; Aufgabe; **nine-to-five job** Bürojob *(mit fester Arbeitszeit)*; **job centre** Arbeitsamt

jogger ['dʒɒgə] Jogger/Joggerin

jogging ['dʒɒgɪŋ] Jogging

join [dʒɔɪn] beitreten, Mitglied werden

joke [dʒəʊk] Witz, Scherz; **practical joke** Streich

joking ['dʒəʊkɪŋ]: **You must be joking!** Du machst wohl Witze!

journalism ['dʒɜːnəlɪzəm] Journalismus

journey ['dʒɜːni] Fahrt, Weg, Reise

joyrider ['dʒɔɪraɪdə] *Fahrer/in eines für eine (Vergnügungs-)Fahrt gestohlenen Autos)*

joyriding ['dʒɔɪraɪdɪŋ] *Fahren eines gestohlenen Autos (zum Vergnügen)*

judo ['dʒuːdəʊ] Judo

juggle ['dʒʌgl] jonglieren

juice [dʒuːs] Saft

July [dʒu'laɪ] Juli

jump [dʒʌmp] springen

junction ['dʒʌŋkʃn] Kreuzung

June [dʒuːn] Juni

junior ['dʒuːniə] Junior

just [dʒʌst] **1.** gerade, soeben; **2.** nur; **3.** einfach

K

keep [kiːp] halten, behalten

Kenya ['kenjə] Kenia

kept [kept]: **I kept** ich (be)hielt / ich habe behalten, gehalten; **I've kept** ich habe behalten, gehalten

ketchup ['ketʃəp] Ketchup

key [kiː] Schlüssel

kick [kɪk] kicken; treten

kill [kɪl] töten, umbringen

kilometre ['kɪləmiːtə] Kilometer; **kilometres per hour (km/h)** [pər'aʊə] Kilometer pro Stunde

kilt [kɪlt] Kilt *(Schottenrock)*

kind [kaɪnd] Art

king [kɪŋ] König

kiss [kɪs] **1.** (sich) küssen; **2.** Kuss

kit [kɪt]: **first-aid kit** Verbandskasten; **sewing kit** Nähzeug

kitchen ['kɪtʃɪn] Küche

kiwi ['kiːwiː] Kiwi

knee [niː] Knie

knee-pad ['niːpæd] Knieschoner

knew [njuː]: **I knew** ich wusste, kannte / ich habe gewusst, gekannt

knife, knives [naɪf, naɪvz] Messer

know [nəʊ] wissen; kennen; **You know, …** Du weißt schon, …

known [nəʊn]: **I've known** ich habe gewusst, gekannt

L

ladies ['leɪdiz]: **Ladies and gentlemen!** Meine Damen und Herren!

lake [leɪk] (Binnen-)See

land [lænd] Land

language ['læŋgwɪdʒ] Sprache

large [lɑːdʒ] groß

lasagne [lə'zænjə] Lasagne

last [lɑːst] letzte/letzter/letztes

late [leɪt] spät; zu spät, verspätet; **I'm late.** Ich bin spät dran; Ich habe mich verspätet. **I'm late for school.** Ich komme zu spät zur Schule.

latest ['leɪtɪst] neueste/neuester/neuestes

Latin America ['lætɪnə'merɪkə] Lateinamerika

laugh [lɑːf] lachen; **laugh at** lachen über; auslachen

law [lɔː] Gesetz

lay [leɪ]: **I lay** ich lag / ich habe gelegen

layout ['leɪaʊt] Layout *(Gestaltungsskizze)*

lead [liːd] führen

leader ['liːdə] Führer/Führerin

leaf, leaves [liːf, liːvz] Blatt, Blätter

learn [lɜːn] lernen

least [liːst] wenigste/wenigster/wenigstes; am wenigsten; **at least** zumindest; mindestens

leave [liːv] (liegen/stehen) lassen; verlassen, weggehen von, abfahren; **leave behind** zurücklassen, hinter sich lassen

led [led]: **I led** ich führte / ich habe geführt; **I've led** ich habe geführt

left [left] linke/linker/linkes; (nach) links; **on the left** links, auf der linken Seite

left [left]: **I left** ich ließ / ich habe gelassen (usw.); **I've left** ich habe gelassen (usw.)

leg [leg] Bein

legal ['liːgl] gesetzlich, legal

lemonade [lemə'neɪd] Limonade

lend [lend] leihen, verleihen

less [les] weniger

lesson ['lesn] (Unterrichts-)Stunde

let [let]: **Let's go!** Lass/Lasst uns gehen. / Gehen wir!

letter ['letə] **1.** Buchstabe; **2.** Brief

library ['laɪbrəri] Bücherei

lie[1] [laɪ] liegen

lie[2] [laɪ] Lüge

life, lives [laɪf, laɪvz] Leben

lifestyle ['laɪfstaɪl] Lebensstil

lift [lɪft] Aufzug

light [laɪt] Licht, Lampe
lights [laɪts] Ampel
like[1] [laɪk] mögen, gern haben;
like to swim / like swimming
gern schwimmen; **I'd like …**
Ich möchte … / Ich hätte gern …;
I'd like to go. Ich möchte gehen.
What do you like about …?
Was gefällt dir an …? **Would you
like …?** Möchtest du / Möchten
Sie …?
like[2] [laɪk] (ähnlich) wie; **like this**
so, auf diese Weise; **What's it
like?** Wie ist es?
line [laɪn] 1. Linie; 2. Zeile
list [lɪst] Liste
listen ['lɪsn] zuhören; **listen to**
hören, sich anhören
listener ['lɪsnə] Zuhörer/Zuhörerin
litre ['liːtə] Liter
little ['lɪtl] wenig; **a little** ein wenig;
Little Italy [lɪtl'ɪtəli] „Klein-Italien"
live [lɪv] wohnen, leben; **live on
little money** von wenig Geld leben
living-room ['lɪvɪŋruːm] Wohnzimmer
load [ləʊd] (be)laden; einräumen
local ['ləʊkl] örtlich; Lokal-; Regional-
logo ['ləʊgəʊ] Logo *(Firmenzeichen)*
lonely ['ləʊnli] einsam
long [lɒŋ] lang; **a long way** weit;
How long? Wie lange? Wie lang?
look [lʊk] 1. schauen, sehen;
2. aussehen; 3. Blick; **look after**
sich kümmern um, aufpassen auf;
look at (sich) ansehen; **look for**
suchen; **look forward to** sich
freuen auf; **I'm looking forward
to meeting you.** Ich freue mich
darauf, Sie kennen zu lernen.
lorry ['lɒri] Lastwagen
lose [luːz] verlieren
lost [lɒst] 1. **I lost** ich verlor / ich
habe verloren; **I've lost** ich habe
verloren; 2. **I'm lost** ich habe mich
verlaufen, verirrt
lot[1] [lɒt]: **a lot (of) / lots (of)** viele;
viel
lottery ['lɒtəri]: **lottery ticket** Los
loud [laʊd] laut
love [lʌv] lieben, sehr mögen; **love
to sing / love singing** sehr gern
singen; **fall in love** sich verlieben;
in love (with) verliebt (in); **Lots of
love from, …** Viele liebe Grüße …
loyal ['lɔɪəl] treu
luck [lʌk] Glück; **Good luck!** Viel
Glück!
lucky ['lʌki]: **you're lucky** du hast
Glück / ihr habt Glück; **Lucky you!**
Du Glückliche/Glücklicher!

lunch [lʌntʃ] Mittagessen; **for lunch**
zum Mittagessen; **have lunch**
zu Mittag essen; **lunch break**
Mittagspause
luxury ['lʌkʃəri] Luxus

M

machine [mə'ʃiːn]: **fax machine**
Faxgerät
madam ['mædəm]: **Dear Sir or
Madam, …** Sehr geehrte Damen
und Herren, …
made [meɪd]: **I made** ich machte /
ich habe gemacht; **I've made** ich
habe gemacht; **it was made in
Japan** es (er/sie) wurde in Japan
hergestellt; **made of plastic** aus
Plastik
magazine [mægə'ziːn] Zeitschrift
mailbox ['meɪlbɒks] Mailbox *(eine
Art Computerbriefkasten)*
mailman ['meɪlmæn] (AE) Briefträger, Postbote
make [meɪk] machen, herstellen;
(Geld) verdienen; erzielen;
make friends Freundschaft(en)
schließen; **I've had to make up
my mind** ich habe mich entscheiden müssen
make-up ['meɪkʌp] Make-up
mall [mɔːl] Einkaufszentrum
man, men [mæn, men] Mann,
Männer
manager ['mænɪdʒə] Manager/in
manic ['mænɪk] manisch; verrückt
many ['meni] viele
map [mæp] Stadtplan, Landkarte;
subway map (AE) U-Bahn-Plan
maple syrup ['meɪpl'sɪrəp] Ahorn-
sirup
March [mɑːtʃ] März
market ['mɑːkɪt] Markt
married ['mærɪd]: **get married**
heiraten
marry ['mæri] heiraten
marshal ['mɑːʃl] Marshal
match [mætʃ] Spiel, Wettkampf
maths [mæθs] Mathe(matik)
matter ['mætə]: **What's the matter?**
Was ist los?
May [meɪ] Mai
maybe ['meɪbi] vielleicht
mayonnaise [meɪə'neɪz] Majonäse
me [miː] mir/mich; **older than me**
älter als ich; **Me, too.** Ich auch.
meal [miːl] Mahlzeit, Speise, (zube-
reitetes) Essen
mean [miːn] bedeuten; meinen

meant [ment]: **I meant** ich meinte /
ich habe gemeint; **I've meant** ich
habe gemeint
meat [miːt] Fleisch
mechanic [mə'kænɪk] Mechaniker/in
media ['miːdiə] Medien
medium ['miːdiəm] mittel(groß)
meet [miːt] (sich) treffen (mit);
kennen lernen
megaphone ['megəfəʊn] Megaphon
member ['membə] Mitglied
membership ['membəʃɪp] Mitglied-
schaft
mention ['menʃn] erwähnen
menu ['menjuː] Speisekarte
message ['mesɪdʒ] Mitteilung;
Botschaft, Aussage
messy ['mesi] schmutzig, dreckig;
unordentlich
met [met]: **I met** ich traf / ich habe
getroffen (usw.); **I've met** ich habe
getroffen (usw.)
metal ['metl] Metall
metre ['miːtə] Meter
Mexican ['meksɪkən] mexikanisch;
Mexikaner/Mexikanerin
Mexico ['meksɪkəʊ] Mexiko
microwave ['maɪkrəweɪv] Mikrowelle
middle ['mɪdl] Mitte
might [maɪt]: **I might ask her …**
Vielleicht bitte ich sie …
mild [maɪld] mild
mile [maɪl] Meile *(= ca. 1,6 km)*;
miles per hour (mph) [pər'aʊə]
Meilen pro Stunde
military ['mɪlətri] Militär
milk [mɪlk] Milch
million ['mɪljən] Million
millionaire [mɪljə'neə] Millionär/in
mind [maɪnd]: **I've changed my
mind** ich habe meine Meinung
geändert; **I've had to make up my
mind** ich habe mich entscheiden
müssen
mine [maɪn] meine/meiner/meines
minority [maɪ'nɒrəti]: **minority
group** Minderheit
minute ['mɪnɪt] Minute
mirror ['mɪrə] Spiegel
miss [mɪs] vermissen; versäumen,
verpassen; **missing** fehlend
mistake [mɪ'steɪk] Fehler
mobile ['məʊbaɪl] 1. mobil, beweg-
lich; 2. **mobile (phone)** Mobil-
telefon, Handy; **mobile job** *Arbeit,
bei der man viel unterwegs ist*
model ['mɒdl] Modell; Nachbildung
modem ['məʊdem] Modem
modern ['mɒdən] modern
mom [mɒm] (AE) Mama, Mutti

moment ['məʊmənt]: **at the moment** zurzeit, im Augenblick

Monday ['mʌndeɪ, 'mʌndi] Montag; **on Monday** am Montag; montags

money ['mʌni] Geld

monster ['mɒnstə] Monster

month [mʌnθ] Monat

monument ['mɒnjumənt] Denkmal

moose [muːs] amerikanische/r Elch/e

moped ['məʊped] Moped

more [mɔː] mehr, weitere; **one more** noch ein/eine; **not any more** nicht mehr; **more expensive** teurer

morning ['mɔːnɪŋ] Morgen, Vormittag; **Sunday morning** Sonntagmorgen; **Good morning.** Guten Morgen. **in the morning(s)** morgens, vormittags; am Morgen; **this morning** heute Morgen

most [məʊst] der/die/das meiste, die meisten; **most dangerous** gefährlichste/gefährlichster/gefährlichstes, am gefährlichsten; **most of the year** der größte Teil des Jahres

motel [məʊ'tel] Motel

mother ['mʌðə] Mutter

motor bike ['məʊtəbaɪk] Motorrad

motto ['mɒtəʊ] Motto, Wahlspruch

mountain ['maʊntən] Berg; **mountain bike** Mountainbike; **mountain biking** Mountainbikefahren

"Mountie" ['maʊnti] *Angehörige/r der berittenen Polizei Kanadas*

mouse, mice [maʊs, maɪs] Maus, Mäuse

move [muːv] **1. move (to)** umziehen (nach), ziehen (nach); **2.** (sich) bewegen; **move cattle** Vieh treiben, Rinder treiben; **move on** weitergehen; weiterkommen

movement ['muːvmənt] Bewegung

movie ['muːvi] (AE) Film

Mr ['mɪstə] Herr *(vor Namen)*

Mrs ['mɪsɪz] Frau *(vor Namen bei verheirateten Frauen)*

Ms [məz] Frau *(vor Namen bei unverheirateten oder verheirateten Frauen)*

much [mʌtʃ] viel; **like/... very much** sehr mögen/...; **How much is/ are ...?** Was kostet/kosten ...?

mug [mʌg] Becher, große Tasse

mum [mʌm] Mama, Mutti

museum [mju'ziːəm] Museum

music ['mjuːzɪk] Musik

musician [mju'zɪʃn] Musiker/in

must [mʌst] müssen; **mustn't** ['mʌsnt] nicht dürfen

my [maɪ] mein/meine

myself [maɪ'self] mir/mich (selbst); selbst

myth [mɪθ] Mythos

N

name [neɪm] Name

nation ['neɪʃn] Nation

national park ['næʃnəl'pɑːk] Nationalpark

nationality [næʃə'næləti] Staatsangehörigkeit, Nationalität

"native" ['neɪtɪv] „Eingeborene/Eingeborener"; **Native American** amerik. Ureinwohner/Ureinwohnerin, Indianer/Indianerin

nature ['neɪtʃə] Natur

near [nɪə] in der Nähe (von); nah

nearest ['nɪərɪst] nächste/nächster/nächstes

neat [niːt] ordentlich

need [niːd] brauchen

needn't ['niːdnt] nicht brauchen, nicht müssen

neighbour ['neɪbə] Nachbar/in

nervous ['nɜːvəs] nervös, ängstlich

net [net] Netz

never ['nevə] nie, niemals

new [njuː] neu

New Yorker [njuː'jɔːkə] New Yorker/in

New Zealand [njuː'ziːlənd] Neuseeland

news [njuːz] Nachricht(en); Neuigkeit(en)

newspaper ['njuːspeɪpə] Zeitung

next [nekst] nächste/nächster/nächstes

next to ['nekstu, 'nekstə] neben

Niagara Falls [naɪ'ægərə'fɔːlz] Niagarafälle

nice [naɪs] nett; schön

night [naɪt] Nacht, (später) Abend; **at night** nachts, in der Nacht; **Good night.** Gute Nacht.

nine-to-five job [naɪntə'faɪvdʒɒb] Bürojob *(mit fester Arbeitszeit)*

nineteentwenties (1920s) [naɪntiːn'twentiz] zwanziger Jahre

no [nəʊ] **1.** nein; **2.** kein/keine

nobody ['nəʊbədi] niemand

noisy ['nɔɪzi] laut, lärmend

non [nɒn]: **non-members** Nicht-Mitglieder

north [nɔːθ] Nord-; (nach) Norden; nördlich

North Sea [nɔːθ'siː] Nordsee

northern ['nɔːðən] Nord-, nördlich

Northern Ireland ['nɔːðən'aɪələnd] Nordirland

Northern Irish ['nɔːðən'aɪrɪʃ] nordirisch; Nordire/Nordirin

nose [nəʊz] Nase

not [nɒt] nicht; **not ... till** erst; **not ... yet** [jet] noch nicht

note [nəʊt] Notiz; Briefchen

nothing ['nʌθɪŋ] nichts; **for nothing** umsonst

notice ['nəʊtɪs] bemerken

notice-board ['nəʊtɪsbɔːd] Anschlagbrett, schwarzes Brett

November [nəʊ'vembə] November

now [naʊ] nun, jetzt

number ['nʌmbə] Nummer; Zahl; Ziffer

nurse [nɜːs] Krankenpfleger/Krankenschwester

O

ocean ['əʊʃn] Ozean; Meer

o'clock [ə'klɒk]: **at 6 o'clock** um 6 Uhr / 18 Uhr

October [ɒk'təʊbə] Oktober

of [ɒv, əv] von; **a cup of tea** eine Tasse Tee; **of course** natürlich, selbstverständlich; **of the right age** im richtigen Alter

off [ɒf]: **get off the train/bus/...** aus dem Zug/Bus/... aussteigen

office ['ɒfɪs] Büro; **office worker** Büroangestellte/Büroangestellter

officer ['ɒfɪsə]: **(police) officer** (Polizei-)Beamter/Beamtin, Polizist/in

official [ə'fɪʃl]: **official language** Amtssprache

often ['ɒfn] oft

oil [ɔɪl] Öl

OK [əʊ'keɪ] okay, (schon) gut, in Ordnung; **I'm OK.** Mir geht's gut.

old [əʊld] alt

on [ɒn] **1.** auf; **2.** an, eingeschaltet; **on March 20th** am 20. März; **on Monday** am Montag; montags; **on Tuesdays** dienstags; **on duty** im Dienst; **on foot** zu Fuß; **on holiday** in/im Urlaub; **on the beach/ ocean** am Strand/Meer; **on the bus/train/plane** im Bus/Zug/Flugzeug; **on the corner** an der Ecke; **on the first floor** im ersten Stockwerk; **on the left/right** links/rechts, auf der linken/rechten Seite; **on the road** unterwegs; **on the stall** am Stand; **on TV / on the radio** im Fernsehen / im Radio; **live on little money** von wenig Geld leben; **When's the programme on?** Wann läuft die Sendung?

once [wʌns] einmal, einst
one [wʌn] ein/eine; eine/einer/eines;
one day eines Tages; **the green
one** der/die/das grüne
online [ɒn'laɪn] online
only ['əʊnli] nur, bloß; erst; **the only**
der/die/das einzige
onto ['ɒntu, 'ɒntə] auf (... hinauf/her-
auf)
open ['əʊpən] 1. (sich) öffnen, aufma-
chen; eröffnen; 2. offen, geöffnet;
open day Tag der offenen Tür
opinion [ə'pɪnjən] Meinung; **in your
opinion** deiner Meinung nach
opposite ['ɒpəzɪt] 1. gegenüber
(von); 2. Gegenteil
or [ɔː] oder
orange ['ɒrɪndʒ] Orange, Apfelsine
order[1] ['ɔːdə] bestellen
order[2] ['ɔːdə] Reihenfolge
ordinary ['ɔːdnri] gewöhnlich, normal
organic [ɔː'gænɪk] biodynamisch,
Bio- *(natürlich behandelt)*
organise ['ɔːgənaɪz] organisieren,
veranstalten
origin ['ɒrɪdʒɪn] Ursprung, Herkunft;
Abstammung
other ['ʌðə] andere, weitere;
each other einander, sich
our ['aʊə] unser/unsere
ours ['aʊəz] unsere/unserer/unseres
ourselves [aʊə'selvz] uns (selbst);
selbst
out [aʊt] 1. hinaus/heraus, aus;
2. draußen; außer Haus; **out of**
['aʊtəv] aus (... hinaus/heraus);
out of work [aʊtəv'wɜːk] arbeitslos
outdoor ['aʊtdɔː]: **outdoor centre**
Ferienlager; **outdoor museum**
Freilichtmuseum
outside [aʊt'saɪd] außerhalb (von);
(nach) draußen
over ['əʊvə] 1. vorbei, zu Ende;
2. über; hinüber/herüber; **all over**
überall in/auf; **over there** da drüben, dort drüben
owe [əʊ]: **she owes me a favour**
sie schuldet mir einen Gefallen
own [əʊn]: **my own** mein eigener /
meine eigene / mein eigenes
owner ['əʊnə] Besitzer/Besitzerin

P

package ['pækɪdʒ] Paket
page [peɪdʒ] Seite
paid [peɪd]: **I paid** ich zahlte / ich
habe gezahlt (usw.); **I've paid** ich
habe gezahlt (usw.)

pancake ['pænkeɪk] *(kleiner)* Pfann-
kuchen
papers ['peɪpəz] Papiere
parade [pə'reɪd] Parade, Umzug
parent, parents ['peərənt, 'peərənts]
Elternteil, Eltern
parental [pə'rentl]: **parental
guidance** Begleitung durch die
Eltern
park [pɑːk] 1. parken; 2. Park; **car
park** *(großer)* Parkplatz, Parkhaus
parking ['pɑːkɪŋ] Park-; **parking lot**
['pɑːkɪŋlɒt] (AE) *(großer)* Parkplatz;
parking space ['pɑːkɪŋspeɪs] Parkplatz, Parklücke
part [pɑːt] Teil; Abschnitt; **take
part (in)** teilnehmen (an), mitmachen (bei)
part-time job ['pɑːttaɪm'dʒɒb] Teil-
zeitarbeitsstelle
partner ['pɑːtnə] Partner/Partnerin
party ['pɑːti] 1. Party, Fest, Feier;
2. Partei
pass [pɑːs] bestehen
passenger ['pæsɪndʒə] Fahrgast,
Passagier/Passagierin
passive ['pæsɪv] Passiv
passport ['pɑːspɔːt] Reisepass, Pass
past [pɑːst] 1. nach; **half past two**
halb drei; **quarter past** Viertel
nach; 2. vorbei; **past the house**
am Haus vorbei; 3. Vergangenheit
path [pɑːθ] Weg, Pfad
pavement ['peɪvmənt] Bürgersteig
pay [peɪ] zahlen, bezahlen
PE ['piː'iː] (= **Physical Education**)
['fɪzɪkledʒu'keɪʃn] Turnen, Turn-
unterricht
pea [piː] Erbse
pen [pen] Füller
pen-friend ['penfrend] Brieffreund/
Brieffreundin
pence (p) [pens, piː] Pence *(briti-
sches Geld)*
pencil ['pensl] Bleistift
pencil-case ['penslkeɪs] Federmäpp-
chen, Schreibetui
penknife, penknives ['pennaɪf,
'pennaɪvz] Taschenmesser
people ['piːpl] Leute, Menschen
per [pɜː] pro; **per cent** [pə'sent]
Prozent
perfect ['pɜːfɪkt] vollkommen, perfekt
perhaps [pə'hæps] vielleicht
permit ['pɜːmɪt] Genehmigung,
Genehmigungsschein, (schriftliche)
Erlaubnis; **work permit** Arbeitserlaubnis
person ['pɜːsn] Person, Mensch
persuade [pə'sweɪd] überzeugen

pet [pet] zahmes Tier, Haustier;
pet shop Kleintierhandlung,
Zoohandlung
petrol ['petrəl] Benzin; **petrol
station** Tankstelle
phone [fəʊn] 1. anrufen, telefo-
nieren; 2. Telefon; **phone call**
Anruf; **phone card** Telefonkarte
photo ['fəʊtəʊ] Foto; **in my photo**
auf meinem Foto; **take photos**
Fotos machen, fotografieren
photography [fə'tɒgrəfi] Fotografie
phrase [freɪz] Redewendung,
Ausdruck
physics ['fɪzɪks] Physik
pick [pɪk] wählen, aussuchen
pick up [pɪk'ʌp] abholen
picture ['pɪktʃə] Bild, Foto
piece [piːs] Stück
pig [pɪg] Schwein
pink [pɪŋk] rosa, pink
pitch [pɪtʃ]: **pitch a tent** ein Zelt
aufstellen
pity ['pɪti]: **That's a pity.** Das ist
schade.
pizza ['piːtsə] Pizza
place [pleɪs] Ort, Platz, Stelle;
place of birth Geburtsort;
take place stattfinden
plan [plæn] 1. planen, vorhaben;
2. Plan
plane [pleɪn] Flugzeug
plant [plɑːnt] Pflanze
plastic ['plæstɪk] Plastik
plate [pleɪt] Teller
platform ['plætfɔːm] Bahnsteig, Gleis
play [pleɪ] 1. spielen; **play the guitar** Gitarre spielen; 2. Theaterstück
play-off ['pleɪɒf] Entscheidungsspiel
please [pliːz] bitte
pleased [pliːzd] zufrieden; erfreut;
Pleased to meet you. Freut mich,
dich/Sie kennen zu lernen.
plumber ['plʌmə] Installateur/Instal-
lateurin, Klempner/Klempnerin
plural ['plʊərəl] Plural, Mehrzahl
p m ['piː'em] nachmittags, abends
pocket-money ['pɒkɪt'mʌni]
Taschengeld
point [pɔɪnt]: **point of no return**
Punkt, von dem es kein Zurück
mehr gibt; Umkehrgrenzpunkt
point out [pɔɪnt'aʊt] hinweisen auf;
betonen
Poland ['pəʊlənd] Polen
polar bear ['pəʊləbeə] Eisbär
police [pə'liːs] Polizei; **(police)
officer** (Polizei-)Beamter/Beamtin,
Polizist/Polizistin; **police station**
Polizeiwache

Polish ['pəʊlɪʃ] polnisch; Polnisch; Pole/Polin
polite [pə'laɪt] höflich
politics ['pɒlətɪks] Politik
pollution [pə'luːʃn] (Umwelt-)Verschmutzung
pool [puːl] (Sammel-)Becken; Teich
poor [pʊə] arm
pop [pɒp] Pop(musik)
popular ['pɒpjələ] beliebt; **popular newspapers** Massenblätter
population [pɒpju'leɪʃn] Bevölkerung
port [pɔːt] Hafen, Hafenstadt
post [pəʊst] Post; **post office** ['pəʊstɒfɪs] Post(amt)
postcard ['pəʊstkɑːd] Postkarte, Ansichtskarte
postcode ['pəʊstkəʊd] Postleitzahl
poster ['pəʊstə] Poster
postman ['pəʊstmən] Briefträger, Postbote
pot [pɒt]: **coffee pot** Kaffeekanne
potato, potatoes [pə'teɪtəʊ, pə'teɪtəʊz] Kartoffel, Kartoffeln
potholing ['pɒthəʊlɪŋ]: **go potholing** Höhlen erkunden gehen
pound (£) [paʊnd] Pfund (brit. Geld)
power ['paʊə] Macht
practical joke ['præktɪkl'dʒəʊk] Streich
practise ['præktɪs] üben, trainieren (AE: practice)
prefer [prɪ'fɜː]: **prefer to watch TV** lieber fernsehen
prepare [prɪ'peə] vorbereiten
preposition [prepə'zɪʃn] Präposition, Verhältniswort
present ['preznt] Geschenk
president ['prezɪdənt] Präsident
price [praɪs] (Kauf-)Preis
print [prɪnt] drucken
prison ['prɪzn] Gefängnis
privately ['praɪvətli] privat, als Privatperson
prize [praɪz] Preis, Gewinn
probably ['prɒbəbli] wahrscheinlich
problem ['prɒbləm] Problem
producer [prə'djuːsə] Produzent
professional [prə'feʃənl] Profi-, Berufs-
professionally [prə'feʃənli] berufsmäßig
programme ['prəʊgræm] 1. programmieren; 2. (Radio-, Fernseh-)Sendung
project ['prɒdʒekt] Projekt, Projektarbeit
protect [prə'tekt] (be)schützen
protest[1] [prə'test] protestieren
protest[2] ['prəʊtest] Protest

Protestant ['prɒtɪstənt] Protestant/in
proud [praʊd] stolz; **proud to be Scottish** stolz Schotte/Schottin zu sein; **he's proud of himself** er ist stolz auf sich
province ['prɒvɪns] Provinz
PS ['piː'es] PS (Nachtrag zu einem Brief)
pub [pʌb] Kneipe, Lokal
public ['pʌblɪk] öffentlich; **public holiday** gesetzlicher Feiertag; **The Public Library** Öffentliche Bibliothek (von New York)
publicity [pʌb'lɪsəti] Werbung; Publicity
pudding ['pʊdɪŋ] Nachtisch
pullover ['pʊləʊvə] Pullover
punctual ['pʌŋktʃuəl] pünktlich
punk [pʌŋk] Punk
pupil ['pjuːpl] Schüler/Schülerin
puppet ['pʌpɪt] Handpuppe, Marionette; **puppet show** Puppentheater
Puritan ['pjʊərɪtən] Puritaner/in
push [pʊʃ] schieben, stoßen; drücken; **push out** [pʊʃ'aʊt] hinausdrängen
put [pʊt] stellen; legen; (an einen Platz) tun; **I put** ich stellte / ich habe gestellt (usw.); **I've put** ich habe gestellt (usw.); **put down** niederlegen; **put in** einfügen, hinzufügen; **put on** aufführen (Theaterstück, Show); **Put your hands up.** Hebt eure Hände hoch.
pyramid ['pɪrəmɪd] Pyramide

Q

quality ['kwɒləti] Eigenschaft
qualm [kwɑːm] ungutes Gefühl, Bedenken
quarter ['kwɔːtə] Viertel; **quarter past** Viertel nach; **quarter to** Viertel vor
queen [kwiːn] Königin
question ['kwestʃən] Frage; **ask a question** eine Frage stellen
queue [kjuː] 1. (Warte-)Schlange; 2. Schlange stehen, sich anstellen
quick [kwɪk] schnell
quiet ['kwaɪət] still, ruhig, leise
quiz [kwɪz] Quiz

R

rabbit ['ræbɪt] Kaninchen
radio ['reɪdiəʊ] Radio

rafting ['rɑːftɪŋ] Floß fahren
railway ['reɪlweɪ] (Eisen-)Bahn; Bahnstrecke; **railway station** Bahnhof
rain [reɪn] 1. regnen; 2. Regen
rainy ['reɪni] regnerisch
ran [ræn]: **I ran** ich rannte / ich bin gerannt
ranger ['reɪndʒə] Aufseher/in (in Nationalparks)
rap [ræp] 1. Rap(musik); 2. rappen
rapper ['ræpə] Rapper
rather ['rɑːðə]: **I'd** (= I would) **rather ...** ich würde lieber ...
RE ['ɑː'riː] (= **Religious Education**) [rɪ'lɪdʒəsedʒu'keɪʃn] Religionsunterricht
read [riːd] lesen, vorlesen; **I read** [red] ich las / ich habe gelesen; **I've read** [red] ich habe gelesen
reader ['riːdə] Leser/Leserin
ready ['redi] fertig
real ['riːəl] echt, richtig
reality [ri'æləti] Wirklichkeit, Realität
really ['riːəli] wirklich, eigentlich
reason ['riːzn] Grund
reception desk [rɪ'sepʃndesk] Empfang, Rezeption
record [rɪ'kɔːd] aufnehmen, aufzeichnen
recording contract [rɪ'kɔːdɪŋkɒntrækt] Plattenvertrag
red [red] rot
refill ['riːfɪl] „Nachfüllung" (eine weitere Portion)
refugee [refju'dʒiː] Flüchtling
reggae ['regeɪ] Reggae(musik)
regular ['regjələ] regelmäßig
relative ['relətɪv] Verwandte/r
relax [rɪ'læks] (sich) entspannen
religion [rɪ'lɪdʒən] Religion
religious [rɪ'lɪdʒəs] religiös
remark [rɪ'mɑːk] bemerken, anmerken
remember [rɪ'membə] sich erinnern (an); daran denken
rent [rent] 1. mieten; 2. Miete
repair [rɪ'peə] reparieren
report [rɪ'pɔːt] 1. Bericht; 2. Zeugnis
reporter [rɪ'pɔːtə] Reporter/in
republic [rɪ'pʌblɪk] Republik
reservation [rezə'veɪʃn] (Indianer-)Reservation, Reservat
respect [rɪ'spekt] respektieren
respected [rɪ'spektɪd] geachtet, respektiert
rest [rest] Rest
restaurant ['restərɒnt] Restaurant
retire [rɪ'taɪə] sich zur Ruhe setzen, in Rente gehen

return [rɪ'tɜːn] Rückfahrkarte;
day return Tagesrückfahrkarte;
point of no return Punkt, von dem
es kein Zurück mehr gibt; Umkehrgrenzpunkt

rhythm ['rɪðəm] Rhythmus; **rhythm
and blues** ['rɪðəmənd'bluːz]
Rhythm and Blues *(Musikstil)*

rich [rɪtʃ] reich

ride [raɪd]: **ride a (motor)bike/
moped** (Motor-)Rad/Moped fahren

right [raɪt] **1.** rechte/rechter/rechtes;
(nach) rechts; **on the right** rechts,
auf der rechten Seite; **2.** richtig;
You're right. Du hast / Sie haben
Recht. **3.** Recht; **animal rights**
Tierrechte, Tierschutz

ring[1] [rɪŋ] Ring

ring[2] [rɪŋ] Klingeln, Läuten

river ['rɪvə] Fluss

road [rəʊd] Straße; **on the road**
unterwegs

robot ['rəʊbɒt] Roboter

rock[1] [rɒk] *(großer)* Stein, Fels

rock[2] [rɒk] Rock(musik); **rock'n'roll**
['rɒkn'rəʊl] Rock'n'Roll

rodeo ['rəʊdiəʊ] Rodeo

role-card ['rəʊlkɑːd] Rollenspielkarte

roll [rəʊl] Brötchen

roll up [rəʊl'ʌp] zusammenrollen

romance [rəʊ'mæns] Romanze;
Liebesgeschichte

romantic [rəʊ'mæntɪk] romantisch

room [ruːm] Zimmer, Raum

rope [rəʊp] Seil

rough [rʌf] hart, rauh; **sleep rough**
im Freien übernachten

rubber ['rʌbə] Radiergummi

rubbish ['rʌbɪʃ] Abfall, Müll

rugby ['rʌgbi] Rugby

rule [ruːl] Regel, Vorschrift

ruler[1] ['ruːlə] Herrscher/Herrscherin

ruler[2] ['ruːlə] Lineal

run [rʌn] rennen, laufen; **I've run**
ich bin gerannt; **run a shop** ein
Geschäft führen

Russia ['rʌʃə] Russland

S

sad [sæd] traurig

safe [seɪf] sicher, in Sicherheit

said [sed]: **I said** ich sagte / ich habe
gesagt; **I've said** ich habe gesagt

sailing ['seɪlɪŋ] Segeln

salad ['sæləd] Salat

salespeople ['seɪlzpiːpl]: **travelling
salespeople** Handelsreisende,
Vertreter/Vertreterinnen

salmon ['sæmən] Lachs

saltfish ['sɔːltfɪʃ] *eingelegter Fisch*

same [seɪm] **the same** derselbe/
dieselbe/dasselbe; der/die/das
gleiche

sandwich ['sænwɪtʃ] Sandwich
(belegtes Brot); **sandwich bar**
„Sandwichladen", Stehcafé

sang [sæŋ]: **I sang** ich sang / ich
habe gesungen

sat [sæt]: **I sat** ich setzte mich / ich
habe mich gesetzt

Saturday ['sætədeɪ, 'sætədi] Samstag,
Sonnabend

sauerkraut ['saʊəkraʊt] Sauerkraut

sausage ['sɒsɪdʒ] Wurst, Würstchen

save [seɪv] sparen

saw [sɔː]: **I saw** ich sah / ich habe
gesehen (usw.)

say [seɪ] sagen

school [skuːl] Schule; **after school**
nach der Schule; **at school** in der
Schule; **go to school** zur Schule
gehen

science ['saɪəns] Naturwissenschaft

Scotland ['skɒtlənd] Schottland

Scottish ['skɒtɪʃ] schottisch; Schotte/
Schottin

scream [skriːm] schreien

screen [skriːn] Leinwand; Bildschirm

sea [siː] Meer

seal [siːl] Seehund

seaside ['siːsaɪd] Küste

season ['siːzn] **1.** Jahreszeit;
2. Saison

seat [siːt] Sitz, Sitzplatz

seat-belt ['siːtbelt]: **Fasten your
seat-belts.** Schnallen Sie sich an.

secret ['siːkrət] **1.** heimlich, geheim;
2. Geheimnis

secretarial [sekrə'teərɪəl] Sekretä-
rinnen-/Sekretärs-

security guard [sɪ'kjʊərətigɑːd]
Wachperson, Angestellte/Ange-
stellter beim Sicherheitsdienst

see [siː] sehen; sich ansehen,
besichtigen; **See you.** Bis dann.

seem [siːm]: **he seems nice** er
scheint nett zu sein

seen [siːn]: **I've seen** ich habe
gesehen (usw.)

sell [sel] verkaufen

send [send] schicken, senden; **she
sends her love** sie lässt grüßen

sense [sens]: **a sense of humour**
(Sinn für) Humor

sent [sent]: **I sent** ich schickte / ich
habe geschickt; **I've sent** ich habe
geschickt

sentence [sentəns] Satz

separate ['seprət] getrennt

September [sep'tembə] September

serious ['sɪəriəs] seriös; ernst(haft)

serve [sɜːv] **1.** servieren; **2.** bedienen

service ['sɜːvɪs] Dienst; **emergency
services** Notdienst

session ['seʃn] Treffen; Sitzung

set [set]: **set the table** den Tisch
decken; **I set the table** ich deckte
den Tisch / ich habe den Tisch
gedeckt; **I've set the table**
ich habe den Tisch gedeckt

settle ['setl] sich niederlassen;
sich einleben

settler ['setlə] Siedler/Siedlerin

sewing ['səʊɪŋ]: **sewing kit**
Nähzeug

shabby ['ʃæbi] schäbig

share [ʃeə] teilen; **he shares
Harry's job** er beteiligt sich
an Harrys Job

she [ʃiː] sie

sheep [ʃiːp] Schaf, Schafe

shelf, shelves [ʃelf, ʃelvz] Regal,
Regale

ship [ʃɪp] Schiff

shirt [ʃɜːt] Hemd

shoe [ʃuː] Schuh

shoot (at) [ʃuːt] schießen (auf);
erschießen

shop [ʃɒp] Laden, Geschäft;
go to the shops einkaufen gehen;
shop assistant Verkäufer/in

shopping ['ʃɒpɪŋ]: **go shopping**
einkaufen gehen; **shopping street**
Einkaufsstraße

short [ʃɔːt] kurz; klein

shorts [ʃɔːts] Shorts

shot [ʃɒt] Schuss

shot [ʃɒt]: **I shot** ich schoss / ich
habe geschossen (usw.); **I've shot**
ich habe geschossen (usw.)

should [ʃʊd, ʃəd]: **you should** du
solltest, du müßtest; **When should
we …?** Wann sollen wir …?

shout (at) [ʃaʊt] (an)schreien, laut
rufen

show [ʃəʊ] **1.** zeigen; **2.** Schau,
Show, Vorführung, Aufführung

shower ['ʃaʊə]: **have a shower**
duschen

shown [ʃəʊn]: **I've shown** ich habe
gezeigt

shy [ʃaɪ] scheu

side [saɪd] Seite

sight [saɪt] **1.** Anblick; **2.** Sehens-
würdigkeit

sign [saɪn] Schild; Zeichen

sign [saɪn]: **sign for the package**
den Empfang des Pakets bestätigen

silly ['sɪli] dumm, albern

simple ['sɪmpl] einfach

since [sɪns] seit

sing [sɪŋ] singen

singer ['sɪŋə] Sänger/Sängerin

single ['sɪŋgl] **1.** einfache Fahrkarte; **2.** Single *(Musikstück; Platte)*

single-parent family ['sɪŋgl'peərənt'fæmli] Familie mit nur einem Elternteil

sir [sɜː]: **Dear Sir or Madam, ...** Sehr geehrte Damen und Herren, ...

sister ['sɪstə] Schwester

sit [sɪt] sitzen; sich setzen; **sit down** sich setzen

skate [skeɪt] Inline Skates (Rollschuh/Schlittschuh) laufen

skater ['skeɪtə] Inline Skates (Rollschuh/Schlittschuh)-Läufer/Läuferin

ski [skiː] Ski fahren

skiing instructor ['skiːɪŋɪnstrʌktə] Skilehrer/Skilehrerin

skyscraper ['skaɪskreɪpə] Wolkenkratzer, Hochhaus

slave [sleɪv] Sklave/Sklavin

sleep [sliːp] schlafen; **sleep rough** im Freien übernachten

slept [slept]: **I slept** ich schlief / ich habe geschlafen; **I've slept** ich habe geschlafen

slogan ['sləʊgən] Slogan

Slovakia [sləʊ'vɑːkiə] Slowakische Republik

slow [sləʊ] langsam

small [smɔːl] klein

smell [smel] **1.** riechen; **2.** Geruch

smelly ['smeli] stinkend

smile [smaɪl] **1.** lächeln; **2.** Lächeln

smoke [sməʊk] rauchen

snack [snæk] Imbiss, Snack; **snack bar** Imbissstube, Imbissstand

snow [snəʊ] Schnee

snowmobile ['snəʊməbiːl] Motorschlitten

snowy ['snəʊi]: **it's snowy** es schneit viel

so [səʊ] also, daher; so; **so far** bisher; **so that** [səʊ'ðæt] damit

soccer ['sɒkə] Fußball

society [sə'saɪəti] Gesellschaft

sock [sɒk] Socke, Strumpf

sofa ['səʊfə] Sofa, Couch

soft [sɒft] weich; weichherzig, verweichlicht

sold [səʊld]: **I sold** ich verkaufte / ich habe verkauft; **I've sold** ich habe verkauft

soldier ['səʊldʒə] Soldat/Soldatin

some [sʌm] **1.** einige, ein paar; **2.** etwas

somebody ['sʌmbədi] jemand

someone ['sʌmwʌn] jemand

something ['sʌmθɪŋ] etwas

sometimes ['sʌmtaɪmz] manchmal

somewhere ['sʌmweə] irgendwo

son [sʌn] Sohn

song [sɒŋ] Lied

soon [suːn] bald

sore throat ['sɔː'θrəʊt] Halsschmerzen

sorry ['sɒri]: **I'm sorry.** Tut mir Leid.

sort [sɔːt] Art, Sorte; **what sort of governor** was für ein Gouverneur

sound [saʊnd] klingen, sich anhören

south [saʊθ] Süd-; (nach) Süden; südlich

southern ['sʌðən] Süd-, südlich

souvenir [suːvə'nɪə] Andenken

spaghetti [spə'geti] Spaghetti

Spanish ['spænɪʃ] spanisch; Spanisch; Spanier/Spanierin

speak [spiːk] sprechen; **Spanish-speaking** spanischsprachig

special ['speʃl] besondere/besonderer/besonderes

spell [spel] buchstabieren

spend [spend] verbringen; **spend money (on)** Geld ausgeben (für)

spent [spent]: **I spent** ich verbrachte / ich habe verbracht (usw.); **I've spent** ich habe verbracht (usw.)

split up [splɪt'ʌp] sich trennen; **they split up** sie trennten sich / sie haben sich getrennt; **they've split up** sie haben sich getrennt

spoke [spəʊk]: **I spoke** ich sprach / ich habe gesprochen

spoken ['spəʊkn]: **I've spoken** ich habe gesprochen

sponsor ['spɒnsə] **1.** sponsern; **2.** Sponsor/in, Geldgeber/in

spoon [spuːn] Löffel

sport [spɔːt] Sport, Sportart; **do sports** Sport treiben; **sports centre** Sportzentrum

sportsman, sportsmen ['spɔːtsmən] Sportler

spray [spreɪ] (be)sprühen, sprayen

spring [sprɪŋ] Frühling

stadium ['steɪdiəm] Stadion

stairs [steəz] Treppe

stall [stɔːl] (Verkaufs-)Stand

stamp [stæmp] Briefmarke

stand [stænd] stehen; **stand up** aufstehen; **I can't stand it** ich kann es nicht ausstehen

"standard" ['stændəd] Klassiker, Oldie

star [stɑː] **1.** Stern; **2.** Star *(berühmte Persönlichkeit)*

stare at ['steərət] anstarren

start [stɑːt] **1.** anfangen, beginnen (mit); anspringen; **start a group/...** eine Gruppe/... gründen; **Start here.** Fang/t hier an. **2.** Anfang

state [steɪt] (Bundes-)Staat, Land; **the States** „die Staaten" *(die USA)*

station ['steɪʃn] Bahnhof; **petrol station** Tankstelle; **police station** Polizeiwache; **TV/radio station** Fernseh-/Radiosender

Statue of Liberty ['stætʃuː'ʌv'lɪbəti] Freiheitsstatue

stay [steɪ] **1.** bleiben; **stay out of** sich heraushalten aus; **2.** übernachten

steak [steɪk] Steak

steal [stiːl] stehlen

steel [stiːl] Stahl

steep [stiːp] steil

stepfather ['stepfɑːðə] Stiefvater

still [stɪl] **1.** (immer) noch; **2.** trotzdem

stilt [stɪlt] Pfahl

stole [stəʊl]: **I stole** ich stahl / ich habe gestohlen

stood [stʊd]: **I stood** ich stand / ich habe gestanden; **I've stood** ich habe gestanden

stop [stɒp] aufhören; anhalten, stoppen; **Stop it.** Lass das. Hör auf (damit).

store [stɔː] (AE) Laden, Geschäft

storey ['stɔːri] Stockwerk

story ['stɔːri] Geschichte, Erzählung

straight [streɪt]: **straight ahead** [streɪtə'hed] geradeaus

strange [streɪndʒ] merkwürdig, seltsam

stranger ['streɪndʒə] Fremde/Fremder

stream [striːm] Bach

street [striːt] Straße

strict [strɪkt] streng

strong [strɒŋ] stark

student ['stjuːdnt] Schüler/Schülerin; Student/Studentin

studio ['stjuːdiəʊ] Studio

stupid ['stjuːpɪd] dumm, blöd

style [staɪl] Stil

subject ['sʌbdʒɪkt] (Schul-)Fach

suburbia [sʌ'bɜːbiə] Vorstadt

subway ['sʌbweɪ] (AE) U-Bahn; **subway token** (AE) U-Bahn-Münze, -Marke

successful [sək'sesfl] erfolgreich

suddenly ['sʌdnli] plötzlich

suggested [sə'dʒestɪd] empfohlen

suggestion [sə'dʒestʃən] Vorschlag

suit [suːt] Anzug; Kostüm

summer ['sʌmə] Sommer

sun [sʌn] Sonne
Sunday ['sʌndeɪ, 'sʌndi] Sonntag
sung [sʌŋ]: **it's sung** es (er/sie) wird gesungen
sunny ['sʌni] sonnig; **sunny-side up** [sʌnisaɪd'ʌp] *(bei Eiern)* als Spiegelei/-eier gebraten
sunset ['sʌnset] Sonnenuntergang
sunshine ['sʌnʃaɪn] Sonnenschein
super ['su:pə] super, toll
superhighway ['su:pəhaɪweɪ] Autobahn
supermarket ['su:pəmɑ:kɪt] Supermarkt
support [sə'pɔ:t] unterstützen, fördern
supporter [sə'pɔ:tə] Förderer/Förderin
sure [ʃʊə] sicher
surf [sɜ:f] surfen; **surf the Internet** „im Internet surfen" *(sich im Computerdatennetz umschauen)*
surfer ['sɜ:fə] Surfer/Surferin
surprise [sə'praɪz] Überraschung; Überraschungs-
surprised [sə'praɪzd] überrascht
survey ['sɜ:veɪ] Umfrage
sweatshirt ['swetʃɜ:t] Sweatshirt
Swedish ['swi:dɪʃ] schwedisch; Schwede/Schwedin
sweet [swi:t] 1. süß; lieb; 2. Süßigkeit, Bonbon
swim [swɪm] schwimmen
swimming club ['swɪmɪŋklʌb] Schwimmverein
Switzerland ['swɪtsələnd] Schweiz
system ['sɪstəm] System

T-shirt ['ti:ʃɜ:t] T-Shirt
table ['teɪbl] Tisch
table-tennis ['teɪbltenɪs] Tischtennis
taco ['tɑ:kəʊ] Taco *(knuspriger, gefüllter Teigfladen)*
take [teɪk] 1. (mit)nehmen; annehmen; 2. dauern; **take over** übernehmen; **take part (in)** teilnehmen (an), mitmachen (bei); **take place** stattfinden; **take a driving test** die Führerscheinprüfung machen; **take photos** Fotos machen, fotografieren; **take the dog for a walk** mit dem Hund rausgehen
take-away ['teɪkəweɪ]: **take-away pizza** Pizza zum Mitnehmen
taken ['teɪkən]: **I've taken** ich habe (mit)genommen (usw.)
talent ['tælənt] Talent

talk (to) [tɔ:k] reden, sprechen, sich unterhalten (mit)
tall [tɔ:l] groß (gewachsen); hoch
Tamil ['tæmɪl] tamilisch
taught [tɔ:t]: **I taught** ich brachte bei / habe beigebracht (usw.); **I've taught** ich habe beigebracht (usw.)
taxi ['tæksi] Taxi
tea [ti:] Tee; **(afternoon) tea** Tee *(Nachmittagsmahlzeit)*
teach [ti:tʃ] beibringen, unterrichten
teacher ['ti:tʃə] Lehrer/Lehrerin
team [ti:m] Team, Mannschaft
technology [tek'nɒlədʒi] Technik, Technologie; **design and technology** künstlerisches Gestalten und Werken
teen curfew [ti:n'kɜ:fju:] Ausgangssperre für Teenager
teenage ['ti:neɪdʒ] Jugend-, Teenager-
teenager ['ti:neɪdʒə] Teenager
telephone ['telɪfəʊn] Telefon
tell [tel] erzählen; sagen; angeben
temperature ['temprətʃə] Temperatur
tennis ['tenɪs] Tennis
tent [tent] Zelt
terrible ['terəbl] schrecklich, fürchterlich
terrorism ['terərɪzəm] Terrorismus
test [test] 1. testen, prüfen; 2. Test
than [ðæn]: **nicer than** schöner als
thank [θæŋk]: **Thank you.** Danke (schön). **Thanks.** [θæŋks] Danke.
Thanksgiving [θæŋks'gɪvɪŋ] Erntedankfest
that [ðæt] 1. das; der/die/das (da); 2. dass; 3. der/die/das *(in Relativsätzen)*; **That's £8.45.** Das macht 8 Pfund 45. **That's what friends are for.** Dazu sind Freunde/Freundinnen da. **That's why ...** Deshalb ..., Darum ...; **so that** damit
the [ðə, ði] der/die/das
their [ðeə] ihr/ihre
theirs [ðeəz] ihre/ihrer/ihres
them [ðem, ðəm] ihnen/sie
themselves [ðəm'selvz] sich (selbst); selbst
then [ðen] dann
there [ðeə] da, dort; dahin, dorthin; **there are** da sind, es gibt, es sind; **there's** (= **there is**) da ist, es gibt, es ist
these [ði:z] diese, die (hier)
they [ðeɪ] sie
thief, thieves [θi:f, θi:vz] Dieb/Diebin, Diebe/Diebinnen
thing [θɪŋ] Ding, Sache; **the same thing** dasselbe

think [θɪŋk] finden, meinen; glauben; (nach)denken; **think of** denken an; **think of an answer** sich eine Antwort ausdenken; **I don't think so.** Das finde ich nicht. **I think so, too.** Das finde ich auch.
thirsty ['θɜ:sti] durstig; **I'm thirsty.** Ich habe Durst.
this [ðɪs] dies/das (hier); diese/r/s; **this morning/afternoon/evening** heute Morgen/Nachmittag/Abend
those [ðəʊz] diese, jene, die (da)
thought [θɔ:t]: **I thought** ich dachte / ich habe gedacht (usw.); **I've thought** ich habe gedacht (usw.)
threw [θru:]: **I threw** ich warf / ich habe geworfen
through [θru:] durch, hindurch
throw (at) [θrəʊ] werfen (nach)
thrown [θrəʊn]: **I've thrown** ich habe geworfen
Thursday ['θɜ:zdeɪ, 'θɜ:zdi] Donnerstag
ticket ['tɪkɪt] Fahrkarte, Flugschein; Eintrittskarte; **lottery ticket** Los
tidy ['taɪdi] 1. aufräumen; 2. ordentlich, aufgeräumt
till [tɪl] bis; **not ... till** erst
time [taɪm] 1. Zeit; Uhrzeit; **(for) a long time** lange; **a waste of time** Zeitverschwendung; **at that time** damals; **in time** rechtzeitig; **What time is it?** Wie spät ist es? 2. Mal; **this time** diesmal
timetable ['taɪmteɪbl] Stundenplan; Fahrplan
tip[1] [tɪp] Tipp, Hinweis
tip[2] [tɪp] Trinkgeld
tired ['taɪəd] müde; **get tired of** genug bekommen von
to [tu:, tu, tə] 1. zu, nach; an; in, bei; 2. vor; 3. bis; **to go** um zu fahren; **start to run** beginnen zu rennen
toast [təʊst] 1. toasten; 2. Toast(brot)
toaster ['təʊstə] Toaster
today [tə'deɪ] heute; heutzutage
together [tə'geðə] zusammen
toilet ['tɔɪlət] Toilette
token ['təʊkən]: **subway token** (AE) U-Bahn-Münze, -Marke
told [təʊld]: **I told** ich erzählte / habe erzählt; **I've told** ich habe erzählt
tolerate ['tɒləreɪt] tolerieren, dulden; sich gefallen lassen
tomato, tomatoes [tə'mɑ:təʊ, tə'mɑ:təʊz] Tomate, Tomaten
tomorrow [tə'mɒrəʊ] morgen
tonight [tə'naɪt] heute Abend/Nacht
too [tu:] 1. auch; 2. **too late** zu spät; **too bad** schade

took [tʊk]: **I took** ich nahm (mit) / ich habe (mit)genommen (usw.)

tool [tuːl] Werkzeug

tooth, teeth [tuːθ, tiːθ] Zahn, Zähne

toothache ['tuːθeɪk] Zahnschmerzen

top [tɒp] Spitze, oberes Ende; **the top five** die Top fünf, die wichtigsten fünf *(einer Bestenliste)*

torch [tɔːtʃ] Taschenlampe

tore [tɔː]: **I tore** ich riss, zerriss / ich habe gerissen, zerrissen

totem pole ['təʊtəmpəʊl] Totempfahl

tough [tʌf] hart

tour [tʊə] Tour, Reise; Rundgang

tourist ['tʊərɪst] Tourist/Touristin; **tourist office** Touristeninformation, Fremdenverkehrsbüro

towards [tə'wɔːdz] auf ... zu, in Richtung

towel ['taʊəl] Handtuch

tower ['taʊə] Turm

town [taʊn] Stadt; **go to town** in die Stadt gehen; **in town** in der (Innen-)Stadt; **town hall** Rathaus

toy [tɔɪ] Spielzeug

track [træk] Rennstrecke

tractor ['træktə] Traktor

tradition [trə'dɪʃn] Tradition

traditional [trə'dɪʃənl] traditionell

traffic ['træfɪk] Verkehr

trail [treɪl] Wanderweg; Pfad

trailer ['treɪlə] Wohnwagen

train [treɪn] Zug, Eisenbahn

train [treɪn]: **train to be a ...** eine Ausbildung machen zum/zur ...

trainer ['treɪnə] Sportschuh

tram [træm] Straßenbahn

translate [træns'leɪt] übersetzen

travel ['trævl] reisen, fahren; **travel agency** Reisebüro; **travel agent** Reisebüroangestellte/r

tree [triː] Baum

tribe [traɪb] Stamm

trick [trɪk] Trick

trip [trɪp] Ausflug, Reise

trouble ['trʌbl] Schwierigkeiten, Ärger

truck [trʌk] (AE) Lastwagen

trucker ['trʌkə] (AE) Trucker

true [truː] wahr

trust [trʌst] vertrauen

try [traɪ] versuchen, probieren

Tuesday ['tjuːzdeɪ, 'tjuːzdi] Dienstag

tunnel ['tʌnl] Tunnel

turkey ['tɜːki] Truthahn, Pute

Turkey ['tɜːki] Türkei

Turkish ['tɜːkɪʃ] türkisch; Türkisch; Türke/Türkin

turn [tɜːn] **1.** abbiegen, einbiegen; **turn left/right (into)** nach links/rechts abbiegen (in); **2.** sich dre-

hen; **turn around** sich umdrehen; **turn away** sich abwenden; **3.** (um)drehen, (um)krempeln

turn [tɜːn]: **it's my turn** ich bin dran, ich bin an der Reihe

TV ['tiː'viː] Fernsehen; Fernsehgerät; **on TV** im Fernsehen; **watch TV** fernsehen; **TV programme** Fernsehsendung

twice [twaɪs]: **twice the time** doppelt so lange

typical ['tɪpɪkl] typisch

tyre ['taɪə] Reifen

U

ugly ['ʌgli] häßlich

uncle ['ʌŋkl] Onkel

uncomfortable [ʌn'kʌmftəbl] unbequem; ungemütlich

under ['ʌndə] unter

underground ['ʌndəgraʊnd] **1.** unterirdisch, unter der Erde; **2.** U-Bahn

understand [ʌndə'stænd] verstehen

understood [ʌndə'stʊd]: **I understood** ich verstand / ich habe verstanden

unfair [ʌn'feə] unfair, ungerecht

unfriendly [ʌn'frendli] unfreundlich

unhappy [ʌn'hæpi] unglücklich

uniform ['juːnɪfɔːm] Uniform

United Kingdom [ju'naɪtɪd'kɪŋdəm] Vereinigtes Königreich

United Nations [ju'naɪtɪd'neɪʃnz] Vereinte Nationen

United States of America [ju'naɪtɪd'steɪtsəvə'merɪkə] Vereinigte Staaten von Amerika

unlucky [ʌn'lʌki]: **we were unlucky** wir hatten Pech

unpack [ʌn'pæk] auspacken

unreal [ʌn'rɪəl] unwirklich

untidy [ʌn'taɪdi] unordentlich, unaufgeräumt

up [ʌp] hinauf/herauf

uphill [ʌp'hɪl] bergauf

upon [ə'pɒn] auf

upset stomach ['ʌpset'stʌmək] Magenverstimmung

upside down ['ʌpsaɪd'daʊn]: **turn upside down** auf den Kopf stellen

upstairs [ʌp'steəz] oben (im Haus); nach oben

Urdu ['ʊəduː] Urdu

us [ʌs] uns

use [juːz] benutzen, verwenden

used [juːst]: **get used to** sich gewöhnen an

useful ['juːsfl] nützlich

user ['juːzə] Benutzer/Benutzerin

usual ['juːʒʊəl]: **as usual** wie üblich

usually ['juːʒʊəli] meistens, normalerweise, gewöhnlich

V

Valentine's Day ['væləntaɪnzdeɪ] Valentinstag

van [væn] Lieferwagen

vanilla [və'nɪlə] Vanille

vegetable ['vedʒtəbl] Gemüse

vegetarian [vedʒə'teəriən] Vegetarier/Vegetarierin

verb [vɜːb] Verb, Zeitwort

very ['veri] sehr

video ['vɪdiəʊ] Videofilm, Video

video-recorder ['vɪdiəʊrɪ'kɔːdə] Videorecorder

view [vjuː] Aussicht, Sicht

viewer ['vjuːə] Fernsehzuschauer/in

village ['vɪlɪdʒ] Dorf

vinegar ['vɪnɪgə] Essig

vineyard ['vɪnjəd] Weinberg

violence ['vaɪələns] Gewalt(tätigkeit)

visit ['vɪzɪt] **1.** besuchen; besichtigen; **2.** Besuch, Aufenthalt

visitor ['vɪzɪtə] Besucher/in, Gast

volleyball ['vɒlibɔːl] Volleyball

vote [vəʊt] wählen

W

wait (for) [weɪt] warten (auf)

waiter ['weɪtə] Kellner, Ober

waitress ['weɪtrəs] Kellnerin

wake [weɪk] **1.** aufwachen; **2.** wecken

walk [wɔːk] **1.** (zu Fuß) gehen, laufen; wandern; **walk the streets** durch die Straßen laufen; **2.** Spaziergang, Wanderung; **go for a walk** spazieren gehen; **take the dog for a walk** mit dem Hund rausgehen, spazieren gehen; **Walk of Fame** Weg des Ruhms

walkman ['wɔːkmən] Walkman

wall [wɔːl] Wand, Mauer

want [wɒnt] wollen; **want to go** gehen wollen; **I want them to help.** Ich will, dass sie helfen.

war [wɔː] Krieg

warden ['wɔːdn] Herbergsmutter/Herbergsvater

warm [wɔːm] warm

warning ['wɔːnɪŋ] (Vor-)Warnung

was [wɒz, wəz]: **I was** ich war; **I was invited** ich wurde eingeladen

wash [wɒʃ]: **wash dishes** Geschirr spülen; **wash up** abwaschen, spülen; **have a wash** sich waschen

washing-machine ['wɒʃɪŋmə'ʃiːn] Waschmaschine

waste [weɪst]: **a waste of time** Zeitverschwendung

watch [wɒtʃ] zusehen, sich anschauen, beobachten; **watch TV** fernsehen

water ['wɔːtə] Wasser

way [weɪ] 1. Weg; **a long way** weit; 2. Art; **a good way of learning** eine gute Art zu lernen; **the way she spoke** die Art, wie sie sprach

we [wiː] wir

wear [weə] tragen, anziehen

weather ['weðə] Wetter; **weather forecast** Wettervorhersage

web [web]: **web site** ['websaɪt] Website (Gesamtangebot eines Anbieters im Internet bzw. im World Wide Web); **word web** „Wortnetz"

Wednesday ['wenzdeɪ, -di] Mittwoch

week [wiːk] Woche

weekday ['wiːkdeɪ] Wochentag

weekend ['wiːk'end] Wochenende; **at the weekend** am Wochenende

welcome ['welkəm]: **Welcome to ...** Willkommen in/im/bei ...; **You're welcome.** Nichts zu danken; Bitte.

well [wel] gut; **Well, ...** Nun, ...

Welsh [welʃ] walisisch; Walisisch; Waliser/Waliserin

went [went]: **I went** ich ging, fuhr / ich bin gegangen, gefahren

were [wɜː]: **you were** du warst; ihr wart; Sie waren

west [west] West-; (nach) Westen; westlich

western ['westən] Western

wet [wet] nass, feucht

whale [weɪl] Wal

what [wɒt] 1. was; 2. welche/welcher/welches; **What a ...!** Was für ein/eine ...! **What about ...?** Wie wäre es mit ...? / Was ist mit ...? **What colour is ...?** Welche Farbe hat ...? **What time is it?** Wie spät ist es? **What's it like?** Wie ist es? **What's the matter?** Was ist los? **What's the weather forecast?** Wie ist die Wettervorhersage? **What's this/... in English?** Was heißt dies/... auf Englisch? **What's your name?** Wie heißt du / heißen Sie?

whatever [wɒt'evə] was auch immer, egal was

wheat [wiːt]: **whole wheat toast** Vollkorntoast(brot)

when [wen] 1. wann; 2. wenn; 3. als; **When's the next train?** Wann fährt der nächste Zug?

where [weə] wo; wohin; **Where are you from?** Wo kommst du her?

which [wɪtʃ] welche/welcher/welches

while [waɪl] während

while [waɪl]: **just a while** nur eine Weile lang

whisky ['wɪski] Whisky

whisper ['wɪspə] flüstern

white [waɪt] weiß

White [waɪt] Weiße/Weißer

who [huː] 1. wer; 2. der/die/das (in Relativsätzen)

whole [həʊl] ganz; **whole wheat toast** Vollkorntoast(brot)

why [waɪ] warum, weshalb; **That's why ...** Deshalb ..., Darum ...

wife, wives [waɪf, waɪvz] Ehefrau, Ehefrauen

wigwam ['wɪgwæm] Wigwam

will [wɪl]: **I will** (= **I'll** [aɪl]) ich werde

win [wɪn] gewinnen

window ['wɪndəʊ] (Schau-)Fenster; **go window-shopping** einen Schaufensterbummel machen

windsurfing ['wɪndsɜːfɪŋ] Windsurfen

windy ['wɪndi] windig

winter ['wɪntə] Winter

wish [wɪʃ] wünschen; **I wish he was ...** Ich wünschte, er wäre ...

witch [wɪtʃ] Hexe

with [wɪð] mit; bei

without [wɪ'ðaʊt] ohne

woke [wəʊk]: **I woke** ich wachte auf / ich bin aufgewacht (usw.)

woken ['wəʊkən]: **I've woken** ich bin aufgewacht (usw.); **I've woken her up** ich habe sie geweckt

woman, women ['wʊmən, 'wɪmɪn] Frau, Frauen

won [wʌn]: **I won** ich gewann / ich habe gewonnen; **I've won** ich habe gewonnen

won't [wəʊnt] (= **will not**): **I won't** ich werde nicht

wonder ['wʌndə] sich fragen

wood [wʊd] Holz

wooden ['wʊdn] Holz-, hölzern

word [wɜːd] Wort; **word web** „Wortnetz"; **words** (of a song) Text

wore [wɔː]: **I wore** ich trug, zog an / ich habe getragen, angezogen

work [wɜːk] 1. arbeiten; funktionieren; 2. Arbeit; **at work** bei der Arbeit; **go to work** arbeiten gehen; **out of work** arbeitslos; **work experience** Berufspraktikum; **work permit** Arbeitserlaubnis

worker ['wɜːkə] Arbeiter/Arbeiterin; **office worker** Büroangestellte/r

working hours ['wɜːkɪŋaʊəz] Arbeitszeit

world [wɜːld] Welt; **in the world** auf der (ganzen) Welt

worn [wɔːn]: **I've worn** ich habe getragen, angezogen

worried ['wʌrid]: **he's worried (about)** er macht sich Sorgen (um)

worry ['wʌri] sich Sorgen machen, beunruhigt sein; **Don't worry.** Mach dir keine Sorgen.

worse [wɜːs] schlechter, schlimmer

worst [wɜːst] schlechteste/r/s, schlimmste/r/s; am schlechtesten, am schlimmsten

worth [wɜːθ]: **it's worth it** es lohnt sich

would [wʊd]: **I would** (= **I'd**) ich würde; **I'd like** (= **I would like**) ... Ich möchte / hätte gern ...; **I'd like to go.** Ich möchte gehen. **Would you like ...?** Möchtest du ...?

write [raɪt] schreiben

written ['rɪtn]: **I've written** ich habe geschrieben

wrong [rɒŋ] falsch; **You're wrong.** Du hast / Sie haben Unrecht.

wrote [rəʊt]: **I wrote** ich schrieb / ich habe geschrieben

Y

yeah [jeə] (AE) ja

year [jɪə] Jahr; Jahrgang

yellow ['jeləʊ] gelb

yes [jes] ja

yesterday ['jestədeɪ, 'jestədi] gestern

yet [jet] noch; **not ... yet** noch nicht

yoghurt ['jɒgət] Joghurt

you [juː] 1. du; ihr; Sie; 2. man

young [jʌŋ] jung

your [jɔː] dein/e; euer/eure; Ihr/e

yours [jɔːz] deine/r/s, eure/r/s, Ihre/r/s; **Yours faithfully,...** Mit freundlichen Grüßen ...

yourself [jɔː'self] dir/dich (selbst); selbst

yourselves [jɔː'selvz] euch (selbst); sich (selbst); selbst

youth [juːθ] Jugend-; **youth club** Jugendclub; **youth hostel** Jugendherberge

Z

zoo [zuː] Zoo

List of names

■ BOYS/MEN

Alex ['ælɪks]
Brian ['braɪən]
Charles ['tʃɑːlz]
Chuck [tʃʌk]
Daniel ['dænjəl]
Dave [deɪv]
Drake [dreɪk]
Jay [dʒeɪ]
Jason ['dʒeɪsn]
Jon [dʒɒn]
José [həʊ'zeɪ]
Michael ['maɪkl]
Mohammed [məʊ'hæmɪd]
Paul [pɔːl]
Richard ['rɪtʃəd]
Rod [rɒd]
Ross [rɒs]
Stephen ['stiːvn]
Thomas ['tɒməs]
Vince [vɪns]

■ GIRLS/WOMEN

Amber ['æmbə]
Angie ['ændʒi]
Blanca ['blæŋkə]
Christine ['krɪstiːn]
Clare [kleə]
Donna ['dɒnə]
Ella ['elə]
Gemma ['dʒemə]
Gwen [gwen]
Helen ['helən]
Jody ['dʒəʊdi]
Joyce [dʒɔɪs]
Laura ['lɔːrə]
Lisa ['liːsə]
Liz [lɪz]
Maggie ['mægi]
Marian ['mæriən]
Molly ['mɒli]
Monica ['mɒnɪkə]
Nasreen [næz'riːn]
Paula ['pɔːlə]
Rachel ['reɪtʃəl]
Sarah ['seərə]
Shauna ['ʃɔːnə]
Shellina [ʃe'liːnə]
Stacy ['steɪsi]
Tara ['tɑːrə]
Teresa [tə'riːzə]

■ FAMILIES

Akbar ['ækbɑː]
Barker ['bɑːkə]
Blackburn ['blækbɜːn]
Blake [bleɪk]
Bolt [bəʊlt]
Brain [breɪn]
Bruce [bruːs]
Burton ['bɜːtən]
Butler ['bʌtlə]
Campbell ['kæmbəl]
Carman ['kɑːmən]
Chang [tʃæŋ]
Chong [tʃɒŋ]
Collins ['kɒlɪnz]
Couric ['kʊrɪk]
Delaney [də'leɪni]
DeVille [də'vɪl]
Dobson ['dɒbsən]
Dubois [djuː'bwɑː]
Dupont [djuː'pɒnt]
Fairley ['feəli]
Forrest ['fɒrɪst]
Franklin ['fræŋklɪn]
Gonzalez [gɒn'zɑːlɪs]
Gordon ['gɔːdn]
Gregson ['gregsən]
Hart [hɑːt]
Henley ['henli]
Hooper ['huːpə]
Kellerman ['keləmən]
Kennedy ['kenədi]
Kovak ['kəʊvæk]
Labone [lə'bəʊn]
Langley ['læŋli]
Lewis ['luːɪs]
Logan ['ləʊgən]
Longhurst ['lɒŋhɜːst]
Mace [meɪs]
Madison ['mædɪsən]
McAllister [mə'kælɪstə]
McHugh [mək'hjuː]
Meyer ['maɪə]
Molina [məʊ'liːnə]
Morris ['mɒrɪs]
Murray ['mʌri]
Mushtaq ['mʊʃtæk]
Norton ['nɔːtən]
O'Neill [əʊ'niːl]
Olsen ['əʊlsən]
Palmer ['pɑːmə]
Parr [pɑː]
Patrick ['pætrɪk]

Porter ['pɔːtə]
Proudfoot ['praʊdfʊt]
Rogers ['rɒdʒəz]
Shrimpton ['ʃrɪmptən]
Singh [sɪŋ]
Smart [smɑːt]
Strong [strɒŋ]
Toft [tɒft]
Trent [trent]
Walker ['wɔːkə]
Watson ['wɒtsən]
Watts [wɒts]
Williams ['wɪljəmz]
Woods [wʊdz]
Zemon ['ziːmən]

■ FAMOUS PEOPLE

Al Capone ['ælkə'pəʊn]
Alfred Hitchcock
    ['ælfrɪd'hɪtʃkɒk]
Martin Luther King, Jr.
    ['mɑːtɪn'luːθə'kɪŋ'dʒuːniə]
Presidents
    Jefferson ['dʒefəsən]
    Lincoln ['lɪŋkən]
    Ronald Reagan
        ['rɒnəld'reɪgən]
    Roosevelt ['rəʊzəvelt]
    Washington ['wɒʃɪŋtən]
Rosa Parks ['rəʊzə'pɑːks]

■ MUSIC

Blue Suede Shoes
    [bluː'sweɪd'ʃuːz]
Bob Marley [bɒb'mɑːli]
Bob Mothersbaugh
    [bɒb'mʌðəzbɔː]
Canyon Rockers
    ['kænjən'rɒkəz]
Chrissie Hynde
    ['krɪsi'haɪnd]
Clef [klef]
David Ellefson
    ['deɪvɪd'eləfsən]
Devo ['diːvəʊ]
Elvis Presley ['elvɪs'prezli]
Guns N' Roses
    [gʌnzn'rəʊzɪz]
Joni Mitchell
    ['dʒəʊni'mɪtʃl]

k.d. lang ['keɪ'diː'læŋ]
    (= Kathryn Dawn
    ['kæθrɪn'dɔːn])
Lauryn Hill ['lɔːrɪn'hɪl]
L-Boogie [el'buːgi]
Madonna [mə'dɒnə]
Maria's Musical Madness
    [mə'riːəz'mjuːzɪkl'mædnəs]
Megadeth ['megədeθ]
Miss Chatelaine [mɪs'ʃætəleɪn]
Pras [præz]
Roberta Flack [rə'bɜːtə'flæk]
Slash [slæʃ]
Spice Girls ['spaɪsgɜːlz]
The Beatles [ðə'biːtlz]
The Pretenders [ðəprɪ'tendəz]
The Score [ðə'skɔː]
The Silver Beatles
    [ðə'sɪlvə'biːtlz]
Tori Amos ['tɔːri'eɪmɒs]

■ PLACES

Abbeydale ['æbideɪl]
Alabama [ælə'bæmə]
Alaska [ə'læskə]
Alberta [æl'bɜːtə]
Auckland ['ɔːklənd]
Baldwin Street ['bɔːldwɪnstriːt]
Banff National Park
    ['bænf'næʃnəl'pɑːk]
Birmingham ['bɜːmɪŋəm]
Bleeker Street ['bliːkəstriːt]
Bloor Street ['blɔːstriːt]
Bristol ['brɪstəl]
Brownsville ['braʊnzvɪl]
Calgary ['kælgəri]
Canal Street [kə'nælstriːt]
Chennai ['tʃenaɪ]
Cherry Tree Road
    ['tʃeritriː'rəʊd]
Chicago [ʃɪ'kɑːgəʊ]
China ['tʃaɪnə]
Chinese Theatre
    [tʃaɪniːz'θɪətə]
Clifton School ['klɪftən'skuːl]
CN Tower ['siː'entaʊə]
Denver ['denvə]
Derbyshire ['dɑːbiʃə]
Edmonton ['edməntən]
Empire State Building
    [empaɪə'steɪtbɪldɪŋ]
Flagstaff ['flægstɑːf]

156

Florida ['flɒrɪdə]
Fort Louisbourg
 [fɔːt'luːɪsbɜːg]
Freeport ['friːpɔːt]
French Quarter
 ['frentʃ'kwɔːtə]
Gatwick ['gætwɪk]
Gray's Papaya
 [greɪzpə'paɪə]
Greenwich Village
 ['grenɪdʒ'vɪlɪdʒ]
Grindleford ['grɪndlfəd]
Haiti ['heɪti]
Hamilton ['hæməltən]
Harlem ['haːləm]
Heathrow [hiːθ'rəʊ]
Holland ['hɒlənd]
Hollywood Boulevard
 ['hɒliwʊd'buːləvaːd]
Hollywood Freeway
 ['hɒliwʊd'friːweɪ]
Hong Kong ['hɒŋ'kɒŋ]
Hyder ['haɪdə]
Illinois [ɪlɪ'nɔɪ]
Iowa ['aɪəwə]
Iqaluit [ɪ'kæluːɪt]
Kamloops ['kæmluːps]
Kensington Market
 ['kenzɪŋtən'maːkɪt]
Kingston ['kɪŋstən]
Lake Pontchartrain
 [leɪk'pɒntʃətreɪn]
Lancaster County
 ['læŋkəstə'kaʊnti]
Lankersheim Boulevard
 ['læŋkəʃeɪm'buːləvaːd]
Las Vegas [læs'veɪgəs]
Leopold Street
 ['liːəpəʊldstriːt]
Lopez High School
 ['ləʊpez'haɪskuːl]
Los Angeles [lɒs'ændʒɪlɪz]
Madras [mə'draːs]
Maine [meɪn]
Malta ['mɔːltə]
Miami [maɪ'æmi]
Midland College
 ['mɪdlənd'kɒlɪdʒ]
Milwaukee [mɪl'wɔːki]
Mississippi River
 [mɪsɪ'sɪpi'rɪvə]
Montego Bay
 [mɒn'tiːgəʊ'beɪ]
Montgomery [mənt'gʌmri]

Montreal [mɒntri'ɔːl]
Monument Valley
 ['mɒnjəmənt'væli]
Mount Rushmore
 [maʊnt'rʌʃmɔː]
Nelson ['nelsən]
Nevada [nə'vaːdə]
New Orleans [njuː'ɔːliənz]
Nunavut ['nʊnəvʊt]
Ottawa ['ɒtəwə]
Peak District ['piːk'dɪstrɪkt]
Pennsylvania
 [pensɪl'veɪniə]
Phoenix ['fiːnɪks]
Puerto Rico [pweətə'riːkəʊ]
Quebec [kwɪ'bek]
Quebec City [kwɪbek'siti]
Rocky Mountains
 ['rɒki'maʊntənz]
Roger's ['rɒʒeɪz]
San Diego [sændi'eɪgəʊ]
San Fernando Valley
 [sænfə'nændəʊ'væli]
San Juan [sæn'hwaːn]
Santiago [sænti'aːgəʊ]
Sheffield ['ʃefiːld]
Skydome ['skaɪdəʊm]
Sligo ['slaɪgəʊ]
Stewart ['stjuːət]
Stratford ['strætfəd]
Universal Center Drive
 ['juːnɪvɜːsl'sentə'draɪv]
Universal City Plaza
 ['juːnɪvɜːsl'sɪtiplaːzə]
Vancouver [væn'kuːvə]
Victoria [vɪk'tɔːriə]
Vine Street ['vaɪnstriːt]
Wellington ['welɪŋtən]
White House ['waɪthaʊs]
Woodstock ['wʊdstɒk]
Yonge Street ['jʌŋstriːt]
Zimbabwe [zɪm'baːbwi]

■ OTHER NAMES

Afrikaans [æfrɪ'kaːns]
AIDS [eɪdz]
Alzheimer ['æltshaɪmə]
Aussie ['ɒzi]
Briggs Plumbing
 [brɪgz'plʌmɪŋ]
British Airways
 ['brɪtɪʃ'eəweɪz]

Canada Courier
 ['kænədə'kʊriə]
Canadian National
 Exhibition
 [kə'neɪdiən'næʃnəleksɪ'bɪʃn]
Caribana [kærɪ'baːnə]
Carnival ['kaːnɪvl]
Celsius ['selsiəs]
Chocpops ['tʃɒkpɒps]
Commonwealth
 ['kɒmənwelθ]
Cornison ['kɔːnɪsən]
Cyber Computer Games
 ['saɪbəkəm'pjuːtəgeɪmz]
Cybersoft ['saɪbəsɒft]
Delaware ['deləweə]
Dynamic [daɪ'næmɪk]
Egg McQueen
 ['egmə'kwiːn]
Eskimo ['eskɪməʊ]
Granada Television
 [grə'naːdə'telɪvɪʒn]
Green Card ['griːnkaːd]
Inuit ['ɪnuɪt]
Jurassic Park
 [dʒʊ'ræsɪk'paːk]
Kids' World [kɪdz'wɜːld]
King Kong ['kɪŋ'kɒŋ]
King's Row [kɪŋz'rəʊ]
Malibu Shores
 ['mælɪbuː'ʃɔːz]
Maori ['maʊri]
Maple Leafs ['meɪplliːfs]
Mars [maːz]
McAllister Trucking
 [mə'kælɪstə'trʌkɪŋ]
Navajo ['nævəhəʊ]
Oscar ['ɒskə]
Pronto ['prɒntəʊ]
Psycho ['saɪkəʊ]
Quickserve ['kwɪksɜːv]
Reggae Sunsplash
 ['regeɪ'sʌnsplæʃ]
Roseanne [rəʊ'zæn]
Route 66 ['ruːt'sɪksti'sɪks]
Rover ['rəʊvə]
Sharks [ʃaːks]
Sparkbrook ['spaːkbrʊk]
Star Trek Adventure
 ['staː'trekəd'ventʃə]
Sugar ['ʃʊgə]
Swampy ['swɒmpi]
TeenScene ['tiːnsiːn]
The Big Issue [ðəbɪg'ɪʃuː]

The Financial Times
 [ðəfaɪ'nænʃl'taɪmz]
The Guardian [ðə'gaːdiən]
The Mail [ðə'meɪl]
The Parks Legacy
 [ðə'paːks'legəsi]
The Rosa Parks Institute
 [ðə'rəʊzə'paːks'ɪnstɪtjuːt]
The Samaritans
 [ðəsə'mærɪtənz]
The Weekly News
 [ðə'wiːkli'njuːz]
Ting [tɪŋ]
Trans-Canada Highway
 ['træns'kænədə'haɪweɪ]
Trends [trendz]
Trivial Pursuit ['trɪviəlpə'sjuːt]
US Immigration
 ['juː'esɪmɪ'greɪʃn]
Veggieburger ['vedʒi'bɜːgə]
Warner Brothers
 ['wɔːnəbrʌðəz]
Wheatos ['wiːtəʊz]
Wheels [wiːlz]
Wild West [waɪld'west]
www.levi.com ['dʌblju:'dʌblju:
 'dʌblju:'dɒt'liː'vaɪ'dɒt'kɒm]
Zealis ['ziːliz]

Irregular verbs

INFINITIVE FORM (Grundform)	SIMPLE PAST FORM (Einfache Vergangenheit)	PRESENT PERFECT FORM (Vollendete Gegenwart)	
be	I was, you were, she was	I've been	sein
have	I had	I've had	haben
do	I did	I've done [dʌn]	tun, machen
beat	I beat	I've beaten	schlagen
become	I became	I've become	werden
begin	I began	I've begun	beginnen
bet	I bet	I've bet	wetten
break	I broke	I've broken	brechen, zerbrechen
bring	I brought	I've brought	bringen, mitbringen
build	I built	I've built	bauen
buy	I bought	I've bought	kaufen
come	I came	I've come	kommen
cost	it cost	it has cost	kosten
draw	I drew	I've drawn	zeichnen
drink	I drank	I've drunk	trinken
drive	I drove	I've driven ['drɪvn]	fahren
eat	I ate [et]	I've eaten	essen
fall	I fell	I've fallen	fallen
feed	I fed	I've fed	füttern
feel	I felt	I've felt	(sich) fühlen
fight	I fought	I've fought	bekämpfen
find	I found	I've found	finden
fly	I flew	I've flown	fliegen
forget	I forgot	I've forgotten	vergessen
get	I got	I've got	bekommen; besorgen
give	I gave	I've given	geben; schenken
go	I went	I've gone [gɒn]	gehen, fahren
grow	I grew	I've grown	wachsen; anbauen
hang	I hung	I've hung	aufhängen, hängen
hear	I heard [hɜːd]	I've heard [hɜːd]	hören
hit	I hit	I've hit	schlagen
hurt	I hurt	I've hurt	verletzen; wehtun
keep	I kept	I've kept	halten, behalten
know	I knew	I've known	wissen; kennen
lead	I led	I've led	führen
leave	I left	I've left	lassen; verlassen
lie	I lay	I've lain	liegen
lose	I lost	I've lost	verlieren
make	I made	I've made	machen
mean	I meant [ment]	I've meant [ment]	bedeuten; meinen
meet	I met	I've met	treffen; kennen lernen
pay	I paid	I've paid	zahlen, bezahlen

INFINITIVE FORM (Grundform)	SIMPLE PAST FORM (Einfache Vergangenheit)	PRESENT PERFECT FORM (Vollendete Gegenwart)	
put	I put	I've put	stellen; legen
read	I read [red]	I've read [red]	lesen, vorlesen
ride	I rode	I've ridden	(Rad) fahren
run	I ran	I've run	rennen, laufen
say	I said [sed]	I've said [sed]	sagen
see	I saw	I've seen	sehen; besichtigen
sell	I sold	I've sold	verkaufen
send	I sent	I've sent	senden, schicken
set the table	I set the table	I've set the table	den Tisch decken
shoot	I shot	I've shot	schießen; erschießen
show	I showed	I've shown	zeigen
sing	I sang	I've sung	singen
sit	I sat	I've sat	sitzen; sich setzen
sleep	I slept	I've slept	schlafen
speak	I spoke	I've spoken	sprechen
spend	I spent	I've spent	verbringen
split up	they split up	they've split up	sich trennen
stand	I stood	I've stood	stehen
steal	I stole	I've stolen	stehlen
swim	I swam	I've swum	schwimmen
take	I took	I've taken	(mit)nehmen; dauern
teach	I taught	I've taught	beibringen, unterrichten
tell	I told	I've told	erzählen; sagen
think	I thought	I've thought	finden; glauben; denken
throw	I threw	I've thrown	werfen
understand	I understood	I've understood	verstehen
wake	I woke	I've woken	aufwachen; wecken
wear	I wore	I've worn	tragen, anziehen
win	I won	I've won	gewinnen
write	I wrote	I've written	schreiben

29,80

Quellen

BILDQUELLEN

Action Press, Hamburg (IMA Press S. 63 unten; Sunshine International S. 107 unten); AKG, Berlin (S. 106 Mitte oben links); AP, Frankfurt a. M. (S. 32 oben Mitte; Dave Allocca/DMI S. 9 unten; Eric Draper S. 32 unten rechts; Lisa De Jong/St. Petersburg Times S. 14 unten; NBC/AP S. 21 oben); Apple, Eching (S. 6 Mitte Bild 5); Jose Azel/AURORA, Portland (S. 30 unten); Anna Baker, York (S. 64 oben; S. 92; S. 95 oben; S. 98 oben links; S. 101 oben rechts); Gary Barber, Dallas/TX (S. 28 oben); Bavaria, Gauting (S. 40 Mitte; S. 111 unten links; Benelux Press S. 24 Bild 3 von oben; Masterfile Coorperation S. 110 unten Mitte; TLC S. 110 unten links; VCI S. 70 Bild 5; S. Wind S. 24 Bild 2 von oben; J. Grames, London (S. 95); J. Grames/Bilderberg, Hamburg (S. 46 Bild 2); John Birdsall, Nottingham (S. 54 Bild B, C, D; S. 72/73 Hintergrund); Anthony Blake, London (A. Sydenham S. 109 Mitte oben rechts); Jutta Brendemühl, Toronto (S. 68); British Airways, Frankfurt a. M. (S. 18 oben); Brown Brothers, Sterling/ PA (S. 32 oben rechts); BTA, Frankfurt a. M. (S. 93 oben); Canadian Food Inspection Agency, Toronto (S. 47 Mitte); J. A. Cash, London (S. 64 unten links; S. 70 Bild 4; S. 73 Mitte; S. 81); courtesy of CNN (S. 6 Mitte Bild 2); Comic Relief, London (S. 56 unten rechts; Kevin Cahill S. 56 Mitte; Concept II Ltd S. 56/57 Hintergrund; Imagination Ltd. S. 56 oben; Stay Still Ltd. S. 56 unten links); Colin Quirk/COMSTOCK, Toronto (S. 84 unten); Corbis, London (Nathan Benn S. 106 unten rechts; Kevin R. Morris S. 66 unten; Bob Rowan/Progressive Image S. 101 links; Paul Sanders S. 42; Joseph Sohm S. 36 unten; Jim Sugar Photography S. 73 oben; Nick Wheeler S. 34 unten); Corel-Library (Hintergründe S. 6/7; S. 8/9; S. 22/23; S. 24/25; S. 38/39; S. 40/41; S. 70/ 71; S. 20 rechts; S. 24 unten; S. 30 oben links, Mitte; S. 35 oben; S. 37 unten; S. 38 oben links, oben rechts; S. 39 unten rechts; S. 40 unten; S. 46 oben, Bild 4, 5, 6; S. 47 unten; S. 48 unten; S. 49; S. 51; S. 66 oben; S. 67; S. 70 Bild 2, 3; S. 71; S. 78 unten; S. 82 unten; S. 84 oben; S. 86; S. 88 unten; 108 Mitte links; S. 110 oben rechts); Roderick Cox, Aachen (S. 10 oben; S. 38 unten; S. 41 Mitte; S. 111 oben); DaimlerChrysler, Untertürkheim (S. 100 Bild C links); Paul Dames, Stuttgart (S. 22 oben links); dpa, Frankfurt a. M. (S. 32 unten links; S. 90) ZB/dpa, Berlin (S. 74 oben; S. 91 unten rechts; S. 105 oben); David Dore, Guildford (S. 80); Dover Publications Inc., Minverva/NY (S. 33 Bild B); Kinoarchiv Engelmeier, Hamburg (S. 87; S. 88 oben links; S. 89); Environmental Images, London (S. 57 oben; Chris Martin S. 78 oben); © Europ. Währungsinstitut, 1997/Europ. Zentralbank, 1998; Focus, Hamburg (Mehta, Dilip/Contact S. 110 Mitte rechts; Jochen Keute S. 53 unten; Stuart Nicol/Katz Pictures S. 24 Bild 1 von oben; Magnum S. 32 oben links; Michael Yamashita S. 82 oben); Mike Ford, Sheffield (S. 54 Bild A; S. 60; S. 61; S. 65; S. 72); Fotex, Hamburg (S. 9 Bild 1; S. 91 oben; R. Drechsler S. 39 Mitte; S. 109 oben; Ipol/K. B. S. 105 Mitte unten rechts; M. H./Redferns S. 109 unten Bild 2; Sungria S. 109 unten Bild 1; T. Podlecki S. 109 unten Bild 3; N. K./Redferns S. 54/55 Hintergrund; D. B./Redferns S. 105 Mitte oben Bild 3; Rex/Oliviera S. 109 unten Bild 4; Target S. 109 unten Bild 5/6); Das Foto- archiv, Essen (Dirk Eisermann S. 6 unten; Wolfgang Schmidt S. 111 unten rechts; Jochen Tack S. 44 Mitte; S. 46 Bild 1; S. 50 oben; S. 108 unten links; Bill Wax S. 38 unten links); Dwight Haigh, Flagstaff/AZ (S. 14 oben; S. 28 unten; S. 45 oben); Artslink/ Hong Kong Arts Centre (S. 110 Mitte links); IFA-Bilderteam, Düsseldorf (S. 18 unten; Jacques Alexandre S. 22 oben rechts; Banus-March S. 29 oben; Fotostock S. 98 rechts; International Stock S. 64 Mitte rechts; LDW S. 26 oben links; S. 107 Mitte links; Nowitz S. 20 unten; Selma S. 64 unten rechts); Image Bank, Berlin (W. Bibikow S. 108 Mitte rechts; D. W. Hamilton S. 48 oben rechts; Marks Production S. 22 Mitte Bild 1; Sobel/Klonsky S. 107 Mitte rechts); Images of Africa, Lichtfield (Carla Signorini S. 111 Mitte oben); International Stock, New York (W. Aldridge S. 13; J. Davis S. 40 oben; K. Frick S. 109 Mitte unten; Michael J. Howell S. 34 oben; Jeff Noble S. 22 Mitte Bild 2; Michael Paras S. 33 Bild A, C, D; Patrick Ramsey S. 32 unten Mitte; S. Thode S. 88 oben rechts; P. Thompson S. 111 Mitte unten); Barbara Jung, Berlin (S. 44 oben rechts; S. 56 Bild 2 von oben; S. 57 Bild A-C; S. 63 Bild 1-5); Kobal Collection, London (S. 6 Mitte Bild 4); Mauritius, Mittenwald (S. 29 Mitte); Microsoft GmbH, Unterschleiß- heim (S. 6 Mitte Bild 3); Miller-Freeman Books, San Francisco/CA (S. 8); MSI, London (S. 19 unten); MTV networks GmbH, Hamburg (S. 6 Mitte Bild 1); Musik + Show Lange, Hamburg (S. 9 Bild 2, 3; S. 105 Mitte oben Bild 1, 4); National Centre for Popular Music, Sheffield (S. 93 unten); News America Publications Inc./Radnor/PA (S. 12 oben); John Lally, York (S. 76; S. 77 oben); Parental Guide™, Omaha/NE (S. 12 unten); Pictor, Hamburg (S. 16; S. 26 oben rechts); Photo Press, Stockdorf (Herdt S. 112 oben; Wolf S. 113 oben); Photo Researchers, New York (S. 25; Jim Corwin S. 106 Mitte; Vanessa Vick S. 107 oben); Photoselection, Hamburg (S. 12 Mitte Bild 3, 4; M. Putland S. 105 Mitte unten links); Picture Bank, Kingston (S. 94); ppw-Max Kohr, Berlin (S. 7); Pop-Eye, Berlin (S. 9 Slash; Heinrich S. 110 unten rechts; Ziebe S. 6 unten); Seventeen/Primedia Inc., New York (S. 104); Pro 7, Unterföhring (S. 12 Mitte Bild 1, 2); Redferns, London (S. 14 Mitte; G. A. Baker Archives S. 105 unten; M. Ochs Archives S. 105); Reebok, Oberhaching (S. 30 oben rechts; S. 63 oben); Paul Robson, York (S. 100 Bild A, B links, D; S. 102 oben links; S. 103); Royal Ontario Museum, Toronto (S. 46 Bild 3); Safeway Stores, Hayes/Middlesex (S. 100 Bild B rechts); Sheffield Airport (S. 58 oben); Shout, Northants (S. 96); Skjold Photographs, St. Paul/MN (S. 22 Mitte Bild 3, Mitte Bild 4; S. 31 Mitte; S. 111 unten Mitte); Dr. Wolfgang K. Soldan, Rancho Viejo/TX (S. 106 oben); Spectator, London (S.102 unten); Sportimage, Hamburg (S. 54 oben links; S. 110 unten Mitte; BBS S. 69 oben; Pressesports S. 108 unten rechts); Stockfood Eising, München (S. 109 Mitte oben links, Mitte oben Mitte; Antony Blake S. 54 oben rechts); Tony Stone, Hamburg (Tim Beddow S. 112 unten; Christopher Bissel S. 70 Bild 1; Anne Nielsen S. 23 Mitte; Oliver Strewe S. 113 unten); Superbild, Berlin (Diaphor S. 55); Touch Magazine, London (S. 54 oben); Transglobe, Hamburg (Pawel Kanicki S. 100 Bild C rechts; Richardson S. 110 oben links); U.S. Immigration & Naturalization Service, Washington (S. 31 unten); Walmsley, Guildford (S. 77 Mitte); Zefa, Düsseldorf (Damm S. 53 oben); Dagmar Zimmer, Berlin (S. 38 unten Mitte, unten rechts oben)

Einband S. Wind/Bavaria, Gauting

LIEDQUELLEN

Black and white (Text: David Arkin, Musik: Robinson) © Warner Music UK Ltd. (23)
I want to be free (T. und M.: Toyah Willcox/Joel Bogen) © Mambo Music Verlags + Produktions GmbH + Co KG (Sony Music Publishing) (55)
Manic Monday (T. und M.: Christopher) © Sony Music Entertainment Inc. (71)
Miss Chatelaine (T. und M.: k.d.Lang/Ben Minks) © Bumstead Publishing/Zavion Music SOCAN (39)
Radio ga ga (T. und M.: Roger Taylor) © Queen Productions Ltd. / Raincloud Productions Ltd. (7)

Nicht alle Copyrightinhaber konnten ermittelt werden, deren Urheberrechte werden hiermit vorsorglich und ausdrücklich anerkannt.